Reading Matters 3

SECOND EDITION

Reading Matters ❸

An Interactive Approach to Reading

Mary Lee Wholey

Continuing Education Language Institute
Concordia University

Nadia Henein

Continuing Education Language Institute
Concordia University

▶ For teaching notes, answer key, and other related instructor material, as well as for additional student activities related to this book, go to *college.hmco.com/pic/wholeythree2e*.

▶ To obtain access to the Houghton Mifflin ESL instructor sites, call 1-800-733-1717.

Houghton Mifflin Company

Boston   New York

Publisher: Patricia A. Coryell
Editor in Chief: Suzanne Phelps Weir
Sponsoring Editor: Joann Kozyrev
Senior Development Editor: Kathleen Sands Boehmer
Editorial Assistant: Evangeline Bermas
Senior Project Editor: Margaret Park Bridges
Associate Manufacturing Buyer: Brian Pieragostini
Executive Marketing Manager: Annamarie Rice
Marketing Associate: Andrew Whitacre

Printed in the U.S.A.

Library of Congress Control Number: 2005934055

Student Text
  ISBN-10: 0-618-47514-1
  ISBN-13: 978-0-618-47514-8

Instructor's Examination Copy
  ISBN-10: 0-618-73258-6
  ISBN-13: 978-0-618-73258-6

23456789-CRS-10 09 08 07 06

Contents

Introduction to the Second Edition

The *Reading Matters* series is a four-level reading program comprising texts at the high-beginning/low-intermediate, intermediate, high-intermediate, and advanced levels. It fosters the development of active readers through a multifaceted approach to interaction: interaction with the text, with other readers, and with readings from sources beyond the classroom. This new edition includes new and updated readings as well as additional readings in the "Expanding Your Language" section of each chapter. The *Reading Matters* series features stimulating extensive reading combined with intensive practice provided by well designed tasks that develop both fluency and accuracy at each level. The series incorporates the latest approaches to teaching productive strategies—from understanding the purpose and nature of different texts to guessing meaning from context, learning vocabulary for academic and professional success, and learning how to access information in the media and over the Internet.

In brief the series provides for:

- The development of active readers through interaction with a variety of texts, with other readers through reading-retell tasks, and with authentic reading outside of the classroom.

- Thematic units featuring high-interest, level-appropriate, informative topics that include texts about culture, science, the environment, business, innovation, sports, and entertainment.

- A wide variety of reading types, such as articles, interviews, essays, charts, and graphs.

- A skills and strategies overview of the comprehensive reading skills and strategies in each chapter that feature the development of critical thinking and information processing.

- Opportunities for personal reading, writing, and speaking activities.

- An index of key vocabulary aimed at both academic and professional needs (provided at *college.hmco.com/pic/wholeythree2e*).

- Access to the *Reading Matters* Online Study Center website, which includes individualized learning and testing materials, at *college.hmco.com/pic/wholeythree2e*.

Extensive Reading

To develop fluency in reading, students need significant exposure to text—that is, extensive reading. Extensive reading provides the opportunity to develop automatic text-processing skills. *Reading Matters* offers high-interest reading selections of sufficient length so that readers get the chance to increase the amount of time spent in silent reading. Variety in text styles is an important component of extensive reading. The series features a variety of styles and genres including articles, interviews, graphs, and charts, so that readers develop an awareness of the scope of reading as well as the various purposes for which texts are written. Authentic texts or adapted authentic texts are used at appropriate levels.

Intensive Reading

Reading Matters features thematically-related units on topics of interest and relevancy today. These topics range from social issues, scientific advances, the environment, and the business world to the fields of leisure, entertainment, and culture. The activities in each unit help students develop fluency and accuracy in reading by activating two complementary text processing methods: top-down and bottom-up.

The Process of Reading

Top-Down

Reading Matters enhances the approaches readers use to understand reading globally. In this series, the readers' background knowledge of the topic and critical thinking skills are engaged and readers are encouraged to make predictions about what they expect to find in a text. The reader reads to confirm or modify these predictions and begins to build a mental framework of the information in the reading selection. Awareness of rhetorical patterns, such as chronological ordering, cause and effect relationships, and other discourse features aids in the comprehension of information from the reading. In addition, *Reading Matters* helps the reader develop an awareness of the range of reading strategies, such as skimming, scanning, or previewing, that readers have at their disposal. The ability to apply these strategies appropriately is an important component of reading competency.

Bottom-Up

Knowledge of grammar and vocabulary has an effect on reading ability. Although readers can predict content from their knowledge of text structure or their background knowledge, a certain level of vocabulary recognition is required for processing text. *Reading Matters* introduces and develops vocabulary-building skills through such activities as guessing from context, recognizing meaning, grouping words, and identifying the use of special terms. Well-designed tasks help the reader learn new vocabulary and key words in the text. In the context of thematic units, the reader's vocabulary develops naturally through exposure to a range of texts. Students engage in a gradual process of acquiring key vocabulary by building from a basic level of vocabulary to a wider net of related terms. Students build their understanding through repeated use of language that contains key concepts and information.

In addition to a solid vocabulary, fluent readers have a good knowledge of syntactic structure.

Actively examining the important grammatical features of a text provides a meaningful context for this kind of learning. To build reading competency, the amount of exposure to reading as well as the identification and practice of learning strategies for both vocabulary and grammar are tremendously important. *Reading Matters* provides direction to readers through activities in the "Vocabulary Building," "Expanding Your Language," and "Read On" sections.

Skills Integration and Interaction

Reading is an active process. Interaction between and among students helps to facilitate this process. In exchanging ideas about the information in a text, readers confirm what they have understood. This confirmation process helps to develop accuracy in reading. It also provides a motivation as well as a clear purpose for reading. Interaction with other students can be best accomplished when speaking tasks are an integral part of a reading activity or the activity leads to the undertaking of writing tasks.

The interrelationship of skills integration and interaction requires a holistic approach to task design. The activities in *Reading Matters* are sequenced, and the recycling of tasks in various combinations allows the progressive development of reading competency in ways that are fresh and effective. The tasks are structured so that the learner builds skills and strategies progressively but in ways that offers challenge as well as variety. In *Reading Matters*, the reader uses and reuses the language of the selection both implicitly—to bolster an answer—and explicitly, as in the exchange of information from paired reading selections that provide complementary or contrasting information on a topic. Readers orally explain the information from their reading selection to readers who chose a different selection. Then, together, they apply that information to carry out a new activity.

Text Organization

Reading Matters 3 contains six thematic units with two chapters in each unit. In the second edition, each chapter features three to six reading selections. Many readings have been updated and new readings have been introduced. The unit themes feature topics of high interest to both academically-oriented and general audiences. Most importantly, the selections are of sufficient length for students to progressively develop fluency in reading. Through the chapter readings, students are able to build a rich semantic network without sacrificing variety so that interest in the topic is not exhausted. Within each unit, reading selections are structured so that the information from one selection can be compared with another.

You can choose among the chapters of a unit selectively to suit the needs of various program types and teaching approaches. Complexity in both text type and length, and difficulty in task type are structured to build gradually from chapter to chapter and unit to unit. Some overlap in level of language and task is built into each of the texts in the *Reading Matters* series so that you can accommodate the various levels of students within a class.

Unit Organization

Each unit in *Reading Matters 3* features the following components:

▶ Introducing the Topic: This introductory section identifies the theme. It features the unit opener photo and quote, which are designed to stimulate the readers' curiosity about and prior experience with the theme, or its personal relevance. The tasks are interactive and draw on a variety of media: text, photos, and graphics.

▶ Chapters: The two chapters in each unit present various topics loosely related to the theme.

Chapter Organization

For each of the reading selections the following tasks are presented:

▶ **Chapter Openers** include pre-reading reflection and discussion questions, graphs, questionnaires, surveys, or illustrations. The purpose of this section is to stimulate discussion of key ideas and concepts presented in the reading and to introduce key vocabulary. Encourage students to explain their ideas as completely as possible. Teach students strategies for maximizing their interaction, such as turn taking, eliciting responses from all group members, and naming a group leader and reporter. Whenever possible, re-form groups to give students a chance to talk more until they feel comfortable with the topic. Elicit key ideas and language from the students.

▶ **Exploring and Understanding Reading** contains content questions of varying levels of complexity. These questions guide students in the development of their reading strategies for improving general comprehension, developing an awareness of text structure, and evaluating the content of a text in detail. Emphasize the purpose of the activity and how it is tied to the development of a particular strategy. Point out the ways in which students can apply their skills to reading assignments. Help students build their tolerance for uncertainty. Point out that the purpose of comparing and checking their answers with the information in the reading is to verify as well as to become familiar with the information in the reading. Act as a resource to help students find the accurate information. An answer key that the instructor can use as needed is provided on the *Reading Matters* website at *college.hmco.com/pic/wholeythree2e.*

▶ **Paired Readings** include interactive Recapping, Retelling, Reacting to the Reading, and Discussing the Story activities that involve oral presentation of information from the readings, oral exchanges of information, and discussion that involves critical evaluation of ideas, including comparison/contrast and debate. At this level, talking about the reading they do is crucial for improving students' language use. Emphasize the importance of explaining the information in as natural and conversational a style as possible. Help students to develop their skill at extracting important information from a text by pointing out the purpose of note taking, highlighting, and underlining key information. Emphasize the importance of practicing at home for in-class presentations.

▶ **Vocabulary Building** comprises tasks that introduce vocabulary-building strategies such as the understanding of key terms, the interrelationship of grammatical structure and meaning, using context cues, and developing other aids to the fluent processing of reading selections. This edition adds exercises in each chapter that focus on learning the meaning of verbs and working with word form and function to foster the understanding of academic and general vocabulary.

▶ **Expanding Your Language** presents activities that offer students additional opportunities to use the material and strategies in the chapter. This section often includes additional extended readings. Encourage students to use these activities to further their own comprehension of the readings. Through these activities, students can improve their speaking and writing fluency.

▶ **Read On: Taking It Further** presents opportunities for personal reading and related activities, including suggestions for further reading as well as reading and writing journal entries, keeping a vocabulary log, and word play. Although most of this work will be done outside of class, time can be found in the class schedule to report on some of the activities. This gives students a purpose for the work and practice in developing their reading skills and strategies.

Reading Matters Online Study Center Website

Students gain confidence in their reading abilities as they discover how to access information more easily from the press, over the Internet, and in their professions or fields of study. The Internet activities give students a chance to consolidate and extend their reading skills. Using the *Reading Matters* website offers students the opportunity for productive work on an individual basis at any time of day or night that's convenient for them. Students are directed to the Online Study Center website at the end of each chapter.

Reading Matters Online Teaching Center Website

As with all Houghton Mifflin textbooks, there is a specific website devoted to necessary teaching tools that come in handy while using the text. Instructors using *Reading Matters* can access useful chapter notes and the answer key at the site. In addition, there are downloadable chapter tests that instructors can administer to students. These tests focus on comprehension skills and important vocabulary. Finally, a sample syllabus is included for instructors who need some guidelines about how to use the text effectively throughout the semester. To access the Online Teaching Center, go to *college.hmco.com/pic/wholeythree2e.*

Acknowledgments

We are grateful to Susan Maguire, who first suggested the idea for the series. A special thanks goes to Kathy Sands Boehmer, who has been an invaluable help throughout the lengthy process of bringing this manuscript into its present form. Thanks also to Margaret Bridges and the rest of the production and editorial staff at Houghton Mifflin.

Our gratitude to the people who read the manuscript and offered useful suggestions and critical comments: Marsha Abramovich, *Tidewater Community College*, Sushmita Chatterji, *Hudson Valley Community College*, Mary Ann Davey, *University of Nebraska*, Jim Epstein, *University of Arizona*, Gretchen Godfrey, *Mission College*, Joy Lane, *Tidewater Community College*, Phoebe Rivera, *Los Angeles Mission College*, Richard Skinner, *Hudson County Community College*, Cynthia Thornburgh, *Portland Community College*, Elizabeth Winkler, *University of Arizona*, and Ellen Yaniv, *Boston University*.

We would like to acknowledge the support and inspiring work of colleagues and students at the Continuing Education Language Institute (CELI) of Concordia University in Montreal. A special thanks goes to Adrianne Sklar for her advice and suggestions after reading drafts of the material. The continuing support of Lili Ullmann and Phyllis Vogel has been invaluable to us. Thank you also to Ioana Nicolae, who helped in the preparation of the answer key and the student online study activities, and to Gyl Mattioli, who helped in the preparation of the instructor website.

Finally, thanks to our families—Jerry, Jonah, and Yael and Sherif, Ghada, and Dina.

Mary Lee Wholey and Nadia Henein

Reading Matters 3: Overview

Unit	Skills	Activities	Vocabulary	Expansion
UNIT 1 **Fun Matters**	• previewing: using sidebars (1), using titles (2) • predicting (1, 2) • skimming (1, 2) • scanning for details (1) • getting information from a chart (2) • note taking: understanding reasons (2), pro/con (2) • understanding examples (2) • using evidence to support ideas (2) • inferring ideas (2)	• quotations (2) • personalizing (1, 2) • using evidence to support ideas (1) • using introductions to predict organization (2) • retelling: making a profile (1) • answering a questionnaire (1, 2) • summarizing opinion (2) • using quotes (2)	• using punctuation: commas (1) • word form (1, 2) • vocabulary in context (1, 2)	• interviewing (1, 2) • personal writing (1) • reaction writing (1) • two-minute taped talk (2) • topic writing (2) • reading journal (2) • vocabulary log (2) • personal dictionary (2) • studying online (1, 2)
UNIT 2 **Weather Matters**	• brainstorming (3) • previewing (3) • surveying (3) • getting main ideas (3) • understanding details (3) • skimming (3, 4) • scanning for specific information (4) • highlighting (4) • understanding special terms (4)	• compare and contrast (3) • presenting information in note form (3) • applying information: problem solving (3) • matching (4) • recapping, reacting to, and discussing information (4) • using evidence to support ideas (4) • questionnaire (4) • applying an explanation (4)	• synonyms (3) • word form (3, 4) • vocabulary in context, using context to guess meaning (3, 4) • adjective and noun forms (3, 4) • compound nouns (4)	• newspaper article presentation (3) • reaction writing (3, 4) • studying online (3, 4) • role-playing the expert (4) • report writing (4) • reading journal (4)
UNIT 3 **Time Matters**	• chunking and outlining (5) • understanding different points of view (5) • understanding introductions (6)	• compare and contrast (5) • matching meanings (5, 6) • using examples to support ideas (5) • personalizing (6)	• word form (5, 6) • vocabulary in context (5) • using descriptive phrases (5) • words with symbolic meaning (5) • matching general information with specific facts (6) • reference words (6)	• oral presentation (5) • reaction writing (5, 6) • studying online (5, 6) • explaining a different point of view (6)

Unit	Skills	Activities	Vocabulary	Expansion
UNIT 4 **Technology Matters**	• predicting and using knowledge (7, 8) • skimming (7, 8) • using the introduction (7) • tellback (7) • scanning: tracing development of ideas (7, 8) • note taking: finding evidence (7, 8) • prioritizing (8)	• giving your opinion (7, 8) • using illustrations to explain ideas (7) • retelling and reacting to the story (7) • understanding special terms (8) • definitions (8) • preparing a table (8) • problem solving (8)	• word form (7, 8) • quotations in context (7) • defining special terms (7) • grouping related terms (8)	• oral presentation (7, 8) • studying online (7, 8) • expository writing (7) • reaction writing (7, 8) • argumentative writing (8) • reading about unintended consequences (8)
UNIT 5 **Health Matters**	• scanning for important information (9) • getting information from a chart (9) • note taking: following a chronology (9) • getting information from a time line (10)	• analyzing proverbs (9) • applying information: making a decision (9, 10) • discussion (9, 10) • note taking (9) • giving an opinion (10) • retelling and reacting to the story (9)	• word form (9, 10) • using signal words (9) • matching ideas and details (9) • specialized vocabulary (9) • expressions in context (10) • using quotes (10)	• discussion (9) • writing an opinion (9) • free writing (9, 10) • studying online (9, 10) • analyzing magazine articles (9, 10) • persuasive writing (10) • debate (10) • journal writing (10)
UNIT 6 **Attitude Matters**	• previewing (11) • surveying (11) • scanning for examples (11) • predicting (12) • understanding inference (12)	• readings in the news (11) • evaluating ideas (11) • underlining facts to support opinion (12) • stating opinions (12) • free writing (12) • brainstorming from quotes (12) • charting results (12)	• word form (11, 12) • language of examples (11) • vocabulary in context (11, 12) • suffixes (11) • verb phrases (11) • adverbs (12)	• questionnaire (11) • discussion (11, 12) • narrative reading (11, 12) • topic writing (11, 12) • studying online (11, 12) • journal writing (11, 12) • critical reading for key ideas (12) • role play (12)

Fun Matters

One half of the
world cannot
understand the
pleasures of
the other.

—*Jane Austen*

Introducing the Topic

To relax and have fun is a very important part of life. The way we do it, however, varies from age to age and culture to culture. This unit is about how our concept of leisure has changed and about the kinds of activities that are becoming more popular these days. It also discusses the impact that our activities can have on the environment.

Points of Interest

Questionnaire

▷ Read the following list of reasons for taking time off. Check (✔) the ones that are important to you. Mark their order of importance from 1 (very important) to 5 (least important). Add any ideas of your own.

Reasons to Take Time Off	Importance
_____ To have time with family and friends	_____
_____ To be more efficient at work	_____
_____ To improve the economy	_____
_____ To stay healthy	_____
_____ To give others a chance to work	_____
_____ To learn something new	_____
Other: _____	_____

▷ Discuss your list with a partner or in a small group.

Quotations

Read the following quotations. Decide whether they support the idea of leisure, are against the idea of leisure, or are neutral.

Check (✔) the category you decide on.

	For	Against	Neutral
1. "Pleasure is the object, the duty and the goal of all rational creatures."	_____	_____	_____
2. "There are toys for all ages."	_____	_____	_____
3. "Play so that you may be serious."	_____	_____	_____
4. "It is a good talent to know how to play."	_____	_____	_____
5. "More free time means more time to waste."	_____	_____	_____
6. "In our play, we show what kind of people we are."	_____	_____	_____

Work with a partner. Explain what each quote means and try to agree on the best category for each. Discuss whether or not you agree with the quote, and give reasons for your opinion.

1 Challenges in Your Free Time

Chapter Openers

Discussion Questions

▶ Think about these questions. Share your ideas with a partner or a small group.

1. Why do you think that the number of people participating in challenging or risky activities is increasing?
2. What are the characteristics of risk takers?
3. Is it important to take risks?

Personalizing

▶ Look at the following list of sports. Check *T* for the ones you have tried, check *WLT* for the ones you would like to try, and check *WNT* for the ones you would never think of trying.

	T	WLT	WNT
Alpine skiing			
Rock climbing			
Skydiving			
White water rafting			
Snowboarding			
Race car driving			
Deep sea diving			
Bungee jumping			

▶ Work with a partner or in a small group.

- Describe the activities you checked in the *T* column and say what you liked about them.
- Explain why you want to try the activities in the *WLT* column.
- Give reasons for not wanting to try the activities in the *WNT* column.

Exploring and Understanding Reading

Previewing

> Reading Tip

In addition to looking at the pictures and reading the title and subtitle, **previewing** includes **reading sidebars** whenever they are included. ▓

▶ **A** The following are sidebars taken from an article on extreme sports. Working with a partner, read each one quickly and take turns telling what each is about.

Mountaineer

I don't remember much about the night I spent alone at Seven Gables in the John Muir Wilderness after falling 100 feet. I was hungry and cold. And I had no feeling in my legs. Since then, I've been in this wheelchair for seventeen years. At first I lay in the hospital feeling sorry for myself. I couldn't see anything positive. Then I began climbing again with customized gear. I'm the first person to climb the 3,000-foot face of Yosemite's El Capitan and the first paraplegic to ski across the Sierra Nevada.

Pro Snowboarder

Every day I get to do something bigger and better than I've ever done. Like taking a trick and going an extra fifteen feet bigger. Of course I'm scared. I don't want to rag doll and hurt myself—that's where I have to conquer my fear. And kids totally respond to that risk taking as part of the appeal. When you go out and try something that's a little bit risky, you feel great about yourself at the end of the day. Because, if you're a pro snowboarder and you don't get hurt, then you're not trying hard enough. I've had two knee surgeries, my latest three months ago. But I do what I do because I want to enjoy life to the max.

Walk Up the Wild Side

Most kids who get locked out of the house wait around for Mom and Dad to get home. Ten-year-old Alain Robert scaled his family's seven-story apartment building near Paris and climbed in a window. Twenty-five years later, the 5-foot 4-inch, 105-pound urban mountaineer known as Spiderman has climbed buildings including the Empire State Building, the 1,482-foot Petronas Towers in Malaysia, and Chicago's 1,454-foot Sears Tower—all without a rope or any other tools. Robert, who has been jailed on four continents for his illegal climbing, spent his teen years perfecting his skills on the cliffs in the south of France. The only climbing aids he uses are rubber-soled shoes and talcum powder for his hands. Dangerous? Sure, but as Robert sees it, "You are born to die one day … I prefer to die in action."

▶ B Answer the following questions with your partner.

1. What qualities/characteristics do these people have?
2. How do they feel about what they do?
3. How do they handle their fear?

Predicting

▶ Read the title and the subtitle of the following article and, using the information from the three sidebars above, list four ideas that you think you will find in the article.

1. _____

2. _____

3. _____

4. _____

▶ Compare your ideas with a partner.

Skimming

 Reading Tip

Skimming is **reading** an article **very quickly** just to get an idea of what it is about. ▪

▶ **A** Read the article quickly and add to or change your predicted ideas.

▶ **B** Answer the question that is asked in the subtitle: Why are Americans seeking risk as never before?

Life on the Edge

Why are Americans seeking risk as never before?

By Karl Taro Greenfield

❶ "Five … Four … Three … Two … One … See ya!" and Chance McGuire, twenty-five, is airborne off a 600-foot concrete dam in Northern California. In one second he falls 15 feet, in two seconds 60 feet, and after three seconds and 130 feet, he is flying at 66 miles an hour. He prays that his parachute will open facing away from the dam, that his canopy won't collapse, that his goggles will be handy, and that no ill wind will slam him back into the cold concrete. The chute snaps open, the sound echoing through the gorge like a gunshot, and McGuire is soaring, carving S-turns into the air, swooping over a winding creek. When he lands, he is a speck on a path along the creek. He hurriedly packs his chute and then, clearly audible above the rushing water, lets out a war cry that rises past those people still sitting on the dam, past the commuters driving by on the roadway, past even the hawks who circle the ravine. It is a cry of defiance, thanks, and victory; he has survived another BASE jump.

❷   McGuire is a practitioner of what he calls the king of all extreme sports. BASE—an acronym for building, antenna, span (bridge), and earth (cliffs)—jumping has one of the sporting world's highest fatality rates: in its eighteen-year history, forty-six participants have been killed. Yet the sport has never been more popular, with more than a thousand jumpers in the United States, and more seeking to get into it every day. It is an activity without margin for error. If your chute malfunctions, don't bother reaching for a reserve—there isn't time. There are no second chances.

❸   Still, the sport may be a perfect fit with the times. As extreme a risk taker as McGuire seems, Americans may have more in common with him than they know or care to admit. America has embarked on a national orgy of thrill seeking and risk taking. The rise of adventure and extreme sports such as BASE jumping, snowboarding, ice climbing, skateboarding, and paragliding is merely the most vivid manifestation of this new national behavior.

❹   The rising popularity of extreme sports speaks of an eagerness on the part of millions of Americans to participate in activities closer to the edge, where danger, skill, and fear combine to give weekend warriors and professional athletes alike a sense of pushing out personal boundaries. According to American Sports Data Inc., a consulting firm, participation in so-called extreme sports is way up. Snowboarding has grown 113 percent in five years and now boasts nearly 5.5 million participants. Mountain biking, skateboarding, scuba diving—their growth curves reveal a nation that loves to play with danger. Contrast that with activities such as baseball, touch football, and aerobics, all of which were in steady decline throughout the 1990s.

❺   The pursuits that are becoming more popular have one thing in common: the perception that they are somehow more challenging than a game of touch football. "Every human being with two legs and two arms is going to wonder how fast, how strong, how enduring he or she is," says Eric Perlman, a mountaineer and film maker specializing in extreme sports. "We are designed to experiment or die."

❻   And to get hurt. More Americans than ever are injuring themselves while pushing their personal limits. In 1997, the U.S. Consumer Products Safety Commission reported that 48,000 Americans were admitted to hospital emergency rooms with skateboarding-related injuries. That's thirty-three percent more than the previous year. Snowboarding emergency room visits were up thirty-one percent; mountain climbing up twenty percent. By every statistical measure available, Americans are participating in and injuring themselves through adventure sports at an unprecedented rate.

❼   Consider Mike Carr, an environmental engineer and paragliding pilot from Denver who last year survived a bad landing that smashed ten ribs and collapsed his lung. Paragliding pilots use feathery nylon wings to take off from mountain tops and float on thermal wind currents—a completely unpredictable ride. Carr also mountain bikes and climbs rock faces. He walked away from a 1,450-foot fall in Peru in 1988. After his recovery, he returned to paragliding. "This has taken over many of our lives," he explains. "You float like a bird out there. You can go as high as 17,000 feet and go for 200 miles. That's magic."

❽   Previous generations did not need to seek out risk; it showed up uninvited and regularly: global wars, childbirth complications, diseases and pandemics from the flu to polio, dangerous products, and even the cold-war threat of mutually assured destruction. "I just don't think extreme sports would have been popular in a ground-war era," says Dan Cady, professor of popular culture at California State University, Fullerton. "Coming back from a war and getting onto a skateboard would not seem so extreme."

❾   But for recent generations, many of those traditional risks have been reduced by science and government, leaving people to face less real risk. Life expectancy has increased. Violent crime is down. Americans are fifty-seven percent less likely to die of heart disease than their parents; smallpox, measles, and polio have been virtually eradicated in the United States.

❿   War survivors speak of the terror and the excitement of being in a death match. "People are taking risks because everyday risk is minimized and people want to be challenged," says Joy Marr, forty-three, an adventure racer who was the only woman member of a five-person team that finished the 1998 Raid Gauloises, the granddaddy of all adventure races. This is a sport that requires several days of nonstop climbing, rafting, and surviving through some of the roughest terrain in the world.

⓫   The question is, How much is enough? Without some expression of risk, people may never know their limits and, therefore, who they are as individuals. "If you don't assume a certain amount of risk," says paragliding pilot Wade Ellet, fifty-one, "you're missing a certain amount of life." And it is by taking risks that one may achieve greatness. "We create technologies, we make new discoveries, but in order to do that, we have to push beyond the set of rules that are governing us at that time," says psychologist Frank Farley of Temple University.

Scanning for Details

▶ Answer these questions. Underline the details in the reading that support your answers.

1. How far does BASE jumper Chance McGuire travel and what is his maximum speed?

_____

2. What other examples of extreme sports are there?

_____

3. What has happened to:

   a. participation in snowboarding over the past five years?

   _____

   b. participation in baseball and touch football?

   _____

4. What does this change in popular sports tell us about Americans today?

   _____

5. What do the activities that are becoming popular have in common?

   _____

6. What happened to Mike Carr as a result of participating in dangerous sports?

   _____

7. Why didn't previous generations have to look for risks?

   _____

8. Why is it important to have a certain amount of risk in life?

   _____

▶ Work with a partner to ask and answer the questions. Look back at the reading if you cannot agree on the answers.

Using Evidence to Support Ideas

It is very important to support ideas with examples, statistics, and explanations. For example, in paragraph 2 the author says, "BASE … jumping has one of the sporting world's highest fatality rates." This is followed by, "in its eighteen-year history, forty-six people have been killed."

▶ Find other examples of supporting information by going through the reading again and completing the following table. The first one has been done for you.

Idea	Support
1. Participation in extreme sports is way up.	Snowboarding has grown 113 percent in five years and now boasts nearly 5.5 million participants.
2. More Americans are getting hurt.	a.
	b.
	c.
3. In the past, life was full of risk.	a.
	b.
	c.
	d.
	e.
4.	a. Life expectancy increased
	b. Violent crime down
	c.
	d.
5.	The example of Joy Marr

▶ Check your answers with a partner. Refer to the article if necessary. Discuss why the evidence is convincing in each case.

Reacting to the Information

▶ The comments on the left were written in response to the article you just read. The statements on the right express different opinions. Read each comment quickly and match it with the opinion that summarizes it the best.

Comment

1. _____ Taking part in risky activities makes us feel alive. It also satisfies our curiosity about our abilities—and how we handle challenge. It can completely focus your mind.

2. _____ Extreme sports are mostly solo activities that fail to teach us the valuable lessons of traditional sports—teamwork, cooperation, good sportsmanship, and friendship. This is not social progress.

3. _____ Although taking part in risky activities may certainly be thrilling for the individual, the dangerous consequences affect the lives of not only the risk takers but also the families and partners.

4. _____ In today's world, millions of people live in fear every single day of their lives, but there are a few who are so bored by their secure, middle-class existence that they jump off bridges to play with death. Why not put that desire for thrill into something meaningful, such as becoming a firefighter or brain surgeon? Or why not volunteer for work in some war-filled country?

Opinion

a. Risk takers are selfish.

b. Risk takers are bored.

c. Risk taking makes us better people.

d. Risk taking teaches us nothing.

▶ Check your answers with a partner. Then discuss the following.

1. Which comments do you agree with or not agree with and why?
2. What is the general opinion of risk takers?

▶ State your own opinion in one or two sentences.

Evaluating the Information

▶ To *stereotype* means to assume that certain people have certain characteristics. Very often that is not the case. So is it really true that people who participate in extreme activities do so only for the thrill and excitement? And is it really true that they are selfish, crazy, and fearless?

❯Paired Readings

▶ Climbing Mount Everest is still the most dangerous adventure known to mankind: for every four people who reach the peak, one dies in the effort. The following readings are personal accounts of two people who made it to the top. Choose one of the accounts and work with a partner who is reading the same one.

❶Meeting the Challenge

Understanding Underlying Ideas

> **> Reading Tip**

Inference The reader sometimes has to **infer** what the writer is feeling or thinking. If the writer says, "The mountain is a mystical, majestic place," he means he really appreciates his surroundings. ■

▶ **Scanning/Highlighting** Read the article and highlight the sections that help you understand the following:

- Jamie's appreciation of his surroundings
- His reasons for climbing Mt. Everest
- How he felt on the way up
- His actions on the summit

▶ Talk to your partner about the article using only the highlighted information.

Jamie Clarke

❶ The mountain environment is a mystical, majestic place. From the top of the tallest mountain in the world—the place the Sherpa people of Nepal call *Sagarmatha*, meaning "Forehead in the Sky"—the world below us curves away across the Tibetan Plateau to the north and across Nepal and Northern India to the south. Above, only a brilliant blue sky lies between us and the heavens.

❷ This is a place among all places to comprehend the power of creation. It is a place that, above all, should elicit our respect and responsible behavior. Everest is not about dying. It is in every sense about being fully alive.

❸ Men and women climb mountains for many reasons, most of them personal. For us, climbing Everest gave us the satisfaction of knowing we had accomplished the most difficult task most people could ever imagine. But personal success, even as we measure it by our climbing, is only meaningful when it leads us to better our performance in everything we do, to be different people today than we were yesterday, and to make a greater contribution to the world around us.

❹   This was our third Everest expedition. In 1991 and again in 1994, we had gone to the mountain but failed to make the summit due to bad weather. After three years of preparation, we and the other members of our team arrived at Everest's southern base camp in early April, 1997, determined to reach the top this time.

❺   On May 5, we were ready to begin our summit push when, with a roar like an express train, jet-stream winds dropped onto the mountain and whipped plumes of snow off the upper slopes of Everest, killing five climbers on the north side. We waited for two weeks. By May 22, we were ready again. Seventy climbers from many countries were on the mountain that night. Suddenly the wind stopped. Under a crystal-clear full moon, we hurriedly ate and dressed. At 11:30 P.M., we stepped out onto the steep southeast shoulder of Mount Everest.

❻   It was like going onstage. We had butterflies in our stomachs and our minds wandered. Was our conditioning suited to the challenge? Would we be distracted by the state of other climbers? Would the winds try to blow us off the ridge?

❼   I knew within the first hour that it was going to be a strong climb when I kept overtaking my Sherpa. I sensed that something extraordinary was happening. By the time we reached the Balcony, I was alone with two Sherpas.

❽   I was transfixed by the rising sun on my right and the setting moon on my left. The immense shadow of Everest played across the clouds, and I imagined myself as a tiny dot trailing on the edge of the mountain. I felt it was a day for which I had been born. I was so filled with joy that I was giggling into my oxygen mask.

9   The most sobering moment in the climb came at the Hillary Step, a rock named for Sir Edmund Hillary that is less than 330 feet below the summit. In the middle of a tangle of ropes hung the body of Bruce Herrod, a South African who died on Everest in the spring of 1996. Pete Atans, an experienced American climber, had already discovered the body and was struggling to free it. I stopped to help. What might have been a simple task at sea level was treacherous and complicated on the rocks at this altitude, but we managed. In our own quiet ceremony, Pete and I committed the body to the mountain.

10   I then moved up onto the Summit Ridge. I can only describe it as a homecoming, even though I had never been there before. I felt I was standing on familiar ground. I knew this place and felt welcome.

11   Seven and a half hours after leaving the camp, Gyalbu and I joined the New Zealand team on the summit. I spent forty-five minutes enjoying the view from the top of the world and taking the obligatory pictures. As the New Zealanders began to drift from the top, three of us remained gazing into the shadow-filled valleys from the only place that earthly shadows could not touch. Soon my Sherpa friends began their descent. I lingered, utterly alone, standing with one foot in Nepal and the other in Tibet. I opened my arms, surrendered to the moment, turned 360 degrees, and saw the edges of the world dropping in all directions.

12   Although I was alone, I felt I was joined by my family, my friends, the people who shared our dream, and the thousands of schoolchildren around the world who had been following our expedition in their classrooms via the Internet. It was a shared achievement because I could not have done it by myself. It was a moment of complete happiness.

❷ Conquering Fear

Understanding Underlying Ideas

▶ **Scanning/Highlighting** Read the article and highlight the sections that help you understand the following:

- How afraid Alan felt and what he did about it
- His unwillingness to risk his life
- His actions on the summit
- Lessons learned

▶ Talk to your partner about the article using only the highlighted information.

Alan Hobson

❶ As we started up the slope above the South Column, I was struck by how steep and hard the ice was. We were not using a fixed rope, and it became clear that the farther we moved from camp, the greater the danger became. As the angle of the slope increased, I focused on what would save my life, rather than on what might kill me.

❷ By 1 A.M., I found myself mysteriously falling behind the rest of our group. Realizing that I might not be thinking clearly, I asked one of my Sherpas, Kami Tsering, to check my oxygen. I suddenly became cold and told him, "We have to go down—now!" But instead of turning around, he walked up to me and announced: "Nineteen ninety-one expedition—no summit. Nineteen ninety-four—no summit. This expedition: very important summit."

❸   Kami discovered I had been drawing on an empty oxygen bottle. He hooked up a new bottle for me, and I felt an immediate psychological and physical boost. I knew that if I could move, I could stay warm. So we trudged on, feeling confident, at least until the wind began gusting again at 2:30 A.M.

❹   The wild, blowing snow stole the moon, which had been lighting our way, and gave me a bad feeling about the mountain. Without warning, one of the gusts blasted me in the face and filled my hood with snow, which slipped down my back. At this point I wondered if I could continue, as I knew how quickly I would get cold up there.

❺   As Kami and I came over the crest of the southeast ridge, a whole new world opened up. I could see the entire ridge and the South Summit. We had enough oxygen left for a decent shot at the top.

❻   My other Sherpa, Tashi Tsering, was waiting on the Balcony—a shelf on the southeast ridge. "You need to let me know whether we can do it safely in the time allowed," I told him. "If we can't, we're going back down—right now." He turned to me and said, "No problem. Still early." I thought, "If the weather holds, we might just pull this off."

❼   But we still had to cross the part that scared me the most—a knife-edged ridge with a 9,000-foot drop on the right into Tibet and a 5,000-foot drop on the left into Nepal.

❽   Cranking my oxygen up as far as it would go, I wanted to make sure that I was in control. Even so, my legs started shaking and I told myself, "This is just horrendous. Don't look down over the edge into the abyss, Alan." Passing an ice hole on the way, I stared down in disbelief—all the way down to the Kangshung Glacier, 9,000 feet below. "Just look at your feet, and follow the footsteps," I told myself.

❾   I finally reached the summit, which is about ten feet long and just wide enough to stand on. Tattered prayer flags and a discarded survey instrument littered the place. It was a bit of an eyesore, but it was also a sight for sore eyes.

❿   Once there, I used my radio and announced, "Base camp: this is Hobson. I confirm arrival on the summit of Tashi Tsering, Kami Tsering, and myself at 9 A.M., May 23, 1997. Half the dream is done. If there is a lesson here, it's that if you hang on to your dreams long enough, you can achieve them." Then I started to cry with joy.

⓫   Within fifteen minutes I had the pictures I needed to prove where I had been. But I had no desire to look at the view because I was still focused on not making any mistakes, on making my country proud—and on making it down alive. On Everest, it only counts if you make the round trip, and I didn't want anyone to be able to say, "I told you he couldn't do it."

⓬   On the way down I removed my mask because of an oxygen flow problem, suffering second-degree burns to my face as a result. I was so tired that my legs gave out and I fell—fortunately, I was clipped to a fixed rope at the time. I took some clexamethasone, a fast-acting anti-inflammatory, and things improved dramatically. By 2:30 in the afternoon, I was back at Camp IV. I was excited, satisfied, and exhausted.

⓭   We went to Everest with the personal goal of attaining the summit, but we also strove for a purpose higher than to simply stand on top of the world. With our adventure safely concluded, our goal will be to demonstrate how the lessons we learned on Everest can be applied to the world of business and the business of life. We want to do more than merely share a story about a couple of guys who climbed a mountain. In many ways, what we did was irrelevant. What is *not* irrelevant are the lessons we learned along the way: how to work as a team, how to overcome setbacks, how to deal with failure, how to push through pain and discomfort, and how to make dreams come true, whatever the obstacles. From Everest, we learned that it is unrealistic to expect to have success without failure. Failure is an integral part of success, because it is from failure that we learn.

◗Comparing the Readings

Retelling the Information

◖ Work with someone who read a different article. Using your highlighting, take turns telling the stories of Jamie Clarke and Alan Hobson. Based on the information from both readings, make a profile (description) of people who participate in extreme activities, such as climbing Mt. Everest. Use the following outline to help you. Write the information in note form.

Reasons for climbing   _____

_____

Feelings during the climb   _____

_____

Reaction to reaching the summit   _____

_____

How the experience will be used   _____

_____

◖ Use the information in the profile to support or destroy the opinions on risk takers discussed on page 11. Reevaluate your own opinion to see if it has changed.

❯Vocabulary Building

Word Form

▶ **A** Study these five words and their forms. Then choose the correct form for each part of speech in the chart below. These words are commonly found in general and academic texts.

survive (v.)	achieve (v.)	function (v.)	minimize (v.)	participate (v.)
survival (n.)	achievable	function	minimal	participant
survivor (n.)	achieving	functional	minimum	participatory
surviving (adj.)	achiever	functionally	minimizing	participation
	achievement	functioning		

Verb	Noun	Adjective	Adverb
achieve	1.	1.	
	2.	2.	
function	1.	1.	1.
		2.	
minimize	1.	1.	
		2.	
participate	1.	1.	
	2.		

▶ Compare your list with a partner.

▶ **B** Write three sentences using words from the list. Use different parts of speech.

Using Punctuation: Commas

Recognizing how punctuation is used can help us make sense of what we are reading. Commas are used to show a list of related terms, which can be nouns, adjectives, or actions in the form of single words or phrases.

Example (from paragraph 8 in the reading "Life on the Edge"): "Previous generations did not need to seek out risk; it showed up uninvited and regularly: *global wars, childbirth complications, diseases and pandemics from the flu to polio, dangerous products,* and even the *cold-war threat* of mutually assured destruction."

The commas indicate that there are five types of risks.

▶ Complete the following exercise. All the examples are taken from the reading on pages 6–8.

1. (Paragraph 1) What four things does Chance McGuire pray for?

   _____   _____

   _____   _____

2. (Paragraph 1) What three actions is he doing?

   _____   _____

   _____

3. (Paragraph 1) What three feelings are expressed in his war cry?

   _____   _____

   _____

4. (Paragraph 4) What are the three characteristics of activities Americans are participating in?

   _____   _____

   _____

5. (Paragraph 4) In which three activities has participation declined?

   _____   _____

   _____

6. (Paragraph 9) What three diseases no longer exist in the United States?

   _____   _____

   _____

▶ Check your answers with a partner. Find other examples of commas in lists in the reading.

Expanding Your Language

Speaking

▶ **A Interviewing** Answer this questionnaire on risk taking. Check (✔) what is true or false for you.

	True	False
1. I do not like my opinions being challenged.	_____	_____
2. I would rather be an accountant than a TV anchor.	_____	_____
3. I believe that I control my destiny.	_____	_____
4. I am a highly creative person.	_____	_____
5. I do not like trying exotic foods.	_____	_____
6. Friends would call me a thrill seeker.	_____	_____
7. I like to challenge authority.	_____	_____
8. I prefer familiar things to new things.	_____	_____
9. I am known for my curiosity.	_____	_____
10. I would rather not travel abroad.	_____	_____
11. I am easily bored.	_____	_____
12. I have never gotten a speeding ticket.	_____	_____
13. I am extremely adventurous.	_____	_____
14. I need a lot of stimulation in my life.	_____	_____
15. I would rather work for a salary than for a commission.	_____	_____
16. Making my own decisions is very important to me.	_____	_____

▶ Go to page 273 to evaluate yourself.

▶ **B** Interview three people who completed their questionnaires. Compare your information. Discuss the following:

- What did the questionnaire show about you?
- Do you agree with the result? Why or why not? Give examples from your experience to support your answer.

▶ Report on the similarities and differences in your group to others in the class.

▶ **C Discussion** Using the information in this chapter and any information of your own, discuss the following:

- Is risk-taking behavior something we are born with, or does it depend on the way we are brought up?
- What are the advantages of risk taking?
- If we feel that we are not taking enough risks, what can we do?

Writing

▶ **A Reaction Writing** Write your reaction to the following: (a) what you now think about risk takers; (b) whether or not you consider yourself a risk taker; (c) whether or not taking risks in general is a good idea.

▶ **B Personal Writing** Think of a time when you were very nervous about doing something, but you still did it. Examples might be going on a journey or changing jobs. Think about why you were nervous, what made you do it anyway, and how you felt afterwards. Make a short outline of your ideas in note form. Use your notes to write a one-page account of this incident.

 *Online Study Center*   For additional activities, go to the ***Reading Matters*** Online Study Center at *college.hmco.com/pic/wholeythree2e.*

2 Taking a Break Responsibly: Eco-Tourism

Chapter Openers

What Do You Think?

▶ Think about the following statements. Circle *T* for true and *F* for false. Be ready to explain your answers.

1. T F   The concept of taking a vacation has existed only for the past 100 years.

2. T F   People take longer vacations now than in the past.

3. T F   People take more frequent vacations now than in the past.

4. T F   Advances in technology are making it hard for people to take time off.

5. T F   Taking a vacation requires a lot of time and money.

▶ Compare your answers with a partner. Give reasons or examples to support what you say.

Personalizing

▶ Answer these questions for yourself.

1. What do you do on weekends or days off?
2. Given the choice, would you rather
   a. watch TV or a movie at home?
   b. go out to a theater or concert?
3. Which of the following is the perfect length for a vacation?
   a. less than 5 days
   b. 5–15 days
   c. 1 month
   d. more than 3 months
4. Where do you like to go for your vacations?

5. Which of the following is important in determining where you go? Why?
   a. food
   b. weather
   c. accommodations
   d. night life
   e. nature activities
   f. historic sites

▶ Compare your answers with a partner or in a small group.

Exploring and Understanding Reading

Previewing

> ▶ Reading Tip

Previewing is a useful reading skill. One way to preview is to **read the title** and **subtitle(s)**, and **look at the pictures** and **captions** (if any). ■

The idea of taking a vacation is a relatively new concept and an evolving one, with the line between work and play now becoming blurred by communications technology. The following reading is about how this concept developed.

▶ Read only the title and the subtitle, and then predict three ideas that will be discussed.

1. _____

2. _____

3. _____

Skimming

▶ Skim the reading and see if your predictions were correct. If you think you were wrong, change your prediction. Check the statement that most accurately reflects the information.

Paid vacations began when

1. _____ people started having more time.

2. _____ there was a change in work style.

3. _____ people started having more money.

The Rise and Fall of Vacations

By Felicia R. Lee

1   Once upon a time, the rich played when the mood struck and almost everybody else worked on their farms all week, relaxing for one day at the end of the week. Although August is now established as top vacation time, few people realize that their paid vacation is a fairly recent phenomenon. The word "vacation" was not even in the dictionary until the middle of the nineteenth century.

2   According to historians, vacation is a reflection of what is happening in society in terms of work and resources available. "You can't have vacations without a certain kind of class with the resources and the time to take vacations," said Cindy S. Aron, an associate professor of history at the University of Virginia. "That did not really happen until the first half of the twentieth century."

3   The popular vacation owes its birth to such factors as the changing nature of work and the rise of the railroad. In the nineteenth century, most people in North America were farmers, artisans, or self-employed in some way. Wealthy people went off to play while others went away primarily for their health. But as the industrial revolution took place, North America was transformed from an agricultural into an urban-industrial society, and by the end of the century more men were working for a salary in the growing corporate world. Working for industry meant working by the clock. People started separating work from life. They started thinking in terms of "after work," weekends, and retirement. Vacation places started to take shape, therefore, as there developed a new middle class that had money in its pockets, some free time, and a taste for amusement.

❹   Interestingly enough, however, this division between work and life is now becoming blurred again. The technological revolution that we are living in at present has brought with it cellular telephones, fax machines, e-mail, and the Internet. This has made people much more available. Combine this with the American anxiety to work harder in order to do more, buy more, and be better, and what happens very often is that people continue to work even while on vacation. Indeed, the trend now seems to be that, although North Americans are getting more paid leave then they did ten years ago, they are taking shorter but more frequent vacations. And sure enough, the computer and the cellular phone go along too.

Note Taking

 Reading Tip

Note taking is a useful way to make a **record** of the **important information** you get from **reading**. You can use notes to explain or write about what you have read. Remember to **use** only **key words** and **phrases** when you write notes. ▪

○ **Understanding Reasons** The article discusses the development of vacations using three different time periods. Complete the following outline to show the development as well as the reasons for it.

Main Points (time period)	Details (reasons)
A. Before industrial revolution	1. Only rich had money & time
	2. No real vacation
B. During and after industrial revolution	1. _____
	2. _____
	3. People ruled by the clock
C. Technological revolution	1. _____
	2. _____
	3. _____

○ **1.** Compare your notes with a partner. If you do not have the same or similar ideas in your outline, check the information in the reading.

2. Use your notes to explain the information. Take turns talking about each stage.

 Tip

When **talking from notes**, try not to read them. **Look quickly at your notes** to remind yourself of the information. Then **look up at your partner** and **relate** the **information** in a conversational way. Use **complete sentences** and add **extra explanations** if necessary. ▪

Applying the Information

▷ **A** Discuss the following questions using both the information you just read and your own personal experience.

1. Are people indeed taking shorter, more frequent vacations?
2. What kind of break would somebody who works hard prefer?

▷ **B** The following is a list of some activities that Americans like to do while on vacation. Rank them in terms of how popular you think each one is. Use *1* for most popular and *5* for least popular. Be prepared to support your choice. Compare your ranking with that of a partner.

Activity	Rank
Gambling	_____
National/State Park	_____
Golfing/tennis/skiing	_____
Museum	_____
Theme/Amusement Park	_____
Shopping	_____
Beach	_____

▷ Check your ranking against the chart at the back of the chapter on page 274. Then discuss the following:

1. How accurate were you?
2. Which activity is actually the most popular?
3. Which activity is the least popular?
4. Why do you think that is the case?
5. Of the activities listed above, which do you think is beneficial for the environment? Which do you think harms the environment?
6. Should the impact on the environment be a consideration when people are deciding on a vacation?

Previewing

▷ The following reading is about a fairly recent type of vacation. Read only the title and the subtitle, and then predict three ideas that will be discussed.

1. _____
2. _____
3. _____

Surveying

❯ Reading Tip

Surveying is another useful reading skill. It means to **read the introduction** and read the **first sentence of every paragraph** after that. It gives the reader a good idea of what the main points of the reading are. ■

◗ Survey the reading. Read the introduction (paragraphs 1–2) and the first sentence of every paragraph after that. Check to see if your preview predictions were correct. If you think you were wrong, change your predictions.

Eco-Tourism

The Eco-Tourism project took off quickly; Spending our money in the world's most threatened areas can help save them.

❶   Imagine a vacation where one day you hike through one of the world's richest rain forests, the next you climb 2,000-year-old Mayan temples while spider monkeys turn somersaults overhead, and the third you sleep late in your $6-a-night hotel room, swim in crystal-clear Lake Peten Itza, or wander the cobbled streets of a hilly city like Flores, in Northern Guatemala, watching mothers deliver their children to school in a dugout canoe as an army of roosters and dogs parades by.

❷   Now imagine doing all that without an ounce of guilt, because you're also helping save the rain forests and soften the effects of global warming. Welcome to the wonderful new world of eco-tourism.

❸   The idea is simple: rain forests and other prized habitats attract tourists, who bring dollars that provide jobs. Governments and local residents quickly realize that if the forests go, so does tourism, which makes a more effective case for preservation than speeches by environmentalists. The ecological rewards are even richer if guides can explain how rain forests absorb carbon dioxide, the chief catalyst in global warming, how industrialized countries encourage deforestation by buying products such as lumber, and how the cutting could end if rich nations helped create economic alternatives for the starving peasants who plunder the forests. Visitors from the United States, Canada, Japan, and Europe presumably would take those lessons home and urge their elected officials to fight against the dangers of pollution.

❹   Although eco-tourism was started by travel agencies to make business, it is now being promoted by environmental groups and environmental officials. They used to see tourists as a growing threat to the land, but now they are welcoming them everywhere—from the jungles of northern Guatemala to the southernmost tip of Costa Rica. That transformation in attitudes is partly because tourists who trek through the jungles and climb the ruins are typically not of the white-shoes-and-fancy-hotels type. Most are there because they appreciate nature and are willing to live in simple lodgings and eat simple fish-and-rice dishes. An even more compelling reason, according to officials from the World Wildlife Fund, the Nature Conservancy, and other international organizations, is that they are losing the battle to save the forests and are willing to try anything. A recent United Nations survey showed that, for every ten acres of trees cut in the tropics, only one new acre is planted. Other attempts to curb the destruction, such as teaching farmers to harvest rather than cut the trees, are being tried, but they take a lot of time. Tourism, on the other hand, is a sure bet to bring in money and, as Costa Rica has proven, it can pick up steam overnight. "Opening parks to tourism obviously has a negative effect on their biological diversity," said Rodrigo Gamez, the Costa Rican environmental advisor during the 80s. "But it is a price we have to pay to guarantee the protection of the whole park system."

❺   Costa Rica's tourism industry has known for years that nature is an exceedingly effective marketing tool, one that encourages North Americans to go to their country rather than somewhere like Jamaica, where packages cost a third as much, said Roberto Morales, North American director of the private Costa Rica National Tourist Bureau. The bureau's ads entice visitors with the prospect of visiting a cloud forest in the morning and an equally exotic but dramatically different dry forest that afternoon. They promote bicycle tours, bird-watching expeditions, and climbs up volcanoes. And they end with jingles like, "Costa Rica: Naturally Thrilling." The variety for eco-tourists is great in Costa Rica. A limited number of rooms are available at and near the La Selva Biological Station, which boasts more than 400 species of birds, 4,000 kinds of insects, and 120 animals, including tapirs, beasts that look like a cross between an elephant and a cow. Tourists can sit in the sun listening to strange birdcalls, watching a clear mountain stream, and being distracted by exotic butterflies. Indeed, one has only to look at the numbers to see how successful eco-tourism in Costa Rica is. In 1980, 60,000 Americans visited the country. Fifteen years later, this number had almost doubled to 102,000.

❻   While Costa Rica is helping to define the current generation of eco-tourism, Bill Garrett, editor of *National Geographic* magazine, is making plans for the next generation. He has proposed carving out a vast network of trails spanning parts of the rain forests of the Yucatan Peninsula in Mexico, northern Belize, and northern Honduras, along with most of the Peten wilderness in northern Guatemala. The trails, called *La Ruta Maya*, or the Route of the Mayas, would take visitors to spectacular ruins of that ancient Indian culture, some of which date to 250 B.C., and to more recent architecture from the Spanish colonial period. They would reach pristine beaches ideal for snorkeling and fishing, as well as dense tropical rain forests and charming villages. And in the middle of the seven-million-acre network would be a three-million-acre Maya Peace Park.

❼   Along the way, research stations would coexist with tourist facilities. And rather than rely on conventional roads, which could also be used by loggers and others to remove the riches of the forests, Garrett envisions a narrow-gauge electric railroad, powered mainly by the sun—"the kind of quiet, non-polluting transportation that would allow tourists to have a good time without harming anything." Revenues from the new enterprises would provide jobs for local *campesinos*, or peasant farmers, and would support the guards, park rangers, and other officials needed to protect parks here and in the three other countries.

❽   Smaller eco-tourism ventures already are being tried across Central America. For instance, tourists can stay in Flores, renting cars by day to visit the ruins in Tikal or nearby rain forests, returning in time for a swim in the lake and enjoying a dinner featuring *petenia esplendia*, a succulent local fish. The strange blend of Third and First Worlds becomes apparent when a short blackout is greeted calmly by local residents but arouses multilingual excitement from French, German, Canadian, and American visitors. Accommodations also are available in Tikal and at the biological preserve halfway between the two towns at a restaurant-lodging house called *Gringo Perdido*—the "Lost Gringo."

❾   Eco-tourism in Costa Rica, Guatemala, and elsewhere faces imposing obstacles, however and has to be implemented very carefully. In the Peten, for instance, an estimated 250 peasants are moving in each day, cutting forests to build thatched houses and to clear land for corn, beans, and other crops. Jobs from tourism must come soon or there will not be much forest left, officials warn. "Eco-tourism can be big business and very good for Costa Rica," said Rebecca Butterfield, who runs a project testing how various species of trees grow in reclaimed farmland. "But you have to be very careful to really use local people as guides, hotel workers, and on other jobs. If the workers are all urban people or foreigners, it won't help at all, and locals won't see the benefit of preserving land."

❿   Eco-tourism itself can pose a threat, especially if it involves massive clearing or building roads that make it easier for cattle farmers, loggers, and others to remove their harvests. Conservationists already are worrying about those issues in the Tikal area, where the Westin chain is planning a large hotel. In Costa Rica, the biggest threat may be tourism's booming success, which leaves many tourists with a bad taste of the country—during peak season, the country is short on hotel rooms, rental cars, and other necessities. Morales, a tourism officer, said his organization is making a concerted effort to convince tourists that the country's natural attractions are as compelling and the accommodations much better after peak season, which runs December through February.

Adapted from *The Boston Globe* and *Edmonton Journal*

Getting the Main Ideas

> **Tip**

Sometimes an idea can cover more than one paragraph. ▪

▶ Write the main idea for each paragraph or group of paragraphs.

Paragraphs 1–2   Introduction – Example of eco-tourism activities

Paragraph 3   _____

Paragraph 4   _____

Paragraph 5   _____

Paragraphs 6–7   Future eco-tourism projects

Paragraph 8   _____

Paragraphs 9–10   _____

▶ Compare your answers with a partner. If you do not have the same or similar ideas, check the information in the reading.

Scanning

▶ **Using Main Ideas to Find Details** Read each question and, using your list of main ideas, predict which paragraph the answer will be in. Look in that paragraph and underline the relevant information. Answer the question in note form and in your own words as much as possible.

1. What are some eco-tourism activities?

    _____

2. Why are governments and local residents interested in keeping the forests?

    _____

3. Who started the idea of eco-tourism?

   _____

4. How did environmentalists initially feel about tourists?

   _____

5. Give two reasons why they changed their minds.

   _____

6. How does Costa Rica attract tourists?

   _____

7. a. How many countries will be involved in Bill Garrett's project?

   _____

   b. What different types of activities will be included in that project?

   _____

   c. What type of transport will tourists have?

   _____

   d. What will be done with the profit?

   _____

8. Why is it important to use local people in the eco-tourism business?

   _____

9. In what way can eco-tourism itself be a problem?

   _____

10. a. What is the biggest problem in Costa Rica? Why?

   _____

   b. What is being proposed as solution?

   _____

▶ Check your answers with a partner or in a small group. Refer to what you highlighted if you disagree.

Using Examples

The author of this article uses many examples in order to support, explain, or clarify a point. Most of the time the author first makes the point and then gives the example(s).

> *Example (paragraph 4):* Environmental groups and officials … are welcoming them (tourists) everywhere—*from the jungles of northern Guatemala to the southernmost tip of Costa Rica.*

The phrases *"jungles of northern Guatemala, southernmost tip of Costa Rica"* are examples of the places where tourists are being welcomed.

▶ Find the examples given for each of the points below:

Points	Examples
1. … they are losing the battle to save the forests (paragraph 4)	
2. The variety for tourists is great in Costa Rica (paragraph 5)	
3. Smaller eco-tourism ventures … across Central America (paragraph 8)	
4. First World (paragraph 8)	
5. Eco-tourism in Costa Rica, … faces imposing obstacles (paragraph 9)	
6. … a bad taste of the country (paragraph 10)	

▶ Check your work with a partner.

Reacting to the Information

◗ Use the information from the article and your own experience to discuss the following questions.

1. Define eco-tourism in your own words.
2. What are the advantages of eco-tourism?
3. Have you ever been an "eco-tourist"? If yes, describe your experience.
4. Explain what you understand from the statement made by Rodrigo Gamez at the end of paragraph 4: *"Opening parks to tourism obviously has a negative effect on their biological diversity. But it is a price we have to pay to guarantee the protection of the whole park system."* Do you agree with him? Why or why not?
5. Do you think eco-tourism is successful today? Why or why not?

Previewing

◗ Read the title and subtitle of the following reading and answer the questions about each.

Title

1. What do you think the word "Paradise" refers to?
2. What is the author implying when he says "Trouble in Paradise?"

Subtitle

1. According to the subtitle, did eco-tourism start as a big or small idea?
2. What is it now?
3. What is implied about the effect of eco-tourism on the Earth?
4. What is the author trying to do by asking a question?

◗ Compare your answers with a partner. Together, decide on what the article will be about.

Predicting

◗ **Predicting the Organization from the Introduction** Some authors use examples in the introduction that help the reader determine the organization of the article. Knowing the organization makes understanding the article much easier.

◗ Read the examples in paragraphs 1–2 and answer the following:

1. According to paragraph 1, is eco-tourism a good thing or a bad thing?
2. According to paragraph 2, is eco-tourism a good thing or a bad thing?
3. What does that tell you about how the article is organized?

Surveying

> **Tip**

Sometimes the first sentence of one paragraph can help you identify the idea of the previous paragraph as well. *Example (paragraph 4): "Yet with that tremendous growth has come a mounting backlash, and complaints that maybe eco-tourism isn't such a good idea for the environment after all."* *"Yet"* means that paragraph 4 gives a different position from paragraph 3; *"maybe eco-tourism isn't such a good idea for the environment"* indicates that paragraph 3 was about the benefits, so paragraph 4 is about problems. ◼

▶ **A** Read the first sentence of paragraphs 3–12. Use key words to help you identify the main idea of each paragraph.

▶ **B** Complete the following to make an outline of the main ideas of the article.

Main Idea	Paragraph(s)
Benefits of eco-tourism	3
_____	_____
Debate: Pros/Cons of eco-tourism	_____
The origin of eco-tourism	_____
_____	_____
Negative consequences	_____
Solution	_____
Conclusion	12

▶ Compare your outline with a partner. Make any changes you think are necessary.

Trouble in Paradise

A modest concept pushed by idealists is now the fastest-growing sector of the tourism industry. Can the Earth survive eco-tourism?

❶   For twenty years John Gray was just another unknown tour operator guiding customers through remote jungle rivers by sea kayak, pointing out monkeys and rare birds. That all changed when Gray discovered a series of exquisite tidal sea caves and isolated lagoons about a mile off the coast of Phuket, Thailand. Stunned by their crystalline waters, delicate stalactite formations, and exotic fish stocks, he launched a classic eco-tourism operation, hiring local tour operators and giving them control of the company. He limited the number of tourists taken in daily, making sure not to upset the fragile local ecosystems. The tours were a hit, and word began to spread.

❷   That's when the trouble started. Soon greedy businessmen arrived from as far away as Bangkok. Eventually no fewer than nineteen competitors had set up shop. "These places were absolutely pristine—it was like a time machine to before humans were on the planet," says Gray. "Now it's like a popular ski resort where you have to wait to get on a lift. The place is

mobbed." Armed collectors of highly prized edible birds' nests moved in, claiming it was their turf. Tourists began to rip down cave stalactites as souvenirs. In 1999, Gray started receiving death threats from local gangs demanding bribes for the bird's-nest collectors. Gray resisted—until one day a gunman pulled up and shot his local operations manager, severely wounding him. "I'm not going to talk about that," Gray says. "We're trying to put it behind us." But, according to press reports, he gave in and is now paying the extortion money to avoid more trouble from the nest collectors.

❸ Running an eco-friendly tour operation nowadays is not always as easy as it sounds. "Eco-tourism" started more than a decade ago as a dubious concept to protect fragile ecosystems by marketing them to governments and local people as profit-making assets. The goal was to develop tourism not by destroying the environment but by inviting foreign visitors to experience it as if they were natives. By some measures, it has surpassed the expectations of even the most devoted idealists. Eco-tourism today is one of the world's fastest-growing industries; Francesco Frangialli, secretary general of the World Tourism Organization, estimates eco-tourism is growing at a rate "maybe double, even triple" the rest of the industry. In May 2003, 1,100 representatives from more than 130 countries convened at a special United Nations conference in Quebec, Canada, to celebrate the International Year of Ecotourism. Aid agencies were on hand to discuss its development possibilities.

❹ Yet with that tremendous growth has come a mounting backlash, and complaints that maybe eco-tourism isn't such a good idea for the environment after all. Sure, governments now have more incentive to protect fragile environments. But indigenous groups from Indonesia to Brazil complain of being forced off these areas by ruthless developers. So many travelers are eager to get back to nature that they end up destroying it in the process. In parts of Nepal, hikers and campers have cut down so many trees for Himalayan campfires that the area is becoming deforested. There's even a growing movement of anti-globalization protesters and NGOs—non-governmental organizations—that have set up their own campaign called the "International Year of Stopping Eco-Tourism." Eco-tourism, says Anita Pleumaron of the Tourism Investigation and Monitoring Team in Bangkok, "has led to more environmental destruction, and harm to communities in the destinations. We are highly concerned that eco-tourism promotion and the U.N. endorsement of the International Year of Eco-Tourism will make the situation worse in the Third World."

❺   There's a lot at stake in this debate. With tourist trips expected to rise from 688 million in 2001 to more than 1.55 billion by 2020, many see eco-tourism as one of the best hopes for development in poor countries and the only path toward tourism that can be sustained in the long term—if it's done right. If it's done wrong, one need look no farther than the slopes of Mount Everest for a preview of what's to come: years of accumulated garbage and discarded equipment greet aspiring climbers like broken-down road signs all the way up the trail. "We have to find a direction to eco-tourism before any more damage is done," says Roger Wheelock, executive vice president and CEO of the Canadian Tourism Commission. "There's been a lack of understanding about what it is. And there are a lot of tourist enterprises that have gone into fragile environments that have not adopted any standards."

❻   It was never supposed to be this way. Eco-tourism grew out of the environmental movements of the 1970s and 1980s. A young Mexican architect crystallized the pitch. On weekend bird-watching expeditions, Hector Ceballos Lasurain noticed that scores of foreigners were also traveling to the same reserves. So when private developers unveiled a plan to move into pristine flamingo habitats in the Mexican Yucatan, the architect began selling a new concept he called "eco-tourism." "I argued that tourists would come and it would help the local people," he recalls. "I convinced the governor of the state of Yucatan, and it has been turned into a very successful nature reserve in Mexico. There used to be fishermen complaining. Now they make income as guides. This story could be repeated in many countries around the world."

❼   Indeed the benefits could. In the years that followed, eco-tourism became the basis for national tourism plans. In Ecuador, bitter battles used to be fought over Charles Darwin's famed Galapagos Islands, with fishermen at times spiting environmentalists by cutting the throats of endangered sea turtles. But when a national policy was put into effect to protect the endangered habitat and the area was marketed, tourists flocked from around the globe. Many of those same fishermen now work as guides—or have been chased away with security funded by park proceeds.

8   In southern India's Lake Periyar, poachers and impoverished locals were gradually destroying the state of Kerala's ancient wildlife sanctuary, which boasts some of the nation's older stands of cinnamon and sandalwood trees as well as wild elephants. With the population exploding, almost fifty percent of the jungle disappeared in just fifteen years. Then NGOs hired poachers—whose years in the jungle had made them highly attuned to animal tracks and smells—as guides and guards and began promoting the spot as a tourist destination. In the past four years, there has been no known case of successful poaching and more than 150 people have been arrested by their reformed colleagues.

9   The potential for other success stories is virtually unlimited. For many poor countries, tourism may offer the best hope for development. "Even a country like Saudi Arabia is opening up," says the World Tourism Organization's Frangialli. "I was in North Korea talking to them. Iran is working on a master plan for their tourism. Libya paid $1 million for a study. They all want tourists. And people like to discover the world; they are tired of mass tourism. And many countries don't have beaches. They can offer mountains and desert and unique cultures. Eco-tourism is the logical solution."

10   Yet if something isn't done, eco-tourism might become a victim of its own success. There seems no end to the exploitation of the trend: in the Philippines, Malaysian businessmen are already promoting an "eco-tourism casino." Even naturalists have begun to debate what exactly eco-tourism connotes. Take East Kootenay, British Columbia, for example, a 20,000-square-mile pristine wilderness area in the Canadian Rockies. The government there has granted concessions to six backcountry eco-lodges, eleven heli-skiing and heli-hiking operators, and scores of other naturalists referring to themselves as eco-tourists. A good thing, right? Tourists can get back to nature and develop an appreciation for the area's rugged beauty. Not necessarily, says Katarina Hartwig of the East Kootenay Environmental Society. She claims the local caribou population has plummeted from 2,300 to 1,885. Rare local wolves are disappearing, too. Nobody knows where they have gone. But Hartwig suspects it is the roar of the helicopters that is wreaking chaos. "It's endangering mountain caribou," Hartwig complains.

11   Solutions to the problems seem a long way off. In a series of meetings around the world, community representatives have complained about being left out of the planning process and of the problems caused by environmental damage. The result has been growing support among NGO types and activists for devising a uniform definition of eco-tourism that encapsulates both local involvement and a respect for nature. Some countries are already working to set up some sort of accreditation process for tour operators that would force them to prove they are eco-friendly. "Tourism is not a smoke-free industry," says Oliver Hillel of the United Nations Environmental Program. "It is exactly as polluting as any other major industry. Eco-tourism should be the response to that."

⓬   But how would such a system be enforced? Even with such a scheme, can fragile environments survive the armies of tourists expected to flood the trails in the coming years? To many it seems unlikely. Just ask John Gray, who readily acknowledges he has had second thoughts about his decision to make a foray into his "timeless" tidal caves. He says, "If I had known then what I know now, I would never have taken people into some of those caves." In hindsight, perhaps environmental groups, too, might have thought a little harder about what exactly it was they were trying to sell.

"Trouble in Paradise" by Adam Piore. From *Newsweek,* July 2, 2002. © Newsweek, Inc. All rights reserved. Reprinted by permission.

Note Taking

▶ **Pro/Con** Using your outline, group together the paragraphs that discuss:

a. the benefits of eco-tourism.
b. the negative consequences of eco-tourism.

▶ Read the paragraphs corresponding to each and highlight the important information.

▶ Use what you highlighted to make notes on both the benefits and the negative consequences.

Benefits	Negative Consequences
•	•
•	•
•	•
•	•
•	•
•	•

▶ Use your notes to talk about the benefits and negative consequences of eco-tourism. Take turns presenting the information.

Applying the Information

▷ **Making a Decision** Using the readings in the chapter, as well as your own knowledge and experience, discuss the following questions.

1. Do you agree with John Gray when he says, "If I had known then what I know now, I would never have taken people into some of those caves."?

2. Which of the following do you agree with the most and why?
   • Eco-tourism is harmful and should be stopped.
   • Eco-tourism is neither good nor bad. It depends on how it is being managed.

3. What can individuals like you and me contribute to ensuring that tourism does not destroy our environment?

Skimming

▷ The following article is about an individual, Bob Hoffman, who is trying to make a difference. Read through the article quickly and highlight the information about each of the following:

Background information on Bob Hoffman

Situation on Mount Everest

Bob's goal

How he reached his goal

People's reaction to his goal

Other benefits besides cleaning Mount Everest

▷ Discuss what you highlighted with a partner.

Everest: From Mountain to Molehill of Litter

❶   Bob Hoffman is the garbage man of Mount Everest, a title he's proud of and not quite ready to give up. Having already reached the top of the mountain in 1998, he returned in 2000 to attempt a full-scale cleanup of what had become known—because of increased traffic and fatigued climbers—as the world's highest garbage dump. Because of bad weather, Hoffman and his team had come up a bit short, clearing 650 of an estimated 800 discarded oxygen tanks at and above 21,000 feet. Pushing sixty, tired and injured with two frostbitten hands, Hoffman felt his Everest days were through. And then came the simple comment that would bring him back. "A reporter said, 'So, you'll let someone else finish the job?'" Hoffman recalls with a wide grin. "Now, that got me. It may not be glamorous being the garbage man of the high mountains, but it reminded me you have to see things through until the job is done."

❷   Hoffman returned to Nepal to lay the bureaucratic foundation for a 2002 Everest expedition referred to as "The Final Sweep," which should restore the mountain to its pristine state for the fiftieth anniversary of Edmund Hillary's first ascent in 1953.

❸   Not everyone approved of the mission. "That sort of money and effort could be better spent on things like education and cleaning up the area leading to Everest base camp, where tens of thousands of tourists come through each year, as opposed to the dozens who climb Everest," says Christine Boskoff, owner of the Seattle-based guide company Mountain Madness (formerly led by climber Scott Fischer, who died during the disastrous 1996 Everest season). "Everyone's doing their part up there already. I'm at fault for leaving trash sometimes, because maybe the risk was too high to bring it down," she says. "But overall, we try to leave the place better than we found it."

❹   Hoffman has no grand ideas about the importance of his efforts. "Sure, the world has far bigger problems than litter on Mount Everest," says Hoffman, "But we just hope to show people that if you can do something for the environment in the harshest conditions on the planet, you can do a little better right where you live."

❺   Hoffman smiles often and talks incessantly. He has a modest home with a green shag carpet, plaid couches, and wood paneling. Still, out in the yard is a playhouse. The sign above the door reads "Ali's House." Daughter Ali, or Alison, is now twenty-three. About the only luxury seems to be a massive Sony television; the main personal touch is a series of rocks suspended in Lucite—rocks from Everest's summit. Tents, oxygen masks, and even some of the older (circa 1960) oxygen bottles that he removed from Everest are stashed throughout his house.

❻   Hoffman says he got into climbing because it was "a way out of the boredom of my day-to-day job." (He just retired after decades as a United Airlines maintenance expert at nearby San Francisco International Airport.) He started climbing only in his mid-40s, and over the ensuing years reached the highest peaks on seven continents.

❼   Hoffman's passion for a cleaner Mount Everest began in 1992. Although he didn't make the summit on that trip, he did come away with a sense of despair at the sight of thousands of yellow and gray oxygen canisters that had accumulated over the years. Returning to Everest in 1995, this time as team leader, Hoffman told his group that they would be taking down more than they brought up. Other climbing teams followed suit, and gradually a reversing trend was set in motion. (Now climbers can be fined if they leave trash behind.) "It wasn't a moment too soon," Hoffman says. "There were hundreds of batteries, piles of fuel canisters, and mounds of pure garbage."

❽   Three years later, Hoffman and his teammates set a higher standard for themselves, starting when they began packing in the United States. Dry goods such as pudding and pancake mixes were emptied into zip-lock bags and placed into plastic storage drums. Climbing gear was cushioned not with Styrofoam peanuts, but with clothing to be donated to village children. "Years later now, I still see the zip-lock bags and drums used by villagers for keeping their food dry and the duffel bags they use to harvest crops," he says. "You wouldn't believe how primitive the conditions are there (in Nepal). We're talking about a village not even having a wheel. So you can imagine what these things mean to them."

❾   The Sherpas play a key role in Hoffman's treks: Picking up eight- to fifteen-pound oxygen tanks at Everest's famed Camp IV, a 26,000-foot "death zone" where the human body deteriorates by the minute, helped net many Sherpas upward of $5,000 each for their efforts—in a country where salaries average $300 a month.

❿   Hoffman doesn't take payment for his efforts, and insists that those climbing with him pay $30,000 for the trip, which includes a summit attempt. "If I have to pay out of my own pocket," Hoffman says, "so be it." Anything to get the job done.

Adapted from *USA Today*

Quotes   ▶ Comment on the following quotations.

1. "It may not be glamorous being the garbage man of the high mountains, but it reminded me you have to see things through until the job is done."

2. "That sort of money and effort could be better spent on things like education and cleaning up the area leading to Everest base camp, where tens of thousands of tourists come through each year, as opposed to the dozens who climb Everest."

3. "But we just hope to show people that if you can do something for the environment in the harshest conditions on the planet, you can do a little better right where you live."

Vocabulary Building

Word Form   ▶ **A** Study these five words and their forms. Then choose the correct form for each part of speech in the chart below. These words are commonly found in general and academic texts.

pollute (v.)   enforce (v.)   estimate (v.)   initiate (v.)   promote (v.)
pollutant (n.)   enforcement   estimation   initiation   promotion
pollution (n.)   enforcing   estimate   initiator   promotional
polluted (adj.)   overestimated   initiative   promoting
                                                                                 promoter

Verb	Noun	Adjective	Adverb
enforce	1.	1.	
estimate	1.	1.	
	2.		
initiate	1.		
	2.		
	3.		
promote	1.	1.	
	2.	2.	

▶ Compare your list with a partner.

▶ **B** Write three sentences using words from the list. Use different parts of speech.

Vocabulary in Context

 Tip

If you follow this procedure, you will find that you will remember word meanings much better than if you consulted the dictionary right away. ▪

▶ Words you already know can help you understand the meaning of a new word. Circle the words that help you guess the meaning of the word in boldface. Write your definition of the word. Then consult a dictionary to check your definition. Use each word in a sentence of your own making.

1. Eco-tourism itself can **pose** a threat, especially if it involves massive clearing or building roads that make it easier for cattle farmers, loggers, and others to remove their harvests.

   _____

2. Now it's like a popular ski resort where you have to wait to get on a lift. The place is **mobbed**.

   _____

3. But, according to press reports, he gave in and is now paying the **extortion** money to avoid more trouble from the nest collectors.

   _____

4. But when a national policy was put into effect to protect the endangered habitat, and the area was marketed, tourists **flocked** from around the globe.

   _____

5. Even naturalists have begun to debate what exactly eco-tourism **connotes**.

   _____

6. She claims the local caribou population has **plummeted** from 2,300 to 1,885.

   _____

7. "The final sweep" should restore the mountain to its **pristine** state.

   _____

8. The result has been growing support among NGO types and activists for devising a uniform definition of eco-tourism that **encapsulates** both local involvement and a respect for nature.

   _____

9. Other attempts to **curb** the destruction, such as teaching farmers to harvest rather than cut the trees, are being tried, but they take a lot of time.

   _____

▶ Check your answers. Work with a partner and take turns reading your definitions and the sentences you made.

Expanding Your Language

Speaking

▷ **A** Work with a partner or a small group. Tell each other whether the information you have read has made a difference in how you will plan your next vacation.

▷ **B** Interview

1. Make 5–7 interview questions to find out what kind of vacations your classmates take.

2. Compare your questions with a partner.

3. Together choose the best five questions.

4. Interview five people and report back to your partner.

5. Prepare a short report on the results of your interview and present it to the class.

Reading

▷ The following article is a guide to how to be a responsible eco-tourist. Read it and check (✔) the questions you would consider asking. Put a cross (✗) next to the ones you would not consider asking.

▷ Discuss the article with a partner. Take turns explaining what you think the purpose of each of the questions is. Also explain why you checked some questions and crossed others.

How to Be a Responsible Eco-Tourist

❶ The Maasai tribespeople of East Africa have been evicted from their traditional lands in order to accommodate safari tours and lodges. The Sioux of the American Black Hills often work as low-wage laborers in the white-owned tourism industry profiting from Sioux culture and lands. Large hotel chain restaurants often prevent local farmers and workers from reaping the benefits of tourism by importing food products to satisfy foreign visitors. In resort areas of Mexico and Hawaii, overbuilt beachfront hotels contribute to beach erosion and destruction of natural wetlands, and generate large amounts of garbage without adequate means of disposal. The fragile coral reefs of the Philippines and the Maldives have been significantly damaged, and dynamiting and mining for coral used to build resort facilities have depleted fisheries that sustain local people.

❷ Perhaps these sad facts don't put you in the holiday spirit. Reducing your footprint while traveling isn't always easy. Becoming an eco-tourist means looking at travel from a different perspective—seeing it not just for pleasure, but also for a purpose. The following guide should help you make some informed choices when planning your next vacation.

❸   Questions you can ask to help preserve *the environment* of the places you visit:

- Is the destination overcrowded or overdeveloped?
- Is the tour operator or guide aware of environmental concerns?
- Does the tour operator or guide contribute financially to conservation and preservation efforts?
- Are available accommodations environmentally sensitive?
- Are there any advisories, rules, or regulations regarding protected areas, water sources, or wildlife habitats?
- What behavior is appropriate when viewing wildlife?
- Will the trip support the work of conservation and preservation organizations?

❹   Questions you can ask to help preserve *the culture* of the places you visit:

- Are the tour operator and accommodations sensitive to the local culture?
- What are the host country's customs?
- What are the local conventions in regard to dress? (Remember that you are a guest and behave accordingly.)
- Where, how, and when should you take photographs?
- How well do you know the language? (Speaking to local people in their language demonstrates your respect for their culture.)
- Are there any local cultural events? Your support helps local performers preserve their heritage.
- How does tourism affect the local culture?

❺   Questions you can ask to help *sustain local economies:*

- Are the lodges, hotels, tour guides, and transportation services locally owned and operated?
- Do the tour company and accommodations employ local people and purchase local products?
- What are the local restaurants and local markets?
- Are the souvenirs you're buying made by local craftspeople and artisans?
- Are there access fees to protected sites? (Such fees may support local efforts to conserve those areas.)
- What is a fair price for the goods or services offered by the local people? (You should make every effort to offer a fair price.)

❻   Questions you can ask to familiarize yourself with an outfitter's *level of eco-responsibility*.

- What is the outfitter's travel philosophy and under what standards does it operate?

- How does the outfitter work with local authorities to manage the impact of tourism on the environment and the community?
- What role do local people play in the organization and what training do they receive?
- Is the organization involved in community projects or in supporting local not-for-profit organizations? Is it possible for travelers to be involved in those projects?
- What education is provided to travelers before and during the trip about local culture and the environment? For example, does the outfitter provide guidelines travelers need to follow to minimize their impact on the communities they're visiting?

❼   Your trip will be influenced by how connected you feel to the local culture and the environment. That connection will depend on the type of restaurants that you eat in, the neighborhood in which you are staying, the interactions you have with the local community, and your understanding of local traditions. Your experience of the local environment will be greatly enriched if you feel you are in an unspoiled site and if you sense that you are leaving it intact for others to enjoy. Bon voyage!

Earth Island Journal

Writing

▶ Think of a vacation that you particularly enjoyed. Write a short report describing your vacation and explaining why you enjoyed it.

Read On: Taking It Further

Reading Questionnaire

▶ Researchers have found that the more you read, the more your vocabulary will increase and the more you will understand. A good knowledge of vocabulary will help you to do well in school and in business. To find out more about making reading a habit for yourself, answer the following questionnaire.

▶ Rank the activities that you think help you to increase the language you understand. Mark *1* beside the one that helps you the most when learning a new language, *2* beside the second, and so on. Mark the same number if you find two activities that help you equally.

_____   Memorizing word lists

_____   Reading texts that are assigned for class

_____   Reading texts that I choose for myself

_____   Talking about the texts that we read for class

_____ Talking about the texts that I choose for myself

_____ Learning how to guess the meanings of words that are new

_____ Doing vocabulary exercises for readings that we study in class

_____ Doing extra vocabulary exercises for homework

_____ Studying the dictionary to find out the parts of words

_____ Using the dictionary to look up new words I don't understand

▶ Discuss your questionnaire with a partner. Do not change your answers. Explain the reasons for your rankings and your experiences with reading. Are there other activities that help you to increase your vocabulary? Explain what these are and how they help you.

Reading Journal

> **Reading Tip**

Keep a notebook to write your reading journal and vocabulary log entries in. ▪

▶ An important way to improve your reading skills and increase your vocabulary is to find material that you choose to read. This activity is called "reading for pleasure." Here are some ideas to start you out.

▶ **Reading** Find some readings on the topics in this unit that you are interested in and that are at your level. Your teacher can help you find some stories to read for your pleasure. For example, you could read *Into Thin Air* in which the author describes one of the trips to Mt. Everest.

Another source of reading material is your bookstore or library's magazine and newspaper section. Discuss what you would like to read with others in a small group. Your group members could recommend something good for you to read. Try to work with a reading partner. Select a reading that your partner or partners will read as well. Make a schedule for the times when you plan to do your personal reading and a time when you would like to finish.

▶ **Writing** At the end of each week, complete a journal report about what you read. Explain the important ideas and what you learned from this reading. Write about what you liked or found interesting. Explain whether or not you would recommend the reading to others.

▶ **Speaking** Each week, be ready to talk about what you read with a partner or with others in a small group. You can use your journal report to help you to recall what is important for the others to know.

Reading Journal Report

▶ Include the following information in your journal entry.

Title of the reading: _____

Author: _____

Subject of the reading:

_____

_____

_____

_____

Summary of the important ideas:

_____

_____

_____

_____

Personal reaction:

_____

_____

_____

_____

Recommendation:

_____

_____

_____

_____

Vocabulary Log

 Choose five important words that you learned from each chapter. Write the words and a definition in your notebook, as in the example below. Check your definition with the teacher.

Chapter 1

Word	Definition
1. *attain*	*achieve or reach*
2. _____	_____
3. _____	_____
4. _____	_____
5. _____	_____

 **A Personal Dictionary**   A personal dictionary is a good way to record the new words you learn as you read. To create your dictionary, divide a notebook into sections for each letter of the alphabet. Then write the word and the definition on the appropriate page. You can also write the way to use the word in a sentence (as a verb, noun, adjective, adverb, or in more than one way). Look for the word in the reading or write the word in a sentence of your own. You can also find synonyms (words that mean the same) or antonyms (words that have an opposite meaning) and write them in your dictionary.

Online Study Center   For additional activities, go to the **Reading Matters** Online Study Center at *college.hmco.com/pic/wholeythree2e*.

UNIT 2

Weather Matters

We shall never
be content until
each man makes
his own weather ...

—*Jerome K. Jerome*

Introducing the Topic

Weather has always played an important role in our lives. Recently, however, our understanding of Earth's climate and its effects has become more detailed. In Chapter 3, we will look at why people are attracted to studying climate change at the ends of the earth and also at the newest tools with which scientists study the weather and climate today. In Chapter 4, we will look at the connection between the weather and our health.

▶Points of Interest

Discussion Questions

▶ Think about these questions. Share your ideas with a partner or in a small group.

1. Check (✔) as many different weather conditions as you know from the list below.

   _____ windstorms   _____ rainstorms

   _____ thunderstorms   _____ snowstorms

   _____ ice storms   _____ sandstorms

   _____ heat waves   _____ typhoons

   _____ cold waves   _____ hurricanes

   Which have you experienced? When and why do they occur? What are the consequences of severe or unusual weather?

2. Do you think the weather can have an effect on our health? Our moods? Give examples from your own experience.

3. Can weather forecasters accurately predict what the weather will be like over the course of a few days, a few weeks, a few years, or in the future? Why is it important to have accurate weather forecasting?

4. Describe the weather conditions you like most or least. Give reasons for your choices.

3 Poles Apart: Climate Research in Antarctica and the Arctic

Chapter Openers

What's the Weather Like?

▶ Every time we open a newspaper, we find news about the weather. Meteorology, the study of the weather and weather conditions, is an area of study that has developed quite dramatically. List some common weather terms that you know.

rainfall   _____

_____   _____

_____   _____

▶ Some examples of weather reports are given below and on page 53. Read each one quickly and underline the following:

- Location
- Type of weather
- Result of the weather

Global Warming Bad for Rice

Philippines—Increased nighttime temperatures are thought to be the cause of significant declines in crop yield at the Research Institute Farm in the Philippines. According to researchers, an average daily temperature increase of 1° Celsius resulted in a ten percent reduction in the rice crop. Other researchers are concerned because rice production has not improved throughout some key rice-producing areas in Asia. This could result in a price increase for this key food commodity throughout much of the world.

Camel Drowning

Rajasthan, India—At least forty-eight camels drowned in northern India's state of Rajasthan due to flash floods triggered by monsoon rains. Incessant rainfall broke an embankment, causing water to gush from the breach and form a huge lake in the Thar Desert.

Deadly Brazilian Chill

Sao Paulo, Brazil—Two people died in southern Brazil from one of the worst cold waves to hit the region in recent history. Up to five inches of snow fell on some rural areas, but fatalities occurred in the slums of Sao Paolo, where temperatures dropped to 37° Fahrenheit. Temperatures in several communities of the southern state of Rio Grande do Sul dropped to 14° as the region had snowfall for the first time since 1994. Beaches in Copacabana, Ipanema, and Leblon were deserted due to the frigid conditions.

Hurricane Charley Hurts Farmers

Kissimmee, Florida—Hurricane Charley ripped through some of the richest agricultural land in Florida and caused hundreds of millions of dollars in damage to the state's second largest industry. The hurricane uprooted orange and grapefruit trees, smashed greenhouses and barns, and destroyed fields and farm equipment. The total loss to farmers could reach higher as the state struggles to return electricity needed to operate the machinery for milking cows on their dairy farms. Experts expect that the price for citrus fruit could increase by up to thirty percent.

Vicious Hail Storm Kills Sixteen in China

Zhengzhou, China—A violent storm with big wind, thunder, and hail hit central China's Hunan province last Friday evening. It killed sixteen people and injured about 200 as buildings collapsed under the force of the storm. The storm lasted for about 25 minutes as the wind speed reached up to 75 kilometers per hour. The streets were filled with broken tree trunks and electricity, telecommunications, and water were cut off.

Discussion Questions

▷ Using what you underlined, discuss these questions with a partner or in a small group.

1. What kind of weather conditions do these articles report?
2. What are the consequences in each case?

Note Taking

▷ **A Presenting Information in Note Form** The next article explains the improvements in making accurate models of the forces that affect the world's climate. Before reading, discuss what you know about these questions with a partner or in a small group.

1. What is global warming?
2. Why is it happening?
3. Do you think that global warming will be a more important or less important issue in the future? Why?
4. How do scientists know what forces are affecting our climate?

▷ **B** Complete the following outline with information from the article.

▷ **1.** Read the main ideas of the outline and see what information to look for. The first main idea and details and the conclusion are provided to show how to select key words for the notes.

   2. Skim the article and underline facts to complete the outline.

   3. Complete the outline.

Main Ideas	Details
A. Reasons to model weather and how models work	• Fact: more carbon dioxide (CO_2) in atmosphere than in 420,000 yrs. Why? • Reality: weather is variable • Are changes due to CO_2 or just natural occurrences? • Models imitate past, present, future climates by building physical laws governing atmosphere, land, oceans, and interactions between them.
B. History of climate modeling	1. In 1980s—present
	2. A decade later
	3. Since then
	4. Next challenge

C. Present day challenges	1. Clouds
	2. Prediction from best models
D. Conclusion	• Modeling more successful than imagined • Producing forecasts with accuracy and on a large scale • Continue to look to future improvements

▷ Use the information in the outline to talk with a partner about the state of weather modeling today, then answer the following question.

What kinds of improvements in weather forecasting would you like to see in the future?

Modeling the Weather Gets Better

❶   Summers feel hotter and winters feel warmer. Just four years ago the thermometer rose higher than any temperature recorded since 1861. With the current amount of industry-produced carbon dioxide in the atmosphere, there is more CO_2 in our sky than there has been for at least 420,000 years and, probably, for the last twenty million years. Coincidence? Because weather is inherently variable, this question cannot be answered simply by considering the facts at hand. Weather must be modeled using computer simulations to see if changes in climate patterns are due to CO_2 and other greenhouse gases, or if they are occurring naturally. Such models imitate past, present, and future climates by building in the physical laws governing the atmosphere, land, and the oceans, as well as the interactions between them.

❷   Climate models have become more complicated since the early versions were introduced. They draw on a combination of physics, chemistry, oceanography, and geology along with other sciences. In the 1980s, independently-developed ocean and sea-ice models were coupled together and added to the global climate models. A decade later aerosols—airborne particles—were thrown into the mix. Since then, natural carbon cycling on land and in the oceans has been added to climate models, but the work is far from complete. An even bigger challenge is understanding the effects of human industry on this system. Burning fossil fuel emits about 5.4 gigatons of carbon dioxide a year. Over short time scales (which for CO_2 means hundreds of years), this greenhouse gas can only be partially absorbed by the oceans and forests, leaving some 3.3 gigatons of man-made CO_2 in the atmosphere. More is added every year.

3   Now, if modelers sometimes feel their heads are in the clouds, they have every right to be there. Clouds are difficult. They are the biggest single physical uncertainty in climate modeling at the present time. Depending on their type and height, clouds can either make the earth warmer or cooler. High clouds tend to act as blankets, trapping heat in; lower clouds are better reflectors of solar energy, keeping heat out. The best models from around the world, including Canada, the United States, and the United Kingdom, predict an increase in the average global temperature of 1.5° to 4.5°C by 2100. Most predictions fall in the middle of this range.

4   Given these many uncertainties, it is remarkable that climate modeling can be helpful at all. But, despite the difficulties, it has been beneficial. Climatologists never imagined modeling would be so successful in producing forecasts on the scale and with the accuracy it has. And as tools and understanding improve, they can only imagine how far they will be able to go in the future.

Adapted from Cathy Nangini, *National Post*

Exploring and Understanding Reading

Brainstorming

> **Reading Tip**

Brainstorming is to **say** or **write everything** that **you know** about a topic. It is a useful technique to use before reading because it helps you prepare for the information. ■

Scientists are looking for evidence of global warming and trying to find out what the future of climate change could be. Interestingly, that search is taking them to the ends of the earth. Find out what important climate information scientists are gathering from their study of the polar regions.

▶ Share what you know about the similarities and differences between the Arctic and the Antarctic. List five facts that show the similarities and five that show the differences. Consider the following types of information (one has been given as an example).

Temperature   Animal and Plant Life
Native Population   Geography
Exploration   Climate Study

Similarities	Differences
1. Scientific research goes on in both places	1. Native populations found only in Arctic
2.	2.
3.	3.
4.	4.
5.	5.

Previewing

Reading Tip

Previewing is a useful reading skill. One way to preview is to **read the title** and **subtitle**(s) and **look at** the **picture**(s). ▪

▶ Look at the pictures, title, and subtitles of this article. List three ideas you think will be discussed in the reading.

1. _____

2. _____

3. _____

▶ Compare your ideas with a partner.

Surveying

Reading Tip

Surveying is another useful reading skill. It means to **read the introduction** and **read the first sentence of every paragraph** after that. ▪

▶ Survey the reading. Read the introduction (paragraphs 1–3) and the first sentence of every paragraph after that. Check to see if your preview predictions were correct. If you think you were wrong, change your predictions.

▶ After surveying the information, look for other information from paragraphs 1 and 2 to add to the brainstorming chart.

Studying the Climate at the Ends of the Earth

For climatologists, the poles are a global research lab.

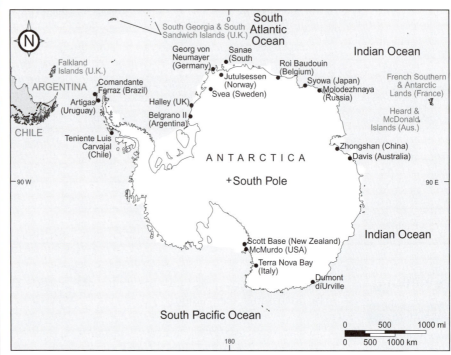

The Antarctic

The Polar Environments

❶   The top and bottom of the world are both the most forbidding and most fascinating areas of the world. Until the 1840s, people hadn't realized that Antarctica was actually an island continent. The land area covers 7 million square kilometers (sq. km.) but, with its ice cap, it covers an area twice that size—14 million sq. km. in all, making it the fifth largest continent in the world. The wild, stormy, ice-filled waters of the Southern Ocean surround the continent. The ice measures about 2.65 million sq. km. in the summer and then grows to 18.8 million sq. km. as the waters freeze in the winter. People think of the continent as a flat, snow-covered, wind-swept land but it is, in fact, covered in high mountains—the highest is 5,140 meters high—and sits on an ice cap that contains ninety percent of the Earth's fresh water. It has the thickest ice in the world, reaching down some 4,800 meters. In contrast, the Arctic is an ocean area of cold and frozen water that is sprinkled throughout with islands claimed by eight different countries. Mirroring the Antarctic continent that caps the Southern Hemisphere, the

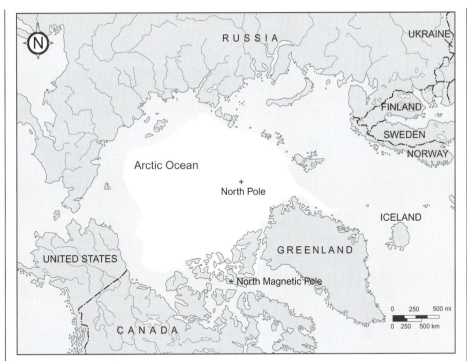

The Arctic

Arctic Circle crowns the top of the Northern Hemisphere. The total area measures 14.056 million sq. km. The Arctic is covered by an ice pack that averages three meters in thickness and is surrounded by open water during the summer. But the ice pack more than doubles in size during the very long sunless winter. Then, the maximum depth of the ice can reach 4.665 meters. The ice that locks these polar regions in bitter cold contains clues to the history of the Earth's climate stretching back hundreds of thousands of years into the last ice age and beyond.

❷   The opportunities that attract those who come to the polar regions to experience the particular beauty and unique features of these stark environments are limited. For much of the year, the polar regions are unwelcoming lands of unrelenting cold that seems to last forever. In the winter, Antarctica has the world's coldest temperatures, dropping to –89° Celsius, the lowest temperature ever recorded on Earth. The seasons are reversed in the Southern Hemisphere—winter is in July and summer is in December—and for five months of the year, the continent is plunged into total darkness. The seasons in the Arctic are the same as in the rest of the Northern Hemisphere, but the weather makes living conditions very difficult. In the winter, temperatures never rise above freezing and can reach near –60°C. Nonetheless, the Arctic Circle islands have been home to the Inuit people for countless generations. The natives successfully adapted themselves to the Arctic environment. It is in the summer that the coasts of Antarctica and the islands of the Arctic Circle are most accessible to researchers, adventurers, and tourists. In the summer, Antarctica is bathed in almost constant sunshine and temperatures on the coast sometimes reach 0°C. Summers in the Arctic are warmer than on Antarctica. Here, too, the sun never sets in the summer and in some parts the temperatures can reach 18°C.

❸   In the last few decades, the polar regions have attracted more visitors—partly because more people are looking for adventure in a challenging environment, but mostly because of increased concern over the effects of global warming. Average temperatures around the world have been rising gradually but steadily for the past fifty years. In recent years, scientists have spent more time and devoted more financial and material resources to the effort to understand global climate change. Many believe that, by understanding the world's climate history, they will gain some insight into its future. Scientists from around the world are now studying conditions at the poles and monitoring the environmental changes that could affect the global climate. By drilling into the ice and extracting ice cores many meters deep, they are able to gain some insight into the types of climate change that have occurred in the past. What researchers learn from their polar studies could help us better understand how global climate change occurs and how to prevent the possibility of climatic catastrophe. Scientists are eager to investigate the role that global warming plays in the changes we see in these polar regions. For example, there is immediate concern over the break up of ice shelves in the Antarctic and the rise in Arctic temperatures. In the Arctic polar regions where native populations have amassed knowledge about the environment over the centuries, there is an immediate and pressing concern over the effect that rising temperatures are having on their traditional way of life.

Signs of Thaw in Desert of Snow: Scientists Begin to Heed Inuit Warnings of Climate Change

❹   In the Arctic, there is increasing evidence that this desert of snow, ice, and killing cold wind, one of the most hostile and fragile places on Earth, is getting warmer. The ice is thawing. Glaciers are receding. Coastlines are eroding. Fall freezes are coming later. The winters are not as cold. The ice roads aren't freezing as early as they used to. The sky seems to be clapping as thunderstorms roll where it was once too cold for them. The Inuit—the native people of the Arctic—say they are watching their world melt before their eyes. Some scientists predict a rise in sea levels leading to devastating floods, thinning ice, and perhaps even an ice-free Arctic within fifty years.

There is concern that the community of Tuktuujaqtuuq, in the western Arctic, could slide into the sea. The Inuit, many of whom straddle their Ancestral Age and the Space Age, building igloos and surfing the Web, have created a website on which elders and hunters post their observations. "About two years ago, when we were corralling reindeer … the north wind started blowing and there were dead birds and dead hair seals and dolphins; all kinds of sea birds were washed ashore," said Herman Toolie of the community of Savoonga. "One of the elders said that these things never used to happen."

❺   Near the sea's edge, the ice floes are melting. The hunters are heading out on snowmobiles. Natsiapik Naglingniq knows they are headed into danger, unable to rely on the weather or the ice, which is opening and closing, teasing those who walk across it. Recently, a hunter went on the local radio to warn that the ice seemed to be melting from the bottom. Naglingniq says that when she was just a girl, living in an igloo, her job was to take out the garbage and, as she did, take notice of the world. "When I would come back in, my parents would ask, 'So what was the weather like out there?' By explaining the weather to my parents, I learned to be able to tell what the next day's weather would be like." In the dark, she would watch for a ring around the moon. "That meant that it would be a bad day tomorrow." But if she saw a clear night and the stars getting closer and farther, as if they were getting bigger and smaller at the same time, "it meant it would be windy the next day." Naglingniq says the weather today changes so rapidly that people cannot make sense of the ring around the moon or the burning circle around the sun. "We were told by the elders at the time there will be a change," Naglingniq says. Beneath her fur-trimmed parka, her eyes are turning a milky gray, but she says she can see when something is amiss. Last summer, the elders saw insects they had never seen before. "The insect is large," she says. "It has lots of legs and it is quite big. As soon as it observes humans, it curls up in a ball. It's strange." She cannot say its name. There is no word in Inuktitut for this insect.

❻   In the Arctic Circle, scientists are studying evidence from ice cores that have been extracted from the ice in Greenland. That evidence suggests that the process of global warming could act as a trigger for global cooling that would alter the climate of the Northern Hemisphere, particularly the northern parts of the United States and Europe. Europeans, whose agriculture could no longer feed even a tenth of their current population, would be hit hardest of all. The key to the whole cycle seems to be the Gulf Stream, which normally delivers huge amounts of warm water to the northern North Atlantic Ocean and Western Europe and moderates the temperatures there. Ocean currents are basically conveyor belts for moving salt around the world's oceans. The warm water of the Gulf Stream is made even more dense and saline by evaporation on its long journey north. If it did not sink to the bottom and flow back south when it reaches the Greenland-Iceland-Norway gap, then the whole conveyor belt would shut

The Earth's Conveyor Belt

An ocean circulation pattern known as the "conveyor" may be affected by global warming

The conveyor moves heat around the earth. It begins in the Arctic and North Atlantic, where water surrounding the ice is cold and salty, hence heavy. This water sinks to the depths of the sea. There, like some unseen river, it flows thousands of miles south, then turns east into the Indian and Pacific Oceans. To replace that sinking water, warm water flows up from the tropics, part of it as the Gulf Stream. Without that flow, Europe and the Northeastern United States would be far colder. If Antarctica melts and the North Atlantic waters grow warmer and less salty, they will no longer sink.

down. What could stop the salty water from sinking? Dilution by too much fresh water on the surface, coming either from increased rainfall over the North Atlantic or from glacial melting and sudden outflows of fresh water from the Greenland fjords. What might cause these events? A rise in temperature in the region. And although average global temperature has risen only about one degree in the past century, the rise in the Arctic region has been several times greater. The evidence in the Greenland ice cores is clear: abrupt, high-speed flips in global climate have happened many dozens of times in historic time. It may be that if we have a couple more centuries of warm-and-wet conditions, we will learn enough about the fine detail of global climate to postpone the next flip indefinitely. But if it goes over the edge now, it would be a calamity for everyone in the Northern Hemisphere.

❼   Terry Fenge, former research director of the Inuit Circumpolar Conference of Canada, said that in the last decade scientists have acknowledged the Arctic as a barometer of climate change. "This is one of those very important areas where traditional knowledge and traditional science are coming together with Western science and they are both in essence saying the same thing: climate change is not a future event. It is happening now."

Scientists Track Changes in Antarctica

❽   In the Antarctic, there are also changes that scientists are concerned about. In 2002, scientists recorded a melting of the ice shelves that caused icebergs to break away from the continent. In 2005, a huge iceberg crashed into the Drygalski ice tongue (that appears on most maps of Antarctica) and broke off a five-kilometer section. The break up of vast ice shelves is seen as an early warning of dangerous climate change that could come as a result of the melting in Antarctica. Since 1950, 13,500 square kilometers of ice shelves have disintegrated. The

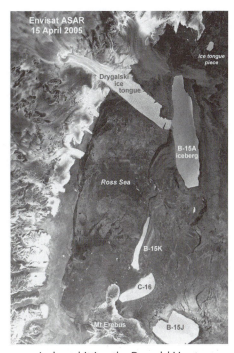

Iceberg hitting the Drygalski ice tongue

retreat didn't attract widespread attention until 1978, when glaciologist John Mercer predicted in *Nature* that if global warming were to occur in Antarctica, the peninsula's ice shelves would be the first to go, melting before any of the continental ice did. By comparing air temperatures above existing and missing shelves, Mercer predicted that average annual temperatures greater than –5°C would render a shelf vulnerable to collapse. In the last fifty years, the average recorded annual temperature has risen 2.5°C (about 4°F). The total loss of ice is more than 8,000 km, and this loss has been quite sudden, occurring within a few years to decades. It is this rate of loss that worries scientists. If, for example, the Ross and Ronne shelves in West Antarctica were completely removed, then the ice melt would increase and it could result in a significant increase in the rate of sea level rise. Melting of a major portion of Antarctica would raise sea levels enough not only to flood many islands but also to inundate China's industrial region and threaten coastal cities in Australia and Asia.

Continued Warming?

9   The warming trend may continue even if human production of carbon emissions is reduced. According to a group of climate and ice experts, there is new evidence that Earth is not even halfway through the current warm era. The evidence comes from the oldest Antarctic ice ever sampled—a piece of ice extracted over five years from Antarctica's deep-frozen core. It is composed of thousands of ice layers that were formed as each year's snowfall was compressed over time. It is the deepest ice retrieved so far and includes layers 3,048 meters deep that date back 740,000 years. The relative abundance of certain forms of hydrogen in the ice reflects past air temperatures. Many ice cores have been cut from various glaciers and ice sheets around the world, but until now, none has reached back beyond 420,000 years. This core sample is the first to capture fully the conditions during that long-lasting warm period. Dr. Jerry F. McManus of the Woods Hole Oceanographic Institution, an expert on oceans and past climates, described the new ice-core record as "spectacular." Dr. McManus said it was particularly important because it gave the first full view of conditions during a past warm period that, in terms of both the planet's orbit and its atmospheric conditions, was most like the current one.

10   Clearly, there are concerns about the fact that CO_2 production is still increasing worldwide and that these levels may be contributing to global warming. But, whatever the causes behind the warming seen in the Arctic and the Antarctic, we are faced with a crucial question. What will be the consequences if the polar regions continue to warm? Data accumulated over the past decade suggest that the possibility of fast climate change is higher than most of the scientific community, and perhaps all of the political community, are prepared to accept. In light of such findings, we should be asking when abrupt change will happen, what the impacts will be, and how we can prepare—and not whether it will really happen. In fact, the climate record suggests that abrupt change is inevitable at some point, regardless of human activity. Action now matters, because we may be able to reduce its likelihood of happening, and we can certainly be better prepared if it does occur. The scientific knowledge taken from the polar ice should not go to waste.

Getting the Main Ideas

▷ Write the main idea for each paragraph.

Paragraph 1   Introduction—Compare and contrast Antarctica and the Arctic

Paragraph 2   Introduction—Summer and winter conditions in the polar regions

Paragraph 3   Introduction—Thesis: Investigating climate change in polar regions

Paragraph 4   Effect of climate change on life of the Inuit

Paragraph 5   _____

Paragraph 6   _____

Paragraph 7   _____

Paragraph 8   _____

Paragraph 9   _____

Paragraph 10   Conclusion

▷ Compare your answers with a partner. Then read the text quickly and check your main ideas.

Understanding Details

▷ Look for the answers to these questions. Underline the details in the reading that support your answers. Mark the question number in the margin of the reading.

1. Why are scientists interested in studying ice from the polar regions?

    _____

2. What are scientists doing in order to investigate climate changes that could affect the world?

    _____

3. a. What concerns have led the Inuit to set up a website?

   _____

   b. What is its purpose?

   _____

4. a. What weather signs did the Inuit rely on in the past?

   _____

   b. Why can't they rely on these signs today?

   _____

5. a. What effect does the Gulf Stream have on the Northern Hemisphere?

   _____

   b. How does the Gulf Stream move?

   _____

   c. What would cause the current action of the Gulf Stream to be changed?

   _____

   d. Why would this be a problem?

   _____

6. What changes in the Antarctic most concern some scientists, and why?

   _____

7. a. What does the core sample taken from Antarctic ice contain?

   _____

   b. Why does Dr. McManus think that this core sample is important?

   _____

8. What questions does writer the think are important to take seriously? Explain why.

   _____

   ▶ Check your answers with a partner. If necessary, refer to what you have underlined.

Reacting to the Information

▶ Today the polar regions of the Antarctic are the subject of study and exploration even for some very ordinary high school and college students. Discuss the following questions before reading the next article.

1. How important is it to understand the changes that are taking place in the Antarctic?
2. If you could join an exploration trip to study the Arctic or Antarctica, would you want to go? Why or why not?

▶ Share your ideas with others in a small group. After reading the article, return to question 2 and see if you have any further thoughts to add.

Understanding Details

▶ Before beginning, read the following questions. After reading, answer as many as you can based on the information in the text.

1. What attraction does this trip have for teenagers?

_____

2. What motivated Geoff Green to start the *Students On Ice* program?

_____

3. What is the *Students On Ice* program? How successful has it become?

_____

4. What must students do to take part in this program?

_____

5. What are some difficulties students have faced on the trip?

_____

6. What safety precautions and environmental rules are followed?

_____

7. What kinds of activities do students participate in on Antarctica?

_____

8. How does the trip affect those who have gone?

_____

Students On Ice: Trips to the Poles

❶   Fewer than one-tenth of one percent of all people ever visit the bottom of the world. Antarctica might not seem like the place to go when looking for something meaningful in life, but if you're a teenager, a trip to the South Pole may be exactly what you're looking for. "It totally changes your perspective of the world," says Duncan McNicholl, a sixteen-year-old, eleventh-grade student from Vancouver, B.C., who recently returned from Antarctica after going on a *Students On Ice* expedition. "The place is totally unaffected and untouched by people. The rest of the world seemed so far away and there was no connection to civilization. I have so much more appreciation for the natural world now."

A Trip that Changes Your Life

❷   Fostering an appreciation of our fragile environment is exactly why Toronto native Geoff Green started the *Students On Ice* program in 2000. The program features two fifteen-day expeditions for high school students every year, one to the Arctic and one to Antarctica. Green has been to Antarctica sixty-three times and the Arctic twenty-five times. But the idea behind the *Students On Ice* program goes far beyond the adventure of traveling to the ends of the Earth. "The poles are the corner stones of the global ecosystem," Green says. "In our technology-driven world, the expeditions allow students to connect with nature and understand the profound effect the environment, not just technology, has on their lives."

❸   The Antarctic expeditions take seventy-five students from around the world and the Arctic expeditions take about a dozen. Students have to raise $10,900 for the trip to Antarctica and must be between fourteen and nineteen. Green says the students with the best chance of making it into the program have a sense of adventure and a respect for nature. McNicholl, for example, worked three part-time jobs for more than a year to cover the costs of the trip. Most of the students pay for the adventure on their own and are encouraged to get community and school sponsorship to help them. Students can also win a trip by entering the environmental essay competition sponsored by *Canadian Geographic*, which selects the two best entries each year. Last year, the first group of Inuit students were selected for an expedition and five underprivileged students from each of New York City's five boroughs were chosen by local officials to go along. "Most of them had never been out of New York City," Green says. "They loved it."

A Trip that Tests Body and Spirit

❹   During the first leg of the trip, traveling for two days by icebreaker through the Drake Passage, one of the most treacherous stretches in the world, many of the students experience an emotion far from love. The Drake Passage is the body of water from Cape Horn to the Antarctic Peninsula, where the Atlantic, the Pacific, and the Southern (Antarctic) Oceans converge. Hurricane-strength winds rip through on an average of once every three weeks. "I think it was forty-five-foot waves on the way down," says twenty-year-old Sara Booth, who was part of the first Antarctic expedition in 2000–2001, which began in December and ended in January. The icebreaker "was rocking twenty degrees in either direction. I didn't eat much for those two days," Booth says. "But standing at the bow of the ship (when winds calmed), looking at the icebergs pass by, it was amazing." The trip through the passage clearly leaves an impression. "We spent one whole day pushing through ice," says McNicholl, recalling the experience of traveling on the Polar Star icebreaker. "You felt totally helpless, totally at the mercy of this amazing force. It was very humbling to look out in every direction and see nothing but ice."

❺   *Students On Ice* observes strict safety rules, so if winds or sea currents get too rough, short- and long-term plans are canceled. A doctor and a nurse are present on the expedition and students have to fill out medical forms before they leave. Fortunately, there have been no accidents since the expeditions began. For Valerie Charbonneau, it was the seasickness during the first leg of the trip that marked her initial experience. "But once we got to Antarctica, it was amazing," says the sixteen-year-old, who's in her last year of high school. "We saw huge icebergs, humpback whales, penguins. We saw mountains coming out of the water and we went into a volcanic pool. I want to study globalization and international development when I go to college. The trip inspired me."

❻   Green says the expeditions are set up so students around the world can learn a wide range of natural and environmental sciences, from glaciology to oceanography to marine biology, all in the hope that students will appreciate why Antarctica's special status as an environmentally protected area is so important to the global ecosystem. "The students are broken down. At first, everyone is seasick. So you see the teenagers less concerned with some of their hang-ups. By the time they get to Antarctica they start to be built up again. You see the transformation take place in them. They go from their media-saturated worlds to this barren, absolutely natural place."

Following Environmental Regulations

❼   Because of the strict international treaties governing Antarctica, the team of twenty-five scientists, historians, and expedition leaders who accompany the students make sure that all environmental regulations pertaining to the area are followed. "It's a 'take only photographs, leave only footprints' philosophy," Green says. "Sometimes we even try not to leave footprints. It's a great classroom for the students." While the program has scientific partners, there is not yet any funding assistance from government or corporate sponsors, something Green hopes will change as more people hear about the expeditions. The students get to visit various scientific research stations during the expeditions and are out exploring and helping with experiments throughout the day. Considering that the sun barely sets, it can make for very long hours. Along the way, they have the chance to interact with wildlife that is fearless of human contact.

A Voyage of Discovery

❽   For Booth, who is now in her second year of a wildlife biology program at McGill University, the Antarctic expedition helped focus her career plans. "I wanted to be a doctor, but the *Students On Ice* program helped me make a few life choices. The scientists made me realize that you actually can do things you're interested in and make a good living as well. The whole idea of going down there—it's so pure and I want to keep things that way."

Adapted from *Toronto Star*

Reacting to the Reading

▶ Give your reaction to the following quotations from the reading "Students On Ice: Trips to the Poles."

1. "Being in Antarctica totally changes your perspective of the world."
2. "In our technology-driven world, the expeditions allow students to connect with nature and understand the profound effect the environment, not just technology, has on their lives."
3. "You felt totally helpless, totally at the mercy of this amazing force. It is very humbling to look out in every direction and see nothing but ice."
4. "… I want to study globalization and international development when I go to college. The trip inspired me."
5. "… The scientists made me realize that you actually can do things you're interested in and make a good living as well. The whole idea of going there— it's so pristine and I want to keep things that way."

▶ Share your ideas with others in a small group. Discuss what you think are the greatest benefits of a program like this. Report your ideas to others in your class.

Applying the Information

▶ What effect will global warming have in different areas of the world? From the readings in this chapter as well as your own knowledge, make a list of some potential problems that could result from global warming as well as their consequences. What do you think could happen if the problem occurred? What would you recommend should be done to avoid the problem?

Problem	Result	Recommendation
1.		
2.		
3.		
4.		

▶ Share your ideas with others in a small group. Decide on four ideas you can agree on. Report your ideas to others in your class.

❯Vocabulary Building

Word Form and Meaning

▶ **A** Study these five words and their forms: noun, verb, adjective, and adverb. Then choose the correct form for each part of speech in the chart below. These words are commonly found in general and academic texts.

acknowledge (v.)	occur (v.)	refine (v.)	transform (v.)	vary (v.)
acknowledgment (n.)	occurrence	refinement	transformation	variance
acknowledged (adj.)	occurring	refined	transformative	variably
		refining	transformed	variable
				varied
				variability
				variable

Verb	Noun	Adjective	Adverb
occur	1.	1.	
refine	1.	1.	
		2.	
transform	1.	1.	
		2.	
vary	1.	1.	1.
	2.	2.	
	3.		

▶ Compare lists with a partner.

▶ **B** Write three sentences using words from the list.

▶ **C** In English, the form of the word can change when it is used as a different part of speech. For example, a suffix (ending) can be added to change the adjective *good* to the noun *goodness*. Some common noun suffixes are *-ness, -tion, -ment, -th, -y*. In addition, suffixes can be added to form adjectives. Some common adjective suffixes are *-ful, -al, -ic*.

▶ Read each sentence and circle the correct word to use in the sentence. Write *N* if the word is a noun or *ADJ* if the word is an adjective.

1. _____ The storm ruined some of the richest **agriculture / agricultural** land in the country.

2. _____ Climatologists never expected modeling to be as **successful / success** at producing forecasts as it has been.

3. _____ They were concerned about the **accurate / accuracy** of the reports.

4. _____ Over the past few years we seem to have been experiencing gradual **globe / global** warming.

5. _____ The ice shelves would melt before the **continent / continental** ice.

6. _____ The **atmosphere / atmospheric** conditions may have changed over time.

7. _____ Abrupt climate change is something that the **scientific / science** community thinks is important to research.

8. _____ Students can win a trip by entering the **environment / environmental** essay competition.

9. _____ The students felt completely at home in this barren **nature / natural** place.

10. _____ Booth is in her second year of a wildlife **biology / biological** program.

Vocabulary in Context

> **Writing Tip**

When you are writing about a certain topic, some ideas or concepts may come up repeatedly. It is boring to use the same words over and over again. That is why synonyms are very important. ▪

▶ **A Synonyms/Adjectives** Refer to "Studying the Climate at the Ends of the Earth" to find the words below in context. Match the words in Column A with words that have the same meaning in Column B.

Column A	Column B
_____ 1. unique	a. never ending
_____ 2. unrelenting	b. reachable
_____ 3. abrupt	c. important
_____ 4. inundated	d. particular
_____ 5. accessible	e. sudden
_____ 6. significant	f. flooded

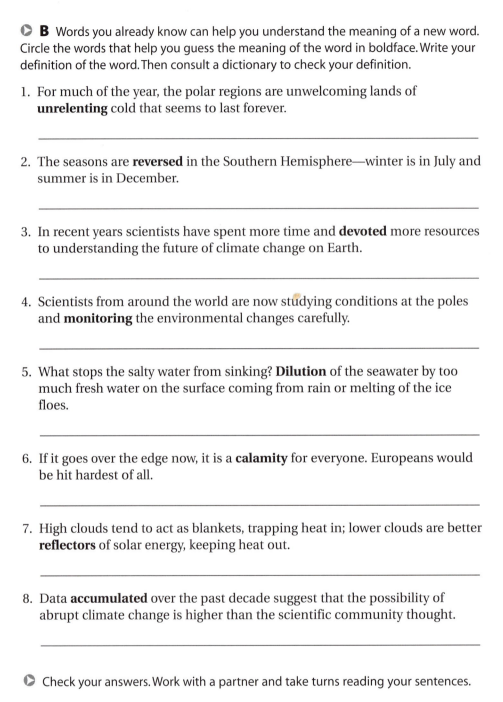

B Words you already know can help you understand the meaning of a new word. Circle the words that help you guess the meaning of the word in boldface. Write your definition of the word. Then consult a dictionary to check your definition.

1. For much of the year, the polar regions are unwelcoming lands of **unrelenting** cold that seems to last forever.

   _____

2. The seasons are **reversed** in the Southern Hemisphere—winter is in July and summer is in December.

   _____

3. In recent years scientists have spent more time and **devoted** more resources to understanding the future of climate change on Earth.

   _____

4. Scientists from around the world are now studying conditions at the poles and **monitoring** the environmental changes carefully.

   _____

5. What stops the salty water from sinking? **Dilution** of the seawater by too much fresh water on the surface coming from rain or melting of the ice floes.

   _____

6. If it goes over the edge now, it is a **calamity** for everyone. Europeans would be hit hardest of all.

   _____

7. High clouds tend to act as blankets, trapping heat in; lower clouds are better **reflectors** of solar energy, keeping heat out.

   _____

8. Data **accumulated** over the past decade suggest that the possibility of abrupt climate change is higher than the scientific community thought.

   _____

Check your answers. Work with a partner and take turns reading your sentences.

€xpanding Your Language

Reading

▶ **Newspaper Article Presentation** Read the following newspaper article and use the information to answer these questions. Discuss your answers with a partner.

1. Why are natural disasters so deadly in the world's poorest nations?
2. What is done in wealthier countries to avoid the deadly effects of natural disasters?
3. What attitude has to change for the situation to improve?
4. What recommendations are made in this article? How could they be put into practice?

Preparing for Disasters: Natural No Longer

A New Age for Weather Forecasting

❶   As 1999 drew to a close, two weeks of continuous rain drummed down the sides of the Avila Mountains in northern Venezuela. The soil was so saturated that landslides and mudflows slid down the mountain, washing away towns, dams, and bridges and claiming thousands of lives. Although this was one of the deadliest natural disasters in recent decades, it was far from unique. In 2003, 700 floods, storms, and other weather catastrophes claimed 75,000 lives worldwide and caused about $65 billion in economic damage. By far, most of the victims—about ninety-eight percent—were in the poorest nations.

❷   But officials at the World Meteorological Organization, the world's weather agency, say that in the future that number can be cut in half. The little-known United Nations agency, with 187 member countries, began a drive in March 2004, to improve early weather warnings and disaster preparations and to build up weather agencies in developing countries. According to the head of this organization, sweeping improvements in forecasting make it possible to notify people of approaching disasters in time to remove them or shore up their defenses. "Five-day forecasts today are as good as two-day forecasts were about twenty years ago, and they can be broadcast almost instantaneously, almost anywhere in the world." China, for example, used such forecasting when its coast was hit by Typhoon Winnie in 1997, said Gao Lanying, a meteorologist with the Chinese weather agency. Accurate forecasting allowed the government to broadcast typhoon information hourly, to recall fishing boats to port, to evacuate 1.4 million people from risky and low-lying areas, and to move grains and other materials. The death toll was 239, rather than thousands, she wrote in a recent paper analyzing China's meteorological disasters.

❸   While forecasting has improved, there has been a worrisome difference between developed countries and developing ones. As was seen in the Southeast Asian tsunami disaster in 2004, poorer nations often lack the means to receive and use weather data to soften the effects of natural disasters and to avoid disruptions to food and water supplies. The cost of natural disasters and their negative effects on development have attracted the attention of the World Bank. Natural disasters can wipe out a country's economy. Venezuela's 1999 mudslides cost the country $3.2 billion. Honduras lost forty-one percent of its annual gross domestic product when Hurricane Mitch barreled through in October 1998, according to the World Bank. The cost of the 2004 tsunami to India, Sri Lanka, and Indonesia is estimated at more than $14 billion. "These are not just natural phenomena and there's nothing to be done about them," said Margaret Arnold, a hazard management official at the bank. "There is a lot you can do."

❹   By contrast, industrialized nations incorporate weather predictions into their emergency preparedness efforts. "We don't have situations as in countries like Bangladesh, where a natural disaster can kill thousands of people," said Dr. Ronald D. McPherson, executive director of the American Meteorological Society. "Those people would have been moved away in advance." One reason the United States loses relatively few lives is experience; it has had to learn to cope with some of the world's worst weather. "We have about as many hurricanes as China, as many winter storms as Russia and Europe, thunderstorms, and virtually all the world's tornadoes—plus big distances here, which make everything vulnerable to disruption," said William Hooke, director of the meteorological society's atmospheric policy program.

❺   But Dr. McPherson noted that developing countries often need preparedness plans. "Part of it is lack of money and lack of experience," he said, "and it's lack of political will." Many politicians do not understand what modern forecasting can do, he said, and some cultures are fatalistic about such catastrophes. Venezuela's government has promised to put a high priority on developing a rainfall monitoring network, coupled with an early warning system for the Avila Mountains, where thousands still make their homes along banks carved out by the mudflows or on crumbling hillsides. "Perhaps we cannot prevent landslides, flash floods, and debris flows," said Dr. Jose L. Lopez, an engineering professor at the University of Central Venezuela who speaks for the government on weather issues. "But we can be much better prepared to prevent these natural hazards from becoming disasters."

❻   The World Meteorological Organization acknowledged that this initiative could not be accomplished overnight. It has set a fifteen-year timeline for improving early warnings and disaster preparedness and strengthening national weather agencies. A first goal is to make sure that all countries have access to observations of extreme weather events that are collected by weather satellites and assistance in incorporating such data into their emergency planning system. It also wants to help train weather service personnel, transfer useful technologies, and educate the public about disaster preparedness. Every nation would benefit from more systematic studies and observations of weather phenomena. The world needs to know more about "how and why natural hazards happen, and how they can develop into disasters."

Adapted from *The New York Times*. Copyright © 2004 by The New York Times Co. Reprinted with permission.

Matching

▷ Look at the following phrases from the article "A New Age for Weather Forecasting." Match the words in Column A with words that have the same meaning in Column B.

Column A

_____ 1. continuous rain

_____ 2. weather catastrophe

_____ 3. sweeping improvements

_____ 4. have access to

_____ 5. worrisome difference

_____ 6. emergency preparedness

_____ 7. systematic studies

Column B

a. the ability to manage in a crisis

b. an organized investigation

c. a troubling discrepancy

d. a meteorological disaster

e. have the use of

f. constant showers

g. a dramatic change for the better

▷ Check your answers with a partner.

Speaking

 Check your local newspaper for the next few days. Find an interesting article on some aspect of the weather. Prepare to talk about it by doing the following things.

▶ **1. Skimming** Quickly read the article to get the general idea and to check whether or not the information is interesting.

2. Highlighting Think of three ideas that the article discusses and highlight information about each.

3. Practice your presentation using the highlighted information.

4. Present your information.

5. Comment on why you found it interesting.

Writing

 Writing Tip

It is useful to have a separate folder in which you can keep all the writing that you do in each chapter. ■

▶ **Reaction Writing** Write what you think about one of the following ideas.

1. The statement "One day we will be able to control the weather."

2. A time when the weather prevented you from doing something you really wanted to do.

3. A time when the weather caused major problems in your city/town/country.

Online Study Center   For additional activities, go to the *Reading Matters* Online Study Center at *college.hmco.com/pic/wholeythree2e.*

4   The Weather and Our Health

Chapter Openers

What is Your Opinion?

▶ Circle *A* if you agree or *D* if you disagree with the statements below.

1. A   D   The psychological effects of weather have a greater impact on people than do the physical effects.

2. A   D   People who say they are depressed because of the weather are just looking for an excuse.

3. A   D   The effect of the weather on our health is greater now than it was in the past.

▶ Compare your answers with a partner or a small group. Give reasons or examples to support your opinions.

Matching

❯ **A** Work with a partner. Match the following conditions with the definitions below.

Conditions

1. _____ migraine headaches

2. _____ allergy

3. _____ the flu

4. _____ asthma

5. _____ depression

6. _____ arthritis

7. _____ hypertension

8. _____ bronchitis

9. _____ appendicitis

10. _____ schizophrenia

Definitions

a. Lung disease that causes tightness of the chest, coughing, and difficulty breathing

b. An unusual physical reaction to certain foods or substances

c. A disease that causes inflammation and stiffness in the joints of the body

d. The condition of feeling sad and sorrowful

e. An inflammation of the small end of the small intestine

f. An infection of the bronchial tubes in the lungs

g. A contagious viral disease that causes fever, inflammation of the respiratory system, and muscle pain

h. A condition of high blood pressure

i. A type of mental disorder characterized by disturbances in thought or speech and inability to function in everyday life

j. A very intense type of headache that causes pain to one or both sides of the head.

❯ **B** Check (✔) the conditions you think are related to the weather and explain the connection.

Exploring and Understanding Reading

Predicting

Many of us might not be aware of how the weather affects us. In this chapter, we will find out about the many effects—both physical and emotional—weather can have on us.

❯ Decide if you think the following statements are true (*T*) or false (*F*) and then share what you think with a partner or small group.

1. T   F   More people are likely to die in the winter than at any other time of the year.

2. T   F   Biometeorology is a well-accepted science everywhere in the world.

3.   T   F   Meteorologists can draw a weather map showing where certain health problems occur.

4.   T   F   Animals have physical reactions to changes in the weather.

5.   T   F   Hospitals would find it useful to have reports that can point out where and when an increase in certain health problems will occur.

▶ In the following article, underline the words that provide support for your answers above. Correct any information that is false.

When the Weather Gets You Down

A meteorologist joined forces with a doctor to create a weather map that predicts health problems.

❶   A study of U.S. cities reveals that death rates are more than twenty percent higher in January than in August. For reasons that remain a deep mystery, winter is the deadliest season. To the surprise of even those scientists who documented the phenomenon, far more people die in winter than at any other time of year—and not necessarily with snow shovels in their hands. In a study of twenty-eight U.S. cities, rates of death from all causes were found to be more than twenty percent higher in January than in August, regardless of climate. Whether Philadelphia or Minneapolis or Miami, the pattern held. "People die not because it's cold, but because it's winter," said Robert E. Davis, a University of Virginia environmental scientist who was the report's lead author. His finding, and the puzzle it presents, caused a strong and surprised reaction from people at the International Congress of Biometeorology in Kansas City, where the study was released. For a week, 200 researchers from around the world convened there to consider potential cause-and-effect connections between weather and health. Some of the topics they touched on included this El Niño winter and a possible run of stomach aches; frigid cold and heart disease; and wind chill and frostbite.

❷   Going back four millennia, ancient medicine linked weather to well-being—laying the foundation for the latter-day science of biometeorology. The science has been well-accepted in Europe for fifty years. And although still dismissed in some U.S. quarters as wackiness, it has been surfacing more and more in the mainstream of American medicine and science— spurred in part by worries over global warming. Biometeorology's disciples have long considered winter to be full of aches and pains. But Davis's study

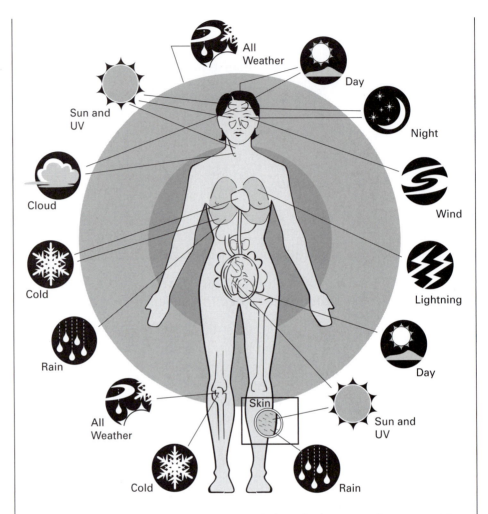

of mortality rates has cast an even darker shadow over the season. Now, other evidence of the weather-health connection has come from Canada.

❸   When Toronto meteorologist Denis Bourque talks about feeling under the weather, he's not just using a figure of speech. After twenty years of research into the connection between weather and health, Bourque and his colleague, Dr. John Bart, have developed a computer-animated weather map that shows not cold fronts and snow flurries, but the medical problems that they can bring. "The family doctors get a lot of people showing up that are having weather-related complaints," said Bourque, sitting in front of a computer terminal that showed his sample weather/health map of North America. "The first step is to get people to realize it's not necessarily a myth."

❹   The weather-disease mapping project began when Bart, a Toronto-area family practitioner, noticed a pattern of people coming into his office. People with migraines, for example, typically came to the doctor under two types of weather conditions. "One is when the weather is becoming more humid and cooler," Bart explained. "The other is when you have a long hot spell. There is a subset of people who get migraines under those conditions." He asked Bourque—an Environment Canada meteorologist who happened to be one of his patients—if he could shed some light on the mystery. It didn't fit into Bourque's full-time job, but he began looking into the question in his spare time. To his surprise, he found that much had been written about the weather and health, not just in dubious sources, but in peer-reviewed, scientific journals.

❺   One study found, for example, that heart attacks peak on the third day after a cold spell. Another found that in people with hypertension, blood pressure rises and falls according to noon temperature. Yet another found that a warm front moving across the country brings with it a wave of migraine headaches. In Germany, the research was so advanced that the German Weather Service regularly issued weather health advisories to medical doctors. There is even a website that allows health-conscious consumers and hypochondriacs alike to click on a map of Germany for the latest weather updates for conditions ranging from appendicitis, bronchitis, and depression to neurosis, thrombosis, and schizophrenia.

❻   The principle underlying bioweather, as the Germans call it, is that all animals, including humans, react to changes in the environment around them. Animals such as bears, for example, change their entire metabolism to hibernate in the winter. So, too, the human body may react to daily changes in things such as temperature, humidity, and barometric pressure. The correlations are not simple, Bourque said, nor are the biological mechanisms well understood. "What the Germans found is that when they tried to zero in on a particular thing—like cold, hot, rainy—it's difficult. They found that if you combined information, you found a much better relationship."

❼   Based on their review of the existing scientific literature, Bart and Bourque—still working together in their spare time—developed an index they called the Mediclim. The index combines eight different measures: temperature, temperature change over the last seven days, humidity, humidity change over the last seven days, atmospheric pressure, pressure change over the past seven days, wind, and vorticity—a measurement of the swirling of air over a large area. Based on these factors, they divided weather into fourteen categories linked to different ailments. They hired a high-tech specialist to write a computer program that crunched the weather data gathered continuously by Environment Canada, correlated it to health information, and produced a computer-animated map showing areas of health risk across North America on any given day.

❽   When the computer program was finished several years ago, Bart felt certain that Environment Canada would soon begin producing a weather health map every day, similar to the UV index. But the department turned a cold shoulder to the project, and potential private investors have likewise proved frosty. "I feel like a kid on a beach with a gold nugget," Bart said. "I keep running up to people saying, 'Look at this, look at this,' and they keep saying, 'Buzz off, kid.'" In theory, they could produce the weather health map every day. But doing so would cost between $60,000 and $100,000 a year, Bourque estimates, because it would require buying the data from Environment Canada and hiring staff to run the computer program. It would cost more to upgrade the graphics and make the map less scientific and more user friendly.

❾   One difficulty with finding an investor, Bourque said, may be that people do not see the utility of such a map. Because they can't do anything about the weather, why worry about its effects on their health? But Bart said patients could use the information to manage their illnesses and plan their daily activities. People prone to migraines could stay away from foods that tend to trigger migraines—for example, red wine and chocolate—on days of adverse weather. Likewise, people suffering from arthritis could take anti-inflammatories as a preventative measure before the adverse weather sets in.

❿   In the United Kingdom, the meteorological office and the Department of Health conducted a pilot study last year forecasting hospital workload based on the weather. The forecasting included such obvious things as falls and broken bones based on ice and snow, but also contained predictions of respiratory ailments based on a combination of weather and virus epidemiology. Results of the pilot study were mixed. Some hospitals found little use for the data, but others, like the Royal Berkshire and Battle Hospitals, gave a sunny response. "These reports were useful. The predictions for increased workload were usually proved correct." Meanwhile, officials within Environment Canada are finally warming to the idea of using weather health forecasting as a tool to improve hospital efficiency, Bourque said. "Because of the U.K. work and the German work, there's now some interest in the department," he said. "I've been asked, 'Could it be done in Canada?'"

⓫   After twenty years of research, Bart and Bourque may finally be convincing others that the connection between weather and health isn't just a snow job.

Adapted from *The Ottawa Citizen* and *The Gazette*

Scanning for Details

▶ Look for the answers to these questions. Underline the details in the reading that support your answer. Mark the question number in the margin of the reading.

1. What were scientists surprised to learn?

_____

2. Where is the weather-health link most accepted?

_____

3. What have Denis Bourque and John Bart developed?

_____

4. What did John Bart notice about patients who came to him with migraines?

_____

5. What information shows how advanced the research into health and weather is in Germany?

_____

6. a. What is the Mediclim?

_____

   b. What does it show?

_____

7. a. What reaction to Mediclim have Bart and Bourque gotten from Environment Canada?

_____

   b. What could explain this reaction?

_____

8. What are some possible ways a weather health report could be beneficial to people with certain health problems?

_____

9. What evidence is there of increased interest in this project?

_____

Using Evidence to Support Ideas

In the reading, examples are often given to support an idea. This is a very common method of organizing information in English. For example, in paragraph 9 the author says, "People prone to migraines could stay away from foods that tend to trigger migraines—for example, red wine and chocolate—on days of adverse weather."

▶ Find other examples of this in the reading. Look for examples to complete the following table. The first has been done for you.

Idea	Support
1. More people die in winter than at any other time of the year.	In a study of twenty-eight U.S. cities, rates of death from all causes were found to be twenty percent higher in January than in August, regardless of the climate.
2. The project began when Bart noticed a pattern of people coming into his office.	
3. Much has been written about health and weather.	• • • •
4.	Bears change their entire metabolism to hibernate in the winter.

▶ Check your answers with a partner. Discuss why the evidence is convincing in each case.

▶ Paired Readings

▶ People have known for a long time that some psychiatric (or mental) disorders are somehow related to changes in seasons. The readings that follow are about two such disorders, SAD (Seasonal Affective Disorder) and Reverse SAD. Choose one of these readings. Work with a partner who is reading the *same* article.

❶ The Wintertime Blues

Skimming

◗ Quickly skim the article and answer the following questions.

1. At what time of the year does this disorder happen?

_____

2. How does this disorder make people feel?

_____

Seasonal Affective Disorder (SAD)

By Gila Lindsley, Ph.D., A.C.P.

As the last of the leaves fall from the trees and the sun sinks lower and lower on the horizon, the spirits of some sink with it. And as the days grow shorter and shorter, many become SAD. That is, many develop **Seasonal Affective Disorder (SAD).**

❶   For those who become SAD with the coming of the cold, dark months, the consequences can be very severe. I'll never forget the first patients I saw with severe SAD. It was in the winter of 1987 or 1988. I was running a Sleep Disorders Center in a New Hampshire psychiatric hospital and had become very interested in SAD as well. The first patient was a woman who was thirty-five or so. She had tried to commit suicide and almost succeeded. I was shaken. I had not realized until then that SAD could be so life threatening. When I talked to her, I found out that she felt SAD every winter, but generally was able to hang on until her kids' February vacation from school, when the family took a vacation in sunny Florida. That immediately lifted her spirits. "What happened this year?" I asked her. "February vacation did not come until the first week of March. I could not hold out any longer." We treated her with bright light. The difference was amazing. We noticed that her room became unusually full of people during the light sessions.

❷   Another patient was a man in his mid-twenties. He was admitted to this same hospital year after year, generally for several months at a time, so severe was his depression. When we looked back at his history, we realized he always came in more or less the same time of year, usually late September, and then was well enough to go home some weeks after New Year's Day. He told us that at other times of the year he was just fine. We also exposed him to artificial light. At first he became more sociable. Then he began to pay better attention to personal hygiene, caring to change his clothes, to bathe himself, and to shave.

❸   Winter depressions can be very, very severe. Even if not severe enough to require hospitalization, as was the case for these two people, the psychological and physical symptoms can still be severe enough to disturb how you function and perhaps even interfere with your personal relationships.

❹   Mood certainly changes. Some people become sad to the point of experiencing real grief at times. Others become more anxious; still others become more irritable. At times the irritability can be so extreme that feelings of violence erupt. This may be one small part of the reason why the incidence of child abuse seems to increase during the dark months.

❺   Physical activity decreases. The person feels very lazy, often sluggish. Physical effort of almost any sort seems to be just too much. On the other hand, appetite—especially a craving for carbohydrates (sugars, starches, or alcohol)—actually increases. Hypersomnia can develop; most people with SAD end up sleeping for very long hours (or wishing they could, if life would allow it). In many ways, it is as if a person were hibernating during the cold, dark months.

❻   Scientists now think that SAD is a result of the decreasing hours of daylight. One of the first studies was done by South African psychiatrist Norman Rosenthal and his colleagues. The investigators found they could predict how many of the people they studied would develop SAD symptoms on the basis of how brief the daylight hours were. As daylight began noticeably decreasing in September, some people were affected. By the time the days close to winter solstice came, almost everyone in the study group was affected. Then, as the season moved away from the solstice toward spring, with lengthening daylight hours, the number of affected people began to decline. By the end of May, almost all were back to their old selves, some unfortunately even switching into what psychiatrists call mania.

❼   To make sure that this connection between change in mood and amount of light was more than just chance, the next step was to supply light to see if it could reverse the SAD mood. Rosenthal's team used two different kinds of light. The dimmer, yellow light had no effect. However, the brighter light that resembled actual sunlight produced a marked change in mood in most (but not all) of the patients who received that treatment.

Diagnosis and treatment of SAD with light therapy should be done by a qualified sleep specialist.

New Technology Publishing, Inc.

Scanning

▶ Look back at the reading for the answers to these questions. Write your answers in note form.

1. a. Why was the first patient admitted to the hospital?

   _____

   b. What made her situation worse this year?

   _____

2. What effect did the light treatment have on the second patient?

   _____

3. a. Name three psychological symptoms of SAD.

   _____ , _____ , _____

   b. What can these symptoms lead to?

   _____

4. Name three physical symptoms of SAD.

   _____ , _____ , _____

5. a. According to the study, when do people start getting SAD symptoms?

   _____

   b. How long can these symptoms last?

   _____

6. a. How many kinds of light did the researchers use to treat the patients?

_____

b. Which kind worked? Why?

_____

▶ Compare your answers with your partner's. Try to agree on the same answers. Look back at the reading if you disagree.

Recapping the Information

 Reading Tip

Highlighting is a useful strategy for finding and remembering facts and important ideas you read. To highlight, use a colored highlighting pen to mark information. Be careful to **mark only the words and phrases that you want to stand out**—not the whole sentence. ■

▶ **A** Highlight the facts you read about SAD that relate to the following ideas.

1. SAD patients
2. Symptoms of SAD
3. Study to show that SAD is a result of lack of light

▶ **B** Working with a partner, compare what you highlighted. Discuss whether you highlighted too much or too little. Add any highlighting you need to.

▶ **C** Using *only* what you highlighted, take turns telling each other the important information in the article. Make sure you explain the information and add any ideas of your own.

Reacting to the Information

▶ Discuss these questions with your partner.

1. How can having SAD affect a person's personal relationships? Give some examples.
2. People who have SAD feel very tired and depressed. Which do you think comes first, the depression or the feeling of being tired?
3. What do you think is the explanation for the link between light and symptoms that SAD people have?

❷ The Summertime Blues

Skimming

> **Reading Tip**

Skimming allows you to get a general idea of what an article is about. When you skim, read quickly. Focus on ideas that you understand. ▪

▶ Quickly skim the article and answer the following questions.

1. At what time of the year does this disorder happen?

   _____

2. How does this disorder make people feel?

   _____

SAD in the Sunshine

Disorder sufferers find good weather depressing.

By David Johnston

❶   As she drove to the mall this week, Audrey Greenway looked up at the strong sun and groaned. "I took an amphetamine pill this morning because I could see it was turning into a bad day," she said. "The sun was shining; it was pure agony."

❷   Greenway, fifty-one years old, has Reverse Seasonal Affective Disorder. As its name implies, this is the opposite of Seasonal Affective Disorder (SAD), or winter depression. Greenway suffers from summer depression. Daylight and warmth are factors. Her mental health begins to deteriorate in the spring. For reasons doctors don't understand, Reverse SAD is more debilitating than SAD. It's also more rare. While four to eight percent of us may suffer from SAD, only .025 percent are believed to suffer from the deeper depressions of Reverse SAD. In Greenway's case, Reverse SAD provokes severe manic depression. Her mania (extreme excitement) happens in winter. With the coming of spring, however, she gradually withdraws from social contact and falls into a depression for which she sometimes takes twenty-seven pills a day.

❸   Greenway is very open about her illness. She has told her story on video for hospital researchers. Her doctor is encouraging her to speak to women's groups about seasonal depression because women are twice as likely to be depressed as men, studies suggest, and four times as likely to suffer from depressions that follow a seasonal pattern.

❹   On the way to the mall, Greenway was upbeat. But as she walked from the parking lot to the doors, her pace slowed. "I feel terrible," she said as she stepped inside the mall. "My body feels like lead. I'm dragging 124 pounds, but it feels like 600. I feel I don't want to be here. My heart is pumping."

❺   Although she lives nearby, Greenway usually shops at a mall that is much farther away because it is the "darkest mall in the city." She pointed to this mall's skylights, then at some indoor trees. "The lights, the trees. They bother me."

❻   Greenway came to this mall only to buy her mother-in-law a present at a special jewelry store. In December and January, when days are shortest, she enjoys shopping—especially on cold nights. Sometimes she enjoys it too much. Her mania provokes expensive shopping. "I've bought truckloads of curtains." On her doctor's advice, she doesn't keep credit cards in her purse. Still, her husband, Ray, sees to it she has two bank accounts—one for when she is manic, the other for when she is not. "When I'm manic, I'm not supposed to touch the non-manic account," said Greenway. "But this winter, I touched both." She smiled. "Emptied them out."

❼   As she approached the jewelry store, her mood suddenly turned fierce. "I can't stand to see these people," she said of the shoppers walking through the mall. "I'd rather be home in bed. I have to make a decision [on what to buy her mother-in-law] and it is impossible. Depression simply does not allow decisions." She spotted a bench. "Here, I have to sit down first." When she sat down, she started to cry. "People are smiling. Don't they know how much it hurts?" She stopped crying, "I don't envy them. What God gave me—there's some good in it, too. I've become a more patient and gentle person. Still, it hurts. I dread clocks moving forward one hour in spring." She looked up at the jewelry store, wiped her eyes, and laughed. "You'd think I was going for surgery the way I'm behaving."

❽ In the store, a saleswoman showed her three varieties of the item she wanted. Greenway chose the first piece. "If I have to make a decision, I'm afraid I might just walk out with nothing," she explained.

❾ As she left the store, the newspaper reporter she had invited to tag along asked whether she would like a coffee. She said she would.

"Where would you like to go?"

"A restaurant with no windows."

❿ She laughed. "My husband says I know all the dark corners in the city." In the restaurant, Greenway chose the darkest spot she could find, even though artificial light doesn't bother her. In five minutes she had brightened considerably. "I really feel I shouldn't hide all I am going through," she said. "When I talk to women, they say, 'Shh! You shouldn't say that.' We have the wrong impression of mental illness. Five percent of all mental illness is manic depression. And ten of every hundred people will experience in their lives a time of deep depression. So why shouldn't we talk about it?"

Scanning

▷ Look back at the reading for the answers to these questions. Write your answers in note form.

1. What kind of medication does Audrey take for her problem?

_____

2. How does the number of people who suffer from Reverse SAD compare to the number who suffer from SAD?

_____

3. Who does Audrey talk to about her disorder? Why?

_____

4. What kinds of malls does she usually shop at? Why?

_____

5. a. What happens to Audrey's shopping habits in winter?

_____

b. What advice does her doctor give her about this?

_____

c. What is her husband's solution to this?

_____

6. Audrey feels that there is some good in her problem. What is it?

_____

7. a. How do people react when Audrey talks about her problem?

_____

b. What is her response?

_____

Recapping the Information

> ▶ **A** Highlight the facts in the reading that relate to the following ideas.

1. General information on Reverse SAD
2. Effect of Reverse SAD on Audrey's behavior
3. How Audrey deals with her problem

 Reading Tip

See page 90 for tips on highlighting. ▪

▶ **B** Working with a partner, compare what you highlighted. Discuss whether you highlighted too much or too little. Add any highlighting you need to.

▶ **C** Using *only* what you highlighted, take turns telling each other the important information in the article. Make sure you explain the information and add any ideas of your own.

Reacting to the Information

▶ Discuss these questions with your partner.

1. How do you think Audrey's condition affects her relationship with her husband and friends?
2. Why would it be useful for her to talk about her problem to other women?
3. What do you think is the explanation for the link between light and symptoms that Reverse SAD people have?

Comparing the Readings

Retelling the Information

▶ Work with a partner who read a different article. Use what you highlighted to retell the information. Explain the ideas clearly in your own words. Encourage your partner to ask questions about the information or write some of the important facts you explain. After you have finished retelling, discuss the questions in the preceding section, "Reacting to the Information."

Reacting to the Readings

▶ Keeping in mind the information in both readings and your own experience, share your ideas about the following questions.

1. Which condition appears to be worse: SAD or Reverse SAD? Why?
2. Why do you think women are more likely than men to have seasonal disorders?
3. According to Audrey (in "SAD in the Sunshine"), people say "Shh! You shouldn't say that," when she talks about her condition. Do you agree with them? Why or why not?
4. Do you or does anyone you know suffer from SAD or Reverse SAD?

Questionnaire

▶ Answer the following questionnaire to confirm your answer to question 4 in the preceding section.

	Yes	No	Sometimes
1. Does work and family life become more difficult for you every winter?			
2. Do you experience constant fatigue or periods of fatigue in winter but not in summer?			
3. Do your eating habits change in winter, with more sweet or starch in your diet?			
4. Does your general feeling of well being tend to decline in the winter?			
5. Do you usually feel fine—or even energized—in late spring and summer without underlying feelings of depression?			

▶ Discuss your results with a partner or in a small group.

A Scientific Explanation

Scientists are always trying to explain what they observe. They do this by asking one question after another until they have a complete picture. The following reading is about the questions that scientists have asked about SAD and what they have found out so far.

▶ Work with a partner. Read the answer to the first question in the reading. Discuss the information with your partner. Take turns doing the same with the remaining questions.

The Biological Clock

By Gila Lindsley, Ph.D., A.C.P.

Which comes first: feeling depressed or feeling tired?

According to research, the first thing that changes with bright light treatment is energy level. People begin to report feeling less sluggish and less tired and, soon after, they report having more energy. Only after this has occurred does the actual depression begin to lift. Working backward, we began to think that the depression is a result of feeling tired and not being able to function properly. And so this turns us once again to light, but with a different kind of question.

What does light have to do with sleepiness and sluggishness?

Here is our current understanding. We are biological creatures and, in general, the human race depends a great deal on being able to see. When primates and then humans were evolving, before electricity was discovered, and also before the discovery of fire, we could not see well when it was dark out. That was the time, then, to sleep so one's batteries could be recharged by sunrise for the next day's hunting and gathering. Therefore we must have developed internal biological clocks that are synchronized to the light-dark cycle in the physical world so that we'd be alert by daylight and become sleepy as the sun began to set.

Where is that internal biological clock?

In recent years, a small cluster of brain cells (i.e., neurons) has been identified as where this master biological clock is. It lies right above an important part of the visual system. One kind of information this "clock" receives has to do with the amount of light coming in through the eyes.

What does the clock do with the information it receives about the amount of light or darkness?

It sends it to a gland at the base of the brain called the pineal gland. This gland releases a hormone, melatonin, into the bloodstream. The amount of light seems to determine how much melatonin is released into the bloodstream. With more light, less melatonin is released; and with less light, more melatonin is released.

What does that mean for the changing seasons?

During those seasons when the light periods are long, in the spring and summer, melatonin release is at its lowest because there are fewer hours of darkness. On the other hand, the closer we move toward the winter solstice, the fewer hours of light there are each day and, correspondingly, the longer the period of time each day when melatonin can be released into the bloodstream.

Once melatonin is in the bloodstream, what is the result?

There are no clear answers right now, for this is quite a new field of research. However, one result found over and over again is that melatonin indirectly causes body temperature to drop. We also know that when we fall asleep, our body temperature drops. The answer could be that, as it gets dark, melatonin is released, causing our body temperature to drop. This then causes us to feel sleepy—a perfect system for prehistoric humans, but not for modern times. Maybe that is why a lot of us find it harder to get up early in the winter.

What we still need to find out is why some people—i.e., those who have SAD—are so much more affected than others.

New Technology Publishing, Inc.

Scanning

▷ **A** The following statements all deal with what happens during dark periods. Read the statements and number them according to the order in which they take place.

_____ a. Clock sends information to the pineal gland.

_____ b. We feel tired and sleepy.

_____ c. Signal about lack of light goes to internal clock.

_____ d. Body temperature goes down.

_____ e. Pineal gland releases melatonin into blood.

▷ Work with a partner to compare the order of the sentences. Locate and underline the information in the article that matches the statements.

▶ **B** Write out what happens during periods of light.

1. _____

2. _____

3. _____

4. _____

5. _____

▶ Compare your answers with a partner's.

Applying the Information

▶ **A** Work with a partner or in a small group. Discuss whether the concept of an internal biological clock can be used to explain the following phenomena.

1. Reverse SAD
2. Feeling hungry in the middle of the night
3. Heart attacks happening more often in midmorning
4. Jet lag
5. Being more likely to feel pain in the morning

▶ **B** One solution for SAD is to expose the person to bright light for a certain number of hours every day. Based on what you have read, try to think of possible solutions for the following.

• Reverse SAD
• Jet lag

❯Vocabulary Building

Word Form

▶ **A** Study these five words and their forms. Then choose the correct form for each part of speech in the chart below. These words are commonly found in general and academic texts.

convene (v.)	expose (v.)	mechanize (v.)	release (v.)	trigger (v.)
convention (n.)	exposure	mechanism	released	trigger
convening (adj.)	exposed	mechanic	releasing	triggering
convened (adj.)		mechanically	release	
		mechanical		

Verb	Noun	Adjective	Adverb
expose	1.	1.	
mechanize	1.	1.	1.
	2.		
release	1.	1.	
		2.	
trigger	1.	1.	

▶ Compare lists with a partner.

▶ **B** Write three sentences using words from the list.

▶ **C Adjectives and Nouns** Choose the correct form of the word for each of the following sentences. In the parentheses ( ), write which part of speech, noun (*N*) or adjective (*ADJ*), is needed to complete the sentence.

1. depressed / depression

   a. In Audrey's case, Reverse SAD causes severe _____ ( ).

   b. Researchers noticed that as the day gets shorter, some people become

   more _____ ( ).

2. ill / illness

   a. Greenway is very open about her _____ ( ).

   b. I got up this morning, took one look at the bright sunlight, and felt

   quite _____ ( ).

3. warm / warmth

   a. Malls can become very ＿＿＿＿＿＿ (　) in summer because of all the modern skylights.

   b. Daylight and ＿＿＿＿＿＿ (　) are some of the factors that lead to certain disorders.

4. biological / biology

   a. ＿＿＿＿＿＿ (　) never used to be one of my favorite subjects at school.

   b. Scientists are still trying to find a complete ＿＿＿＿＿＿ (　) explanation for Reverse SAD.

◉ **D Two Words—One Idea** Some words in English are formed from two separate words that are joined together. Some examples of these words (nouns) are *housebound*, *homemaker*, and *workload*. Some word combinations (adjectives) are hyphenated (-). Some examples are *free-spirited*, *ice-cold*, and *warm-blooded*. Some of these words can be found in the chapter readings.

Find the following words in the readings and give a synonym for each that could replace it in the sentence.

Word	Synonym
1. daylight	＿＿＿＿＿＿＿＿＿＿
2. computer-animated	＿＿＿＿＿＿＿＿＿＿
3. truckloads	＿＿＿＿＿＿＿＿＿＿
4. frostbite	＿＿＿＿＿＿＿＿＿＿
5. full-time	＿＿＿＿＿＿＿＿＿＿
6. health-conscious	＿＿＿＿＿＿＿＿＿＿
7. forecasting	＿＿＿＿＿＿＿＿＿＿

▶ Look for other examples in the readings and highlight them. Compare your answers with a partner.

Vocabulary in Context

▷ You can often understand the meaning of a new word from your understanding of the other words in a sentence. Match the highlighted word in each sentence with one of the words in the following list.

a. appear suddenly
b. disturbed
c. continue
d. follow after
e. weakening
f. causes
g. strong desire
h. fear
i. get worse

1. Her mental health begins to **deteriorate** in the spring. _____

2. Reverse SAD is more **debilitating** than SAD. _____

3. In Audrey's case, Reverse SAD **provokes** severe depression. _____

4. "I **dread** clocks moving forward in the spring." _____

5. The newspaper reporter she had asked to **tag along** asked whether she would like a coffee. _____

6. I was **shaken** when I realized that she had tried to commit suicide. _____

7. At times the irritability can be so extreme that feelings of violence can **erupt**. _____

8. She felt SAD every winter but was generally able to **hang on** until a vacation in Florida in February. _____

9. Appetite and a **craving** for sweets actually increase while a person is suffering from SAD. _____

▷ Check your answers with a partner or with your teacher.

Expanding Your Language

Speaking

▶ **Be the Expert** Work with a partner who read a different article. One person takes the role of a reporter. The other takes the role of someone suffering from SAD or Reverse SAD. Interview each other using the following steps.

▶ **1.** Brainstorm four or five questions you could ask. For example, "What disorder do you suffer from? In what way does it affect your life?"

2. Use your questions to interview your partner.

3. Make notes on the answers you get.

4. Reverse your roles and repeat steps 1–3.

Writing

▶ **Report Writing** Write a report about your interview. Use these steps to help you.

▶ **1.** Read over the notes you made during your interview. Make sure you understand them. If necessary, check the information with the person you interviewed.

2. Write a short introduction in which you mention who you are talking to and why.

3. Using the notes you made, write two to three sentences about each answer.

4. Write a short conclusion in which you can give your opinion about the problem.

▶ **Reaction Writing** Write what you think about one of the following ideas.

1. When people are affected by the weather, what kind of reactions do they have?

2. Is the effect of the weather on our health greater now than in the past? What will it be like in the future?

❶Read On: Taking It Further

Magazine Articles

▶ Find an interesting magazine article about some aspect of the weather or climate change. You could look for an article about global warming or about unusual weather events, such as Hurricane Katrina, which caused an estimated US $34 billion in insurance costs in 2005 when it hit New Orleans and the Gulf Coast areas of the United States. Try to find an article that is one or two pages long. Prepare to present the information to a partner or to a small group.

Follow these steps:

▶ **1. Skimming** Quickly read the article to get the general idea and to check if the information is interesting.

2. Surveying Read the introduction (one or two paragraphs) and the first sentence of every paragraph after that.

3. Find the writer's point of view and the ideas he or she uses to support it.

4. Highlight the important information for each idea. Make notes from your highlighting.

5. Practice your presentation.

6. Make your presentation.

Reading Journal

▶ Write your reactions to the article in your reading journal. You can also include your reactions to articles presented by your fellow students.

Online Study Center For additional activities, go to the *Reading Matters* Online Study Center at *college.hmco.com/pic/wholeythree2e.*

Time Matters

To everything
there is a season
... and a time to
every purpose
under heaven.

—Ecclesiastes 3:1–10

Introducing the Topic

The passage of time is something that we have no control over. The only thing we can try to control is what we do with it. In this unit, you will read about time in the twenty-first century. Is our experience of time the same as it used to be? Chapter 5 looks at what some writers have to say about our fast-paced world and how speed is influencing our lives. Chapter 6 probes the topic of procrastination and its effect on our lives. You'll look at the issue of time management and how to cope with the demands on our time and energy in a positive way.

Points of Interest

Our Experience of Time

Do we have control over our time, or is time out of our control? Check (✔) the category you think fits each of these expressions. Write what you think each expression means. The first one has been done for you.

Expression	Within Our Control	Out of Our Control
1. If you want something done, ask a busy person. *Busy people know how to use their time well.*	✔	
2. Time waits for no one.		
3. A stitch in time saves nine.		
4. Time is money, look to the clock.		
5. Time heals all wounds.		
6. Never put off until tomorrow the things you can do today.		
7. You can't hurry love.		
8. Work expands to fill the time available.		

▶ Work with a partner or a small group. Compare the categories you chose, and explain what the expression means to you. Discuss the following questions.

- Is today's world too fast paced or not?
- Do we have more control over time today than in the past?

5 Are We in a Race Against Time?

Chapter Openers

What's Your Opinion?

▶ Circle *A* if you agree or *D* if you disagree with each statement.

1. A D   Most days I have enough time to do the things I plan to do.

2. A D   Thanks to technology such as computers and cell phones, it takes less time to get work done than it used to.

3. A D   I often feel that I don't have enough time to spend with friends and family.

4. A D   In the future, I expect to have more time to do the things I want to do.

▶ Work with a partner or a small group. Compare your ideas. Explain your ideas using reasons and examples.

Discussion Questions

▶ Think about these questions. Share your ideas with a partner or a small group.

1. What is your typical daily schedule?
2. Has it always been like this? If not, explain the changes that have taken place.
3. Is the pace of life busier here or in your country? Explain.
4. What is the average number of hours you work in a typical workweek?
5. Are there any activities that you would like to do but have no time for?
6. How often do you have free time in which you can do whatever you want?

Exploring and Understanding Reading

Previewing

▶ The following reading is about the busy schedules that most North Americans have. Read only the title and subtitle, then predict three ideas that will be discussed.

1. _____

2. _____

3. _____

▶ Compare and discuss your predictions with your partner or group.

Surveying

▶ **A** Read the introduction (paragraphs 1–3) and the first sentence of every paragraph after that. Change or add to your predictions.

▶ **B Identifying the Focus** Check the statement that most accurately reflects what the reading is about.

1. _____ Busy schedules that most North Americans have

2. _____ Reasons why North Americans have busy schedules

3. _____ Reasons why North Americans have busy schedules and what can be done about the situation

Our Schedules, Our Selves

"We are bigger than our schedules."

❶   John is twenty minutes—no, more like half an hour—late for his breakfast meeting, which he was hoping to get out of early so he could make an 8:30 A.M. seminar across town. And, somewhere in there, there's that conference call. Now, at the last minute, he has to be at a 9:40 A.M. meeting. There is no way he can miss it. The afternoon is totally booked, but he can probably push back his 10:15 A.M. appointment and work through lunch. That would do it. Whew! The day has barely begun and already he is counting the hours until evening, when he can finally go home and happily, gloriously, triumphantly, do *nothing*. He'll skip his game of squash, forget about the neighborhood meeting, ignore the shelves that need to be put up and just relax. Yes! ... No! Tonight's the night of the concert. He promised Nathan and Mara weeks ago that he would go.

❷   Welcome to the daily time squeeze of the 21st century—a grueling 24-7 competition against the clock that leaves even the winners wondering what happened to their lives. Determined and focused, we march through each day obeying the orders of our calendars. The idle moment, the reflective pause, have no place in our plans. Stopping to talk to someone or slowing down to appreciate a sunny afternoon will only make you late for your next round of activities. From the minute we rise in the morning, most of us have our day charted out. The only surprise is if we actually get everything that we had planned done before collapsing into bed at night.

❸   On the job, in school, and at home, increasing numbers of North Americans are virtual slaves to their schedules. Some of what fills our days are boring obligations, some are wonderful opportunities, and most fall in between but, taken together, they add up to too much. Too much to do, too many places to be, too many things happening too fast, all mapped out for us in precise quarter-hour allotments in our Palm pilots or day planners. We are not leading our lives, but merely following a dizzying timetable of duties, commitments, demands, and options. How did this happen? Where's the luxurious leisure that decades of technological progress were supposed to give us?

❹   The acceleration of the global economy—with the associated decline of people having any kind of control over wages and working conditions—is a chief culprit. People at the bottom of the socioeconomic ladder feel the pain most sharply. Holding down two or three jobs, struggling to pay the bills, working weekends, enjoying no vacation time, and with little social safety net, they often feel out of control about everything happening to them. But even successful professionals, people who seem fully in charge of their destinies, feel the pinch. Doctors, for example, who work impossibly crowded schedules under the command of HMOs, feel so overwhelmed that many of them are now seeking union representation.

❺   The onslaught of new technology, which promised to set us free, has instead increased the rhythms of everyday life. Cell phones, e-mail, and laptop computers instill expectations of instantaneous action. Although such direct communication can loosen our schedules in certain instances (it's easier to shift around an engagement on short notice), overall they fuel the trend that every minute must be accounted for. It's almost impossible to put duties behind you now, when the boss or committee chair can call you at the opera or the restaurant where you are having dinner with your family, and documents can be e-mailed to you while you're on vacation in Banff or Thailand. If you are never out of the loop, then are you ever not working?

❻   Our own human desire for more choices and new experiences also plays a role. Like hungry diners gathering around a buffet table, we find it hard not to pile too many activities on our plates. An expanding choice of cultural offerings over recent decades and the sense that each of us can fully play a number of different social roles (worker, citizen, lover, parent, artist, etc.) have opened up enriching and exciting opportunities. Spanish lessons? Yes. Join a volleyball team? Why not? Violin and gymnastics classes for the kids? Absolutely. Tickets to a jazz festival, food and wine exposition, and political fund-raiser? Sure. And we can't forget to make time for school events, therapy sessions, religious services, and dinner with friends.

❼   Yes, all of these can add to our lives. But with only twenty-four hours allotted to us each day, something is lost, too. You don't run into a friend anymore and impulsively decide to get coffee. You can't happily enjoy an experience because your mind races toward the next one on the calendar. In a busy life, nothing happens if you don't plan it—often weeks in advance. Our "free" hours become just as programmed as the workday. What begins as an idea for fun frequently turns into an obligation obstacle course. Visit that new barbecue restaurant. Done! Go to tango lessons. Done! Fly to Montreal for a long weekend. Done!

❽   We've booked ourselves so full of pre-scheduled activities that there's no time left for those magic, spontaneous moments that make us feel most alive. We seldom stop to think of all the experiences that we are eliminating from our lives when we load up our appointment book. Reserving tickets for a basketball game months away could mean you miss out on the first balmy evening of spring. Five P.M. skating lessons for your children fit so conveniently into your schedule that you never realize it's the time when all the other kids in the neighborhood gather on the sidewalk to play.

❾   A few years back, radical Brazilian educator Paulo Freire was attending a conference of Midwestern political activists and heard over and over how overwhelmed people felt about the duties they face each day. Finally, he stood up and, in slow, heavily accented English, declared, "We are bigger than our schedules." The audience roared with applause.

❿   Yes, we are bigger than our schedules. So how do we make sure that our lives are not overpowered by an endless round of responsibilities? Especially in an age when demanding jobs, two-worker households, or single-parent families make the joyous details of everyday life—cooking supper from scratch or organizing a block party—seem like an impossible dream? There is no set of easy answers, despite what the marketers of new convenience products would have us believe. But that doesn't mean we can't make real steps to take back our lives.

⓫   Part of the answer is political. As long as Americans work longer hours than any other people on Earth, we are going to feel trapped by our schedules. Expanded vacation time for everyone, including part-time and minimum-wage workers, is one obvious and overdue solution. Shortening the workweek, something the labor movement and progressive politicians successfully accomplished in the early decades of the twentieth century, is another logical objective. There's nothing fixed about forty hours on the job; Italy, France, and other European nations have already cut back working hours. An opportunity for employees outside academia to take a sabbatical every decade or so is another idea whose time has come. And how about more vacation and paid holidays? Martin Luther King's birthday was a good start. But how about Susan B. Anthony's birthday, and your own! Any effort to give people more influence in their places of work—from strengthened unions to employee ownership—could also help us gain much-needed flexibility in our jobs *and* our lives.

⓬   Another avenue is personal: how you think about time can make a big difference in how you feel about your life. Note how some of your most memorable moments occurred when something in your schedule fell through. The canceled lunch that allowed you to spend an hour strolling around town. Friday night plans discarded in favor of a bowl of popcorn in front of the fireplace. Don't be shy about throwing away your schedule whenever you can get away with it. And with some experimentation, you may find that you can get away with it a lot more than you imagined.

⓭   Setting aside some time in your calendar for life to simply unfold in its own surprising ways can also nurture your soul. Carve out some nonscheduled hours (or days) once in a while and treat them as a firm commitment. And resist the temptation to turn every impulse or opportunity into another appointment. It's neither impolite nor inefficient to simply say, "Let me get back to you on that tomorrow" or "Let's check in that morning to see if it's still a good time." You cannot know how crammed that day may turn out to be, or how uninspired you might feel about another engagement, or how much you'll want to be roller-blading, playing chess, or doing something else at that precise time.

⓮   In our industrialized, fast-paced society, we too often view time as just another mechanical instrument to be programmed. But time possesses its own ever-shifting shape and rhythms, and defies our best efforts to control it within the tidy lines of our Palm pilots or date books. Stephan Rechtschaffen, author of *Time Shifting*, suggests you think back on a scary auto collision (or near miss), or a spectacular night sitting outside under the stars. Time seemed almost to stand still. You can remember everything in vivid detail. Compare that to an over-crammed week that you recall now only as a rapid-fire blur. Keeping in mind that our days expand and contract according to their own patterns is perhaps the best way to help keep time on your side.

Jay Walljasper, *Utne*

Chunking/ Outlining

Reading Tip

Often **one main idea** covers **several paragraphs**, where each paragraph could be a **supporting point**, an **example**, or further **explanation. Chunking** means **identifying** the **main idea** and **grouping the paragraphs** that discuss each. It is a **useful** strategy because it makes **locating and using information** from a reading easier. ▪

▶ Survey the article again, this time underlining key words that help you identify the point of each paragraph. Group the paragraphs according to overall main ideas. List the main ideas, the supporting points, and the paragraph(s) that discuss each idea.

Note: Not every single paragraph needs to be included. Some paragraphs are linking paragraphs.

Paragraph(s)	Main Idea	Supporting Points
1-3	Introduction	example (1)
		schedules/21st century (2, 3)
_____	_____	acceleration/global economy (4)
		_____
		_____
_____	_____	_____
		_____
_____	_____	_____
		_____
14	Conclusion	

▶ Compare your chunking with your partner or group and be prepared to explain what you did.

Scanning

Reading Tip

Using **main ideas** and **supporting points** can help you **locate information** more quickly. ▪

▶ Read the questions and, using your list of main ideas and supporting points from the exercise above, decide which paragraph(s) contain(s) the relevant information. Scan the paragraph(s) to find the answers. Write the answer in note form and include the number of the paragraph where you found the information.

1. a. Give information to show that John has a busy day ahead of him.

_____   _____

_____   _____

   b. What things does he have to give up?

_____

2. Give examples of other things that people in general have to give up because of their busy schedules.

_____

3. a. Who is most affected by the acceleration in the global economy?

   _____

   b. Why?

   _____

4. What is the advantage and disadvantage of new technologies?

   Advantage: _____

   Disadvantage: _____

5. In what way are humans responsible for the busy schedules they have?

   _____

6. What price do we pay for having such busy schedules?

   _____

▶ Check your answers with a partner or small group. Refer to the reading if you do not agree.

Note Taking

▶ **1.** Paragraphs 10–13 give some solutions for our busy schedules. Identify the two main solutions and highlight/underline the important information corresponding to each solution. Use the highlighted/underlined information to make notes.

2. Compare your notes with a partner.

3. Use your notes to explain the information. Take turns talking about each solution.

Main Idea	Details
Solutions	1. _____
	_____
	_____
	2. _____
	_____
	_____

Using Examples to Support Ideas

▷ It is very important to support ideas/points with examples, statistics, and explanations. For example, in paragraph 4 the author says that people who have low social and economic status are the busiest. He then gives examples to support his point of what they have to do: "… two or three jobs, struggling to pay the bills, working weekends, no vacation time … ."

What are the following examples of?

1. Doctors (paragraph 4)

   _____

2. cell phones, e-mail, laptops (paragraph 5)

   _____

3. citizen, parent, artist (paragraph 6)

   _____

4. barbecue restaurant, tango lessons (paragraph 7)

   _____

5. Italy, France (paragraph 11)

   _____

Reacting to the Information

▷ **A** Discuss these questions with your partner or group.

1. Do you feel your schedule is too busy? If yes, what are you doing about it?
2. Do you agree with the solutions proposed in the reading?
3. Who do you think is most responsible for people having busy schedules? The individual? Explain.

▷ **B Different Points of View** At the end of the reading, "Our Schedules, Our Selves," the author says, "… we too often view time as just another mechanical instrument to be programmed." What do you think he means by that?

Discuss your opinion with your partner or group.

❭Paired Readings

▶ The following readings give two different ways of looking at time. Choose one of the readings and work with a partner who is reading the same one.

❶Time Bound

Highlighting

▶ Read the article and highlight the sections that help you understand the following.

1. Type of schedule that the Japanese have
2. The impression that the West has of Japan
3. Western concept of time
4. Japanese concept of time
5. Benefits of the Japanese concept

▶ Compare what you highlighted with your partner.

Living on Tokyo Time

Busy Japanese commuters

❶   It is fair to say that Japanese people are unbelievably busy. Working ten hours a day and often coming in on days off, they rarely take a vacation of more than three or four days. A straight week is an unbelievable luxury.

Students have less than a month for summer vacation, and even then they have all kinds of assignments to do.

❷   As an American working in Japan, I watch people living like this, with almost no time for themselves, and I wonder why they don't have more nervous breakdowns. I seem to have far more anxiety about free time than my Japanese friends do, although, compared to them, I have much more of it. Why doesn't this cradle-to-grave, manic scheduling bother them?

❸   A lot of Westerners make the assumption that Japanese people are simply submissive, unoriginal, or masochistic enough to put up with such a punishing system. I don't think that's it. In Japan, time is measured in the same minutes and hours and days as anywhere else, but it is experienced as a fundamentally different phenomenon. In the West, we save time, spend time, invest time, even kill time—all of which implies that it belongs to us in the first place. We might find ourselves obliged to trade huge chunks of our time for a steady salary, but most of us resent this as something stolen from us, and we take it for granted that our spare hours are none of our teachers' or bosses' business.

❹   The Japanese grow up with a sense of time as a communal resource, like the company motor pool. If you get permission, you can borrow a little for your own use, but the main priority is to serve the institution—in this case, society as a whole. Club activities, overtime, drinks with the boss, and invitations to the boring weddings of people you hardly know are not seen as intruding on your free time—they are the *shikata ga nai* (nothing you can do about it) duties that turn the wheels of society. "Free" time (*hima*) is something that only comes into existence when all these obligations have been fulfilled. This is nicely supported by an expression my boss uses whenever he leaves work a little early: *chotto hima morau* ("I'm going to receive a little free time.").

❺   Although I can't pretend I like living on a Japanese schedule, I try hard not to make judgments. *Oku ga fukai*—things are more complicated than they appear. The Japanese sacrifice their private time to society, but in return, they get national health insurance, a wonderful train system, sushi, the two thousand temples of Kyoto, and traditional culture so rich that every backwater village seems to have its own unique festivals, seasonal dishes, legends—even dialect. All of which are invaluable social goods that I would not trade for a lifetime of free hours.

Lynnika Butler, "The Salt Journal," *Utne*

2 Time Free

Highlighting

▶ Read the article and highlight the sections that help you understand the following:

1. Way of life in the United States
2. Drawbacks of the way of life in the United States
3. Way of life in Guatemala
4. Benefits of the way of life in Guatemala
5. Adjustment to life in the United States

▶ Compare what you highlighted with your partner

The Politics of Spontaneity

1   I've been home for only two days when my good friend A.J. asks if I want to "schedule something." Fresh from Guatemala, where I haven't touched anything even remotely resembling a date book for two months, I find myself on the verge of panicking. The only response I can give is an anguished face, at which point A.J. takes pity on me and we agree to try and connect another time.

2   I am not the first person to return to the United States from a long stay abroad and feel like I'm walking into a strange world. Witnessing my friends and my culture with a temporarily altered perspective, I simply can't make sense of the crammed and sped-up lives that most of us lead. I never before have noticed so many people complaining so often of overload and exhaustion, all the while ready to take out their calendars to see when they can squeeze me in.

3   While my mind is confused by this rush to make unwanted commitments, my spirit still feels like it's wandering through the lakeside village where local people sometimes don't even have pen and paper, let alone phones, computers, or any of the tools we Americans rely on to map our futures. At times I made plans in Guatemala, but never more than my memory itself could hold. This allowed me to feel deeply in touch with my body's true limits, a great gift.

4   I've been back in San Francisco four weeks now and I'm still resistant to the appointment-stuffed lifestyle that characterizes my circles.

5   I'm currently attempting to maintain a more open schedule without being completely isolated. But many of my friends just don't know what to do with me. I commit to almost nothing these days, choosing to leave plenty of time for quality-filled, spontaneous contact. People's initial reactions to my hesitation at setting a time and date for every interaction ranged from curiosity to obvious feelings of rejection. Meanwhile, I'm starting to see more friends more often, with almost no planning, than I have in years. So something must be working! But it's still not easy to maintain the practice. When my friends pull out their appointment books, I have to fight the urge to do the same.

❻   Despite the challenge, I find that this I'm-not-going-to-schedule-every-minute-of-my-life experiment feels like an act of personal resistance to a social system that values efficiency and production over the body's natural rhythms. The constant and greedy speed of our culture hurts me, hurts my exhausted friends in San Francisco, and most of all, hurts the people of Guatemala and other developing countries, who are systematically being forced to keep up with us. For them especially, I'm hoping to find a new way.

Leda Dederich, *Utne*

Comparing the Readings

Retelling the Information

▶ Work with someone who read a different story. Using your highlighting, take turns telling the important information.

Compare and Contrast

▶ Based on the information from all three readings in this chapter, note down the key characteristics of how time is viewed in each of the following societies.

1. American _____

_____

2. Japanese _____

_____

3. Guatemalan _____

_____

▶ **B** Using the above information, discuss the following:

1. Similarities and differences
2. Advantages and disadvantages of each
3. Which one resembles your own the most and why
4. Which one you prefer and why

❯Vocabulary Building

Word Form

❯ **A** Study these five words and their forms. Then choose the correct form for each part of speech in the chart below. These words are commonly found in general and academic texts.

reject (v.)	confer (v.)	contract (v.)	flex (v.)	schedule (v.)
rejection (n.)	conference	contract	flexibility	scheduled
rejected (adj.)	conferring	contractor	inflexible	schedule
	conference	contractually	inflexibility	scheduling
			flexible	
			flexibly	

Verb	Noun	Adjective	Adverb
confer 1.	1.	1.	
contract	1. 2.		1.
flex	1. 2.	1. 2.	1.
schedule	1.	1. 2.	

❯ Compare your lists with a partner.

❯ **B** Write three sentences using words from the list.

Vocabulary in Context

▶ You can often understand the meaning of a new word from your understanding of the other words in the sentence. Guess the meaning of the word in boldface in each of the following sentences. One way of doing this is to cover the boldface word and try to think of another word that would make sense in its place.

1. Welcome to the daily time-squeeze of the 21ˢᵗ century—a **grueling** 24-7 competition against the clock that leaves even the winners wondering what happened to their lives.
2. From the minute we rise in the morning, most of us have our day **charted out**.
3. The decline of people having any kind of control over wages and working conditions is a chief **culprit**.
4. The **onslaught** of new technology, which promised to set us free, has instead increased the rhythms of everyday life.
5. But with only twenty-four hours **allotted** to us each day, something is lost, too.
6. Friday night plans **discarded** in favor of a bowl of popcorn in front of the fireplace.

▶ Compare your guesses with a partner. Use a dictionary to check whether you were right or not.

Using Descriptive Phrases

Writers use several techniques to make their writing interesting and appealing. One way is the use of descriptive phrases that represent an idea in a symbolic way. For example, "squeeze me in" in paragraph 2 in the reading, "The Politics of Spontaneity," does not mean that the writer will really be pushed into a small area. It means that her friends have a hard time finding time to meet her in the middle of all their activities.

▶ Find the following boldface words and expressions in the reading and, using the context to help you, write the symbolic meaning of each in the list on the next page.

Living on Tokyo Time

1. Why doesn't this **cradle-to-grave**, manic scheduling bother them? (paragraph 2)
2. In the West, we **save** time, **spend** time, **invest** time, even **kill** time. (paragraph 3)
3. … they are duties that **turn the wheels** of society. (paragraph 4)

The Politics of Spontaneity

4. … or any of the tools we Americans rely on to **map our futures**. (paragraph 3)
5. The constant and **greedy** speed of our culture hurts me … (paragraph 6)

Our Schedules, Our Selves

6. Determined and focused, we **march through each day obeying the orders** of our calendars. (paragraph 2)

7. We are not leading our lives, but merely following a **dizzying timetable** of duties, commitments, demands, and options. (paragraph 3)

8. But even successful professionals, people who seem fully in charge of their destinies, **feel the pinch**. (paragraph 4)

9. … overall they **fuel** the trend that every minute must be accounted for. (paragraph 5)

Word(s)	Symbolic Meaning
squeeze me in	find time for me in the middle of their many activities
1. _____	_____
2. _____	_____
3. _____	_____
4. _____	_____
5. _____	_____
6. _____	_____
7. _____	_____
8. _____	_____
9. _____	_____

▶ Check your answers with your partner. Find a few more examples and write both the word(s) and the corresponding symbolic meaning.

❰Expanding Your Language

Speaking

▶ **A Personal Experience** Think of a time when you were under a lot of pressure because you had too many things to do. Find a partner and describe the situation, what you did, and how you would avoid the same thing happening again.

▶ **B Oral Presentation** Choose a topic related to time. Some examples are the different types of calendars that are used around the world, the different types of clocks and other ways of keeping time that are used, or the problem of jet lag and how to avoid it when you travel across different time zones.

To prepare your presentation, follow these steps.

▶ **1.** Choose your topic for a three-minute presentation.

2. On your own, brainstorm an outline of the important ideas you want to talk about.

3. Discuss your ideas with another person. Ask for suggestions for ideas to include or exclude.

4. Gather information from your school library, the Internet, or your own sources to complete your outline.

5. Repeat step 3. Show your completed outline to your teacher.

6. Practice delivering your presentation until you are comfortable explaining without reading your notes.

7. Make your presentation to others in a small group.

Writing

▶ **Reaction Writing** Write your reactions to the ideas that you read about in this chapter concerning time and the way it is viewed in different places. What thoughts did you have about the information or in the group discussions that followed?

Online Study Center   For additional activities, go to the ***Reading Matters*** Online Study Center at *college.hmco.com/pic/wholeythree2e.*

6 Procrastination: Can We Manage Our Time?

Chapter Openers

Matching

▶ Match each word with the definition that fits it best.

_____ 1. procrastinator

_____ 2. procrastinate

_____ 3. postpone

a. to put off doing something until a later date

b. person who repeatedly delays completing his or her work

c. to continually delay doing something that we don't want to do

▶ Check your answers with a partner. Use each of these words in an example. Which is worse, to procrastinate or to postpone?

Discussion Questions

▶ Think about these questions. Share your ideas with a partner or a small group.

1. Why do people procrastinate? Give three important reasons.
2. Is procrastination a serious problem? Give three examples to support your opinion.
3. What can procrastinators do to solve their problems? Give three solutions.

Personalizing

▶ In the following list, check the activities/tasks you procrastinate, do on time, or do ahead of time. Be ready to discuss why and what the consequences have been.

	Procrastinate	On Time	Ahead of Time
1. homework	_____	_____	_____
2. cleaning	_____	_____	_____
3. paying bills	_____	_____	_____
4. studying for exams	_____	_____	_____
5. buying holiday gifts	_____	_____	_____
6. shopping for food	_____	_____	_____
7. visiting the dentist	_____	_____	_____
8. exercising	_____	_____	_____
9. completing tax forms	_____	_____	_____

Exploring and Understanding Reading

Previewing

▶ Read the title and subtitle of the reading. Predict what aspect of procrastination the author will focus on and write it below. Underline the key words that enabled you to make that prediction.

_____

▶ Compare your prediction with a partner or small group.

Understanding the Introduction

▶ Read paragraphs 1–5 and answer the following questions.

1. What should Jared have been doing by now?

_____

2. What is he doing instead?

_____

3. Why?

_____

4. Is Jared's situation unique? Explain.

_____

5. What is procrastination? (Use your own words as much as possible).

_____

6. a. What do psychologists believe causes procrastination?

_____

   b. How did they come to this conclusion?

_____

7. Why did psychologists choose to study procrastination among students?

_____

8. What effect does procrastination have?

_____

▶ Compare your answers with a partner or small group.

Analyzing the Introduction

Good introductions are very important for several reasons. They serve to:

- get the reader interested.
- tell the reader what the focus of the article is and/or the point of view of the author.
- give the reader an idea of the type/source of information in the article.

▶ Quickly read the introduction again (paragraphs 1–5) and use the following questions to help you decide if the introduction served its purposes.

1. **Interest**
   a. How does the author get the reader interested?
   b. Do you think this is an effective way to gain interest? Why or why not?

2. **Focus/Point of View: Finding the Thesis Statement** The thesis statement is one or two sentences toward the end of the introduction that clearly states what the article is about.
   c. Underline what you think is the thesis statement. Restate the thesis in your own words.

   _____

   d. Does the thesis statement support the prediction you made about the article after you previewed it? Why or why not?
   e. Is the author expressing his own point of view? If not, whose point of view is he expressing?

3. **Type/Source of Information**
   f. According to paragraph 4, what type of information does the article contain and where does it come from (two sources)?

4. Compare your answers with a partner, then discuss the following.
   g. Was it an effective introduction?
   h. Why does the author restate the thesis again at the end of paragraph 5?

Scanning

▶ Paragraphs 6–14 state the various reasons why people procrastinate and briefly explain each. Read quickly and highlight the important information for each reason. Working with a partner, take turns explaining each reason, using what you underlined. Try to use your own words as much as possible.

Stand and Deliver

❶   At the age of 37, Jared, a would-be professor in New York State, should already have a permanent position at a university and perhaps be publishing his second or third book. Instead, he's working on a paper in sociology that he'd planned to complete a decade ago. He's blown two "drop-dead" deadlines and is worried about missing a third. His girlfriend is losing patience.

No one can understand why a guy they consider brilliant doesn't "just do it." Nor, for that matter, can Jared. "If I could change it, believe me, I would," he swears.

❷   Jared is among the one in five people who chronically procrastinate, endangering careers and throwing away peace of mind, all the while repeating, "I should be doing something else right now."

❸   Procrastination is not just an issue of time management or laziness. It's about feeling paralyzed and guilty as you channel surf, knowing you should be studying or rethinking your investment strategy. Why the gap between incentive and action? Psychologists now believe it is a combination of several factors, some of which are anxiety and false beliefs about productivity.

❹   Tim Pychyl, Ph.D., associate professor of psychology at Carleton University in Ottawa, Canada, tracked students with procrastination problems in the final week before a project was due. Students first reported anxiety and guilt because they had not started their projects. "They were telling themselves, 'I work better under pressure' or 'This isn't important,'" says Pychyl. But as soon as they began to work, they reported more positive emotions; they no longer lamented wasted time, nor claimed that pressure helped. Psychologists have focused on procrastination among students because the problem is rampant in academic settings: some seventy percent of college students report problems with overdue papers and delayed studying, according to Joseph Ferrari, associate professor of psychology at Chicago's DePaul University.

Reprinted with permission from *Psychology Today* Magazine. Copyright © 2003 Sussex Publishers, Inc.

❺   Pychyl also found that procrastination is detrimental to physical health. College students who procrastinate have higher levels of drinking, smoking, insomnia, stomach problems, colds, and flu.

So why can't people just buckle down and get the job done?

❻   *False Beliefs* Many procrastinators are convinced that they work better under pressure, or they'll feel better about tackling the work later. But tomorrow never comes and last-minute work is often low quality. In spite of what they may believe, "Procrastinators generally don't do well under pressure," says Ferrari. The idea that time pressure improves performance is perhaps the most common myth among procrastinators.

❼   *Fear of Failure* "The main reason people procrastinate is fear," says Neil Fiore, Ph.D., author of *The Now Habit*. Procrastinators fear they'll fall short because they don't have the requisite talent or skills. "They get overwhelmed and they're afraid they'll look stupid." According to Ferrari, "Procrastinators would rather be seen as lacking in effort than lacking in ability." If you flunk a calculus exam, better to loudly blame it on the half-hour study blitz than admit to yourself that you could have used a tutor the entire semester.

> Do you check your e-mail 100 times a day, only to answer two messages? Understanding why people really procrastinate is the key to emptying that in-box and getting on with life.

❽   *Perfectionism* Procrastinators tend to be perfectionists—and they're in overdrive because they're insecure. People who do their best because they want to win don't procrastinate; but those who feel they must be perfect to please others often put things off. These people fret that, "No one will love me if everything I do isn't utter genius." Such perfectionism is at the heart of many an unfinished novel.

❾   *Self-Control* Impulsivity may seem diametrically opposed to procrastination, but both can be part of a larger problem: self-control. People who are impulsive may not be able to prioritize intentions, says Pychyl. So, while writing a term paper you break for a snack and see some dirt in the refrigerator, which leads to cleaning the entire kitchen.

❿   *Punitive Parenting* Children of authoritarian parents are more likely to procrastinate. Pychyl speculates that children with such parents postpone choices because their decisions are so frequently criticized—or made for them. Alternatively, the child may procrastinate as a form of rebellion. Refusing to study can be an angry—if self-defeating—message to Mom and Dad.

⓫   *Thrill-Seeking* Some procrastinators enjoy the adrenaline "rush." These people find perverse satisfaction when they finish their taxes minutes before midnight on April 15 and dash to the post office just before it closes.

⓬   *Task-Related Anxieties* Procrastination can be associated with specific situations. "Humans avoid the difficult and boring," says Fiore. Even the least procrastination-prone individuals put off taxes and visits to the dentist.

⓭   *Unclear Expectations* Ambiguous directions and vague priorities increase procrastination. The boss who asserts that everything is high priority and due yesterday is more likely to be kept waiting. Supervisors who insist on "prioritizing the Jones project and using the Smith plan as a model" see greater productivity.

⓮   *Depression* The blues can lead to or exacerbate procrastination—and vice versa. Several symptoms of depression feed procrastination. Decision-making is another problem. Because depressed people can't feel much pleasure, all options seem equally bleak, which makes getting started difficult and pointless.

⓯   It might be comforting for procrastinators to realize that there is a reason for why they procrastinate. But for the situation to change, they have to do something about it. And for a procrastinator, that is not so easy to do.

Maia Szalvitz, *Psychology Today*

Applying the Information

▷ Use the information to discuss the following questions.

1. Do any of the reasons apply to you? If yes, which ones and why?
2. Do you agree with the idea that procrastination is especially a problem among college students?
3. Why do you think this is or is not the case?

Skimming

▷ Many people feel that one important reason why university students procrastinate is that they do not know how to study. The following article gives some suggestions on how to overcome this problem.

Read each of the following statements and, based on your own experience, predict whether it is true or false. Quickly read through the article and verify your predictions.

1. T F   Most students know how to study by the time they start college.

2. T F   Most students expect to do badly on their first set of exams at college.

3. T F   There are many resources available to help students study more effectively.

4. T F   Most students study better at night.

5. T F   Most students cannot concentrate for more than ninety minutes.

6. T F   It is useful to study while waiting at the airport or doctor's office.

7. T F   One of the best ways of learning something is to explain it to someone else.

8. T F   Most students don't know how to take good notes.

▶ Check your answers with your partner or group. Correct any information that is false.

Learning How to Use Your Time

It's not easy but just about everyone can do it. And the rewards—emotional, intellectual and financial—reach well beyond a grade in a college course.

❶   As they begin their first year of college, many students do not know how to study—in no small part because they have not been challenged enough in secondary school.

❷   A nationwide survey by the University of California at Los Angeles of over 364,000 students found that only 31.5 percent reported spending six or more hours a week studying or doing homework in their last year of high school. That was down from 43.7 percent twelve years earlier, when the question was first asked. And 40.2 percent said they studied fewer than three hours a week, while 17.1 percent owned up to studying less than one hour a week.

❸   No surprise then that so many college freshmen who insist they know all the material wonder why their first battery of exams do not go so well. No surprise either that offering courses that teach "learning strategies" or "Student Success" has become a cottage industry.

❹   For the bookish, *How to Study in College* by Walter Pauk, the standard text in the field, is available in its seventh edition, at more than 400 pages. For those inclined to the Internet, hundreds of institutions have established websites with morsels of advice on how to study that also advertise the services of learning strategies centers. The University of St. Thomas, in St. Paul, Minnesota, for example, insists that successful students commit daily MURDER (Mood, Understand, Recall, Digest, Expand, Review).

❺   Over 1.6 million students are enrolled in student success courses in two- and four-year colleges and universities, according to the National

Association for Developmental Education; an additional 900,000 take advantage of tutoring and supplemental instruction, individually or in groups.

❻ At the Learning Resource Centers at the New Brunswick, Newark, and Camden, New Jersey, campuses of Rutgers, about 13,000 students in 34,000 visits a year are supported in a variety of settings. They include workshops with descriptions like "Cramming for exams—and the consequences—in the social sciences" and "Identifying and understanding one's individual learning style for success in ecology courses."

❼ Nonetheless, it is not easy to get the students who most need assistance to use the resources available to them. Doing so, suggests Janet Snoyer, a learning strategies specialist at Cornell University, means "breaking down the relentless high school mind-set that 'help' is designed for laggards and ill-equipped minds." Professionals know that, although they will require those with obviously inadequate preparation to see them and will urge all first-year students to come in early in the semester, many students will not make an appointment until they receive a disappointing grade, and others not even then.

❽ Sometimes, a lack of motivation, procrastination, and difficulty managing time on the part of students are symptoms of emotional or personal distress. For such students, Ms. Snoyer says, "Study skills tips barely reach the tip of the iceberg," and a referral to peer counseling or psychological services is appropriate.

❾ But for many students, learning how to learn is the iceberg. Fortunately, it can be chipped away at, or even melted. Professionals begin by getting students to acknowledge that being an undergraduate is a full-time job, requiring 35 or 40 hours every week including attendance in class and course-related work. Accounting for how they have spent every hour for a week or two helps students assess their ability to set priorities, manage time and, if necessary, to create a new schedule and monitor their adherence to it.

❿ When they hit the books, students should also consider where, how long, and with whom they will study. Will proximity to a telephone, television, refrigerator, friend, or potential date lead to temptation? Can extended exposure to an isolated library cubicle cause sleep disorders?

⓫ A Cornell student, Paul Kangas, discovered that trying to study "while lying in bed was a good antidote for insomnia but not the best way to memorize a list of German vocabulary words." But no matter how conducive to studying their accommodations may be, few undergraduates work more effectively at night than during the day.

⑫   And even fewer can concentrate for more than ninety minutes without a break. That is why, as Michael Chen, an instructor in the Center for Learning and Teaching at Cornell, puts it, "Time between classes is prime time, not face time."

⑬   In his book, Mr. Pauk advises undergraduates to carry pocket work so that they can read an article or memorize vocabulary for Spanish class while waiting at the doctor's office or the airport. Even if this approach seems a bit compulsive, a specific goal—one chapter, three problem sets—and a reward when it is reached, makes study less daunting. That reward, whether it is a coffee break or an update on the soccer game, works only if it lasts no more than half an hour.

⑭   Although students often spend their study time alone, study in groups can be extremely helpful. Carolyn Janiak, a Cornell student, said she found that she always learned more when working with others because discussions "force me to focus on the bigger picture and argument." As she clarified her opinions, she said, she was able to memorize details as well.

⑮   Group sessions work best if each student has already reviewed (and, if necessary, memorized) all the material required for an assignment or exam; dividing up the work and asking each person to learn a part is risky. Leslie Schettino, who teaches learning strategies courses in New York State at Tompkins Cortland Community College and Ithaca College, asks members of study groups to compare lecture notes, read problems aloud, pretend they are tutors in, say, the math lab, and end a meeting only when everyone understands the most important concepts. Often students discover that the best way to master material is to be forced to explain it to someone else.

⑯   But groups are not for everyone. Andrew Janis of Cornell tries to study when his roommate is out because "complaints about organic chemistry distract me." He plays "quiet jazz" or turns his radio to "an AM station that is all fuzz." As he examines notes, handouts, and review sheets, he uses an online encyclopedia to help with dates and other pertinent information.

⑰   Effective note taking is essential. It takes time for students, who are used to high school teachers who signal them with the phrase, "Now this is really important," to recognize the "architecture" of a lecture—the introduction and summary, inflection, emphasis and pause, the use of "therefore," the digression—and to figure out what is worth taking down. Successful students read over their notes nightly, identifying the theme and two or three crucial points. If anything is not clear, they ask the instructor for clarification as soon as possible. To review notes for the first time the night before an exam is to court disaster.

⑱   Notes on a text should be taken on a separate sheet of paper or a computer. Students might begin by skimming to identify the "geography" of the book—its subheadings, graphs, maps and tables, and its main lines of argument. I advise students to throw out their highlighters: those who use them are passive learners who do little more than paint their books yellow. Students who summarize a chapter in their own words, in a few paragraphs, tend to understand the material better and remember it longer. Questions might be recorded in the margin of the book, to be raised in discussions or in office hours.

19   Learning how to learn is not easy. It requires will and discipline, what the nineteenth-century English biologist Thomas Henry Huxley called "the ability to make yourself do the thing you have to do, when it ought to be done, whether you like it or not."

Glenn C. Altschuler, *The New York Times.* Copyright © 2000 by The New York Times Co. Reprinted with permission.

Scanning

▶ Read the article more carefully and answer the following questions in note form and in your own words as much as possible.

1. Why do so many college freshmen not do very well on their first set of exams?

2. What resources are available to these students?

   a.

   b.

   c.

3. Why do students not use these resources?

4. What is the first thing that students have to realize?

5. What factors need to be taken into account when studying?

6. a. Why is it a good idea to work in groups?

   b. When is it most effective?

7. Why do students find it difficult in the beginning to take good notes?

_____

8. What is the best way to learn textbook information?

_____

9. a. What does learning how to learn require?

_____

b. What are the benefits of learning how to learn?

_____

▶ Check your answers with your partner or group.

Vocabulary Building

Word Form   ▶ **A** Study these five words and their forms. Then choose the correct form for each part of speech in the chart below. These words are commonly found in general and academic texts.

challenge (v.)   authorize (v.)   avail (v.)   incline (n.)   instruct (v.)
challenge (n.)   authority   available   inclination   instruction
challenger (n.)   authoritarian   availability   inclined   instructor
challenging (adj.) authorization   availably   incline   instructive
                    authoritative
                    authoritatively

Verb	Noun	Adjective	Adverb
authorize	1.	1.	1.
	2.	2.	
avail	1.	1.	1.
incline	1.	1.	
	2.		
instruct	1.	1.	
	2.		

▶ Compare your lists with a partner.

▷ **B** Write three sentences using words from the list.

Vocabulary in Context

▷ **General Information vs. Specific Facts** In English, general information given in one sentence or clause is often followed by sentences or clauses that contain specific facts about—or examples of—that general idea. Often the language used in the examples helps you understand the ideas in the general statement and vice versa.

▷ Match each general sentence in Column A with one that best follows from Column B.

Column A

_____ 1. The problem of procrastination is rampant among students.

_____ 2. Procrastination is detrimental to physical health.

_____ 3. The main reason people procrastinate is fear.

_____ 4. Ambiguous directions and vague priorities increase procrastination.

_____ 5. Procrastinators tend to be perfectionists because they're insecure.

Column B

a. Those who feel they must be perfect to please often put things off.

b. The boss who asserts that everything is high priority and due yesterday is more likely to be kept waiting.

c. Seventy percent of college students report problems with overdue papers and delayed studying.

d. They get overwhelmed and they're afraid they'll look stupid.

e. College students who procrastinate have higher levels of drinking, smoking, insomnia, stomach problems, colds, and flu.

▷ Check your answers. Work with a partner to read the pairs of sentences.

Reference Words

▶ Words like *this*, *that*, *these*, *those*, *such*, and *so* are used in order to avoid repeating an idea and to provide continuity in reading or writing. The following words/phrases are taken from the reading, "Learning How to Use Your Time," and are listed in the order in which they appear. Locate each word/phrase and note what it is referring to. The first one has been done as an example.

1. That was down from 43.7 percent in 1987.

   The percentage of students spending six or more hours a week studying or doing homework.

2. Doing so, suggests Janet Snoyer …

   _____

3. For such students, Ms. Snoyer says, …

   _____

4. Even if this approach seems a bit compulsive …

   _____

5. That reward …

   _____

Expanding Your Language

Reading

▶ **Different Points of View** Is procrastination always a bad thing? Some people might argue otherwise. The reading that follows makes a few humorous points.

▶ **A** Skim the reading. Find three advantages that you think are valid (believable or true in your opinion or experience) and two that you think are not valid. In the margin, write *V* if you think it is valid, and *NV* if you think it isn't.

Compare your answers with a partner. Be prepared to discuss the reasons for your choices.

▶ **B** What makes a piece of writing fun to read? How do you know that the writer is joking? Reread the selection and highlight phrases or ideas that you think are funny. Work with a partner to confirm your ideas. Be prepared to discuss your ideas with others.

Procrastinate Now

(Original title: Here's Something to Read While You're Not Doing Your Taxes)

By Barbara Brotman

The arrival of spring can mean only one thing: It's time to bring the clay planters inside for the winter. It was supposed to be done six months ago, but blind adherence to a sensible chore schedule is not the way of a practitioner of the art of procrastination.

And art it is. Oh, certainly there are amateurs who dabble in the field, keeping a few unpacked boxes from the last move in the basement or maintaining a modest slush pile of junk mail. But some of us have achieved a higher level of accomplishment in the field of putting off accomplishment. Is it not time to stop upbraiding us with brisk announcements of official desk-cleaning days, and give us credit for the complex delaying tactics we use to avoid answering mail for months at a time?

Never mind the psychological explanations unearthed by scientists—fear of failure, fear of success, perfectionism, avoidance of conflict, or over-reliance on chore completion as a source of self-esteem. ("I pick up the dry cleaning on time, therefore I am good.")

And don't call us lazy; researchers say that laziness is a minor factor because procrastination is so time-consuming. A social worker who led procrastination counseling groups estimates seventy-five percent of procrastinators' work time was spent putting off the work.

Why not consider the advantages of procrastination?

Improved Efficiency If you keep putting off a chore, you may not have to do it at all. Someone else may do your chore or it may become a moot point, streamlining your to-do list while giving you less to do.

Take storm windows. In our guest room, ours are leaning against the wall because we never got around to putting them on for the winter. Now we don't have to. All we have to do is put them away until next winter. Although, frankly— why bother?

Or let's say you owe someone a letter. If you wait long enough, the person may die, pointed out the pasha of postponement, Les Waas, president of the Procrastinators Club of America (bumper sticker: "Procrastinate NOW"). Or you may die, in which case only the most churlish could still hold a grudge.

Moreover, you can do things faster if you put them off, because you have to. Most people take three months to complete their income-tax returns, Waas observed; procrastinators take three hours on April 15.

"A positive procrastinator is … better organized than the average individual," said Waas, an advertising agency owner who founded the club on a lark in 1956 and then found himself getting applications for membership. "Many of the things we put off never have to be done anyway. You save a lot of time."

Simplicity What better way to pare your life down to the essentials than to put off cleaning out your refrigerator?

Let those newspapers and school notices pile up, and repeat: Ommm …

Preservation of Mental Health If we completed all our minor tasks promptly, we would be left with too much time on our hands to consider our major problems, the meaning of life, and what to do when our children become teenagers. Idle hands make mental mischief, but procrastinating hands always have photographs to file.

Excitement Can anything truly compare with the thrill of a last-minute panic? Desperation focuses the mind and jump-starts the creative process.

Cleaning the fishbowl at midnight to avoid imminent piscine death, buying birthday gifts at the all-night drugstore, vacuuming dust bunnies fifteen minutes before guests arrive—these are the things that make the blood course and the mouth swear.

In short, we are to be envied, not reproached. Join us in our off-putting ways, and you, too, can truly taste life, and the bittersweet tang of late-payment fees.

Speaking

▶ **Reporting on a Survey** Together with a partner, brainstorm five questions that you could use to interview someone on how they manage their time, e.g., "Do you make a daily schedule?" Carry out your survey as follows.

▶ **1.** Use your questions to interview 5–7 people and note down their responses.

2. Share your information with your partner.

3. Prepare a brief report (in note form) that summarizes your and your partner's results.

4. Use your report to present your results to your classmates.

Writing

▶ **Reaction Writing** Write in your journal about the topic of procrastination and time management. How do you feel you manage your time? What do you want to be doing in the next year? In two years? In five years?

▶Read On: Taking It Further

**A Different
Point of View**

▷ **A** Madonna sings "This used to be my playground" in a song about her memories of a special place in her past. Download the lyrics of the song and bring them to class.

▷ Discuss the following questions with a partner or in a small group.

1. What place is being referred to in the song?
2. Why would the writer of the song like to go back there?
3. What do you think the message of the song is?
4. What does this story tell us about the nature of time?
5. Imagine that you were to return to your childhood home. Where would you like to go? Why?

▷ **B** There are many songs that deal with the nature of time, the effect of time, or what people would do if they could bring back time, e.g., "Cat's in the Cradle," "The Times They're a Changing," "Time in a Bottle," etc.

▷ **1.** Find a song about time that you like and download the lyrics.
   2. Prepare some questions that you can use to discuss the song.
   3. Use your questions to discuss the song with a partner or in a small group.

Writing

 **Reaction Writing** Write your reactions to the song by Madonna or to one of the songs you discussed. Can you imagine yourself in a similar situation? How would you feel?

Online Study Center   For additional activities, go to the *Reading Matters* Online Study Center at *college.hmco.com/pic/wholeythree2e.*

Technology Matters

Technology made large populations possible; large populations now make technology indispensable.

—*Joseph Wood Krutch*

Introducing the Topic

Man's ability to think and create is one of the main characteristics that separate him from the rest of the animal kingdom. Life today would be very different without all the inventions we have that help us meet our needs for food, shelter, and entertainment. Although man has been inventing for most of his existence on Earth, this unit will focus on those inventions that came into being during the twentieth century; it is then that there has been the biggest explosion. Chapter 7 will look at some of the highlights of technological innovations that are part of our world today. Chapter 8 is about spreading technology from the developed world to the developing world.

Points of Interest

What's Your Opinion?

The following quotations are about technology and/or inventions. Work with a partner or small group and for each:

- discuss what the writer is trying to say.
- decide if the quotation is negative, positive, or neutral.
- discuss whether you agree or disagree and give reasons for your opinion.

1. Name the greatest of all inventors: Accident.
2. The danger of the past was that men became slaves. The danger of the future is that men may become robots.
3. Inventor is a person who makes an ingenious arrangement of wheels, levers, and springs and believes it civilization.
4. It is said that one machine can do the work of fifty ordinary men. No machine, however, can do the work of one extraordinary man.
5. If there is technological advance without social advance, there is almost automatically an increase in social misery.
6. A world technology either means either a world government or world suicide.
7. One has to look out for engineers—they begin with sewing machines and end with the atomic bomb.
8. Technology made large populations possible; large populations now make technology indispensable.

Evaluating What We Have

A The following items were all invented between 1900 and 2003. Put them in order starting from the earliest to the most recent invention. Try to guess which year each invention was made. The first one has been done as an example.

_1909_	instant coffee	_____	photocopier
_____	cellular phone	_____	bubble gum
_____	zipper	_____	vacuum cleaner
_____	airplane	_____	McDonald's
_____	CD (compact disc)	_____	robot
_____	credit card	_____	escalator
_____	computer	_____	atomic bomb
_____	VCR	_____	self-cleaning window

Compare with a partner or small group. See page 275 for the correct order.

B Choose six different inventions (from the list above or any others that you can think of) that have made a big difference in our lives. List them in order of importance.

1. _____   4. _____

2. _____   5. _____

3. _____   6. _____

Share your examples with a partner or in a small group. Discuss the reasons for your choices.

7 Building Our World

Chapter Openers

What Do You Know?

▶ Share what you know about each of the following constructions in terms of:

- where they are.
- who built them.
- when they were built.
- why they were built.

1. The Pyramids
2. The Taj Mahal
3. The Golden Gate Bridge
4. The Eiffel Tower
5. The Great Wall
6. Disneyland

The Taj Mahal

Giving Your Opinion

▶ Choose one of the constructions mentioned above (or any other construction that you know of) and think about what makes it special.

Why do you think humans are so interested in building such huge constructions?

▶ Share your ideas with a partner or a small group.

▶Paired Readings

▶ The following readings are about two different kinds of constructions. Choose one of them and work with a partner who is reading the same one.

❶Bridges: Building Across

Using Illustrations

▶ **A** Are there any famous bridges in your country or where you live? If yes, what are they and why are they famous?

▶ **B** Look at the following information about some of the famous bridges in the world and answer the questions below.

1. When was the first iron bridge built?
2. What is the Golden Gate Bridge famous for?
3. Where is the longest suspension bridge? When was it completed?
4. What was special about the Brooklyn Bridge?

Spanning History

Modern bridge engineering began with the first iron bridge in 1779 and has yielded ever longer, stronger, and more sophisticated structures.

❶ Akashi Kaikyo Bridge

Length: 12,828 feet
Location: Kobe, Japan
Completed: 1998

The longest and tallest suspension bridge ever built, with towers rising more than 900 feet.

❷ **Golden Gate Bridge**

Length: 8,981 feet
Location: San Francisco
Completed: 1937

Set a record for suspension bridge
length in spite of fog, tides, and
the threat of earthquakes.

❸ **Brooklyn Bridge**

Length: 3,460 feet
Location: New York
Completed: 1883

When built, was the longest suspension
bridge; the first to use steel cables.

❹ **Iron Bridge**

Length: 100 feet
Location: Shropshire, England
Completed: 1779

The world's first bridge
made entirely of iron.

Using the Introduction

▷ Read the first two paragraphs of the next reading quickly, then answer the following questions.

1. Who built the Brooklyn Bridge?
2. Why was it built?

Tellback

▷ Read paragraphs 3–4 quickly. Without looking back at the article, tell your partner whatever you remember. Repeat for paragraphs 5–7, 8–9, 10–11, and 12, taking turns in talking first.

▷ Together with your partner, list three or four main ideas that the article discusses.

1. _____

2. _____

3. _____

4. _____

High and Mighty

Soaring structures capture the imagination. Few have a stronger hold than the Brooklyn Bridge, with its grace and human drama.

❶ The New York photographer, Dave Frieder, has actually climbed the Brooklyn Bridge, carrying eighty pounds of camera equipment up the massive steel cables to one of the Gothic towers high above the East River. From that perch, he could see past the opposite tower, over the cityscape, and into New Jersey. "It's such an incredible contrast," he says of the view. "Here's a bridge built in the late 1800s standing above all of downtown Manhattan."

❷ Somehow, the Brooklyn Bridge looks equally at home in Frieder's late-twentieth-century photos and the earliest prints taken 120 years ago, when it connected two separate cities which were then expanding only horizontally. It's still one of the most visible symbols in a town that doesn't lack for them. Behind the symbol is a story of genius, illness, family conflict, and a woman who was ahead of her time.

❸ Brooklyn is now New York City's largest borough, but 150 years ago, although growing quickly, it was considered a village by its neighbors across the river. Although Brooklyn and New York were separated by no more than a mile in places, the journey by ferry could take more than an hour in the winter when the East River froze over and slowed the boats. In 1852, one of those chilled and grumpy commuters was actually in the position to do something about it. John Augustus Roebling, a German immigrant and engineer, was a technical genius—he had introduced iron wire rope to the United States and was using it in his current project, a suspension bridge over the Niagara gorge. He was also not an easygoing man. "His domestic life can be summed up in a few words, domineering tyranny," wrote his son, Washington, in a candid biography, *Life of John A. Roebling*. Washington continued, "It was a fortunate thing that his engineering engagements kept him away for prolonged periods, otherwise his children all would have died young."

❹ John Roebling was chosen as engineer for the bridge in 1867. And despite his feelings toward his domineering father, Washington, also a civil engineer, ended up becoming a key figure in the construction of the bridge. Father and son were surveying the Brooklyn tower site in 1869 when a ferry crashed into the pilings and crushed John's toes. Because he didn't trust medical doctors, he accepted amputation (without anesthetic) but refused any further treatment. He developed tetanus, and as his jaw locked and made speech impossible, he wrote notes about the bridge and his financial affairs. He died of the disease less than a month later.

❺ It fell to Washington, who felt guilty over his failure to warn his father of the ferry's approach, to carry out the ambitious vision. The structure would be the longest suspension bridge in the world, with a span of more than 1,595 feet between the towers. It would use cables woven of steel, stronger than the usual iron but rare in bridges. And its towers would require underwater foundations, built using open-bottomed, airtight wood-and-iron boxes called "caissons" that rested on the river bottom—44 feet below the water's surface for the Brooklyn tower, and 78 feet for the Manhattan side. Workers were literally sealed inside, where they would dig deeply into the riverbed to sink the foundation.

❻ Working in the caissons was like working in a coffin, and not only because of the cramped and stuffy conditions. In 1870, a fire broke out in one, forcing Washington to flood the caisson to put it out. And because of the high air pressure in the underwater work site, ascending too quickly to the surface caused a poorly understood illness, then called caisson disease and now known as the bends. In the spring of 1872, caisson disease—whose symptoms were joint pain, skin rashes, and even paralysis—struck the chief engineer himself.

❼ Washington nearly died, and although he attempted to return to the work site, soon he was simply physically unable to supervise the project. After a recuperative trip to Germany, he and his family moved to Trenton, New Jersey.

❽ How would the chief engineer communicate with his crew? Enter Emily Roebling, Washington's wife. He had fallen in love with her when he was in the Union Army during the Civil War—she was the sister of his commanding officer—and remained so for the rest of his life. Emily, says scholar Vivian Thiele, was athletic, smart, and an absolute model. When her husband fell ill, she wrote letters and read correspondence from the assistant engineers. After the family moved back to Brooklyn, in 1876, she became his on-site representative. Eventually she administered her husband's financial affairs and helped support him during at least two failed attempts to remove him as chief engineer. Some historians have actually elevated her to the level of engineer, but others say that rather than engineering, "she was very good at public relations," always ready to defend her husband's reputation.

❾   There was plenty to challenge Emily's public relations skills. The project was constantly attacked by accusations of bribery, political maneuverings, and plain old doubt. "Every possible accusation was made," wrote Washington. "The bridge would fall down, the wind would blow it down, it would never pay, nobody would ever use it, it damaged the shipping interests, it was too long to walk over it, it would never compete with the ferries, the cost would be so great that the cities would be ruined, etc." In May 1883, a week before the bridge's official opening, Emily asked to cross it in a horse-drawn carriage to demonstrate its safety. She chose an unusual symbol of victory as a traveling partner: a live rooster. On the day itself, the chief engineer watched the festivities from his window in Brooklyn before he and Emily hosted a reception attended by President Chester Arthur.

❿   Nothing was really ever the same after the thirteen-year project was finished. Not for Washington; his firm went on to make wire rope for bridges including the George Washington and the Golden Gate, and he even led the business again for five years toward the end of his life. (He did this all without Emily, who died in 1903.) Not for Brooklyn; it grew to be the country's third-largest city before becoming a borough in 1898. And definitely not for New York City; in his book *The Great Bridge*, historian David McCullough wrote that the bridge could be seen as the gateway to the city's modern era—introducing the steel later used to build the skyscrapers that dwarfed even the bridge's mammoth towers.

Adapted from Katherine Hobson, *US News & World Report*

Scanning

▶ Answer the following questions in note form and in your own words as much as possible.

1. What was Brooklyn considered to be 150 years ago?

   _____

2. Why was it hard to get from Brooklyn to New York?

   _____

3. Describe John Roebling:

   a. as a professional. _____

   b. as a family man. _____

4. a. What happened in 1869?

   _____

   b. What effect did this incident have on John?

   _____

c. What effect did it have on his son, Washington?

_____

5. What two problems did constructing the caissons cause?

a. _____

b. _____

6. What role did Emily, Washington's wife, play in the construction of the bridge?

_____

7. What special skill did Emily have and why was it important?

_____

8. How did Emily show that the bridge was safe?

_____

9. What effect did the building of the Brooklyn Bridge have on:

a. Washington? _____

b. Brooklyn? _____

c. New York? _____

▶ Compare your answers with your partner.

Recapping the Information

> **Tip**

The **information** for **one** main **idea** can be **in more than one place**. One main idea is "problems with building the bridge." Information on "construction problems" is in paragraph 6. Information on "other problems" is in paragraph 10.

▶ **A Note Taking** You are going to talk about this article to someone who read a different article. Before doing so, you need to make some notes and to practice telling the information.

To make notes, follow these steps:

▶ **1.** Make an outline using the main ideas you identified earlier.

2. Identify the supporting points (if any) for each main idea. (See model on pages 54–55.)

3. Highlight the information corresponding to each point.

4. Use what you highlighted to complete your notes.

▶ **B Telling the Information** Working with a partner, compare your notes. Discuss whether your notes have the right amount of detail. (Too much? Too little?)

▶ Using your notes, take turns telling each other the important information in the article. Make sure you explain the information and add any ideas of your own.

❷ Skyscrapers: Building Up

Using Illustrations

▶ **A** Are there any famous buildings in your country or where you live? If yes, what are they and why are they famous?

▶ **B** Look at the following information about some of the famous skyscrapers in the world and answer the questions below.

1. When was the first skyscraper built?
2. Which is the tallest building listed here?
3. Which part of the world used to have the tallest skyscrapers?
4. Why do you think this is no longer the case?

Standing Tall

Modern skyscrapers began being built in the nineteenth century and continue to get taller as time goes on.

❶ Home Insurance Building

Height: 138 feet
Location: Chicago
Completed: 1885

The first modern skyscraper.

❷ Empire State Building

Height: 1,250 feet
Location: New York City
Completed: 1931

Offers an eighty-mile view on a clear day.

❸ Petronas Twin Towers

Height: 1,483 feet
Location: Kuala Lumpur, Malaysia
Completed: 1998

Held the record for world's tallest building
for only seven years (1996–2003).

❹ Taipei 101 / Taipei Financial Center

Height: 1,671 feet
Location: Taipei, Taiwan
Completed: 2003

First building to exceed the 0.3-mile mark.

**Using the
Introduction**

▷ Read the first two paragraphs of the next reading quickly, then answer the
following questions.

1. Who built the Chrysler Building and the Empire State Building?
2. Why were they built?

Tellback

▷ Read paragraph 3 quickly. Without looking back at the article, tell your partner
whatever you remember. Repeat for paragraphs 4–5, 6–8, 9–10, 11–12, and 13, taking
turns in talking first.

▷ Together with your partner, list three or four main ideas that the article discusses.

1. _____

2. _____

3. _____

4. _____

Race to the Sky

Manhattan's glittering towers were created in a frenzy of speculation and self-promotion.

❶   One day in April 1929, an agitated Walter Chrysler called elite architect William Van Alen into his Manhattan office. "Van, you've just got to get up and do something," said the auto magnate, according to a contemporary account. "It looks as if we're not going to be the highest after all." Chrysler's bid to put up the tallest building in the world, a monument to himself and American capitalism, was in jeopardy. In the business offices of Lower Manhattan, George Ohrstrom, a 34-year-old banker nick-named "the kid," was vowing to set the record at 40 Wall Street. "Think up something," Chrysler ordered his architect. "Go to it!" The great skyscraper race had started.

❷   The solution Van Alen concocted in secret would help Chrysler beat Ohrstrom in spectacular fashion. But Chrysler's triumph was short-lived. Later in 1929, John Jakob Raskob, financier for General Motors, announced his plans for an Empire State Building that would dwarf Chrysler's skyscraper. Raskob "wanted to put it up as a sign of the possibility of America," says Neal Bascomb, author of *Higher: A Historic Race to the Sky and the Making of a City*. He wanted a symbol of "what a kid who started as a stenographer can do with a little intelligence and hard work."

❸   The race is long forgotten, and later buildings, including Chicago's Sears Tower and the ill-fated World Trade Center, stole the height crown from the Empire State Building. But the results, especially the Chrysler and Empire State Buildings, still shimmer on the New York skyline as emblems of American optimism. The Chrysler Building's facade, with its shiny metal hubcaps, American eagle carvings, and gleaming steel, pays homage to the capitalist ideal. The sleek geometric lines and massive form of the Empire State testify to American efficiency and commercial dominance. These art deco skyscrapers represent a break with European conventions of architecture, says Mike Wallace, a City University of New York historian, and mark a moment "when New York was reaching for a new kind of cultural supremacy."

❹   The groundwork for the race was laid in the late nineteenth century. Until then, walls had to be thick enough to bear the weight of the floors above, which made erecting tall buildings impractical and expensive. But while designing Chicago's Home Insurance Building in 1883, architect William Jenney came up with the novel idea that a steel skeleton structure—a "cage design"—could support the heavy load of a tower.

❺   Early skyscrapers were decorated with arches, columns, and moldings, as in Cass Gilbert's 1913 Woolworth Building, but gradually American designers stripped away the heavy accents and decorations. "No old stuff for me!" Van Alen, the Chrysler Building architect, once said. "No copyings of arches and columns and moldings! Me, I'm new! Avanti!" A landmark 1916 zoning law in New York City also reshaped the skyscraper. To preserve light and air at street level, the law required buildings to have a "setback" between 9 and 18 stories up and stipulated that towers above that height could occupy no more than a quarter of their site. The result was the familiar "wedding cake" style of 1920s New York skyscrapers.

❻   The push for height was driven by economics as well as the desire for fame. By 1927, oceans of capital were spilling into commercial real estate as well as the stock market. With land prices shooting up, developers began to add stories to their buildings. A 1930 study calculated that a 63-story skyscraper would earn a desirable 10.25 percent return. More stories added to construction costs—but might also fetch higher rents.

❼   At 40 Wall Street, the cold power of money was paramount. Ohrstrom, the investment banker, chose Craig Severance, Van Alen's former partner, to be the architect. The building took form from the inside out, according to Bascomb. Severance figured out how many offices he could fit on a floor, then placed the elevators and the steel columns to determine the shape of the building, which would rise 67 stories and reach 840 feet. Construction started in May 1929, under deadline pressure. In those days, all New York office leases began on May 1. To finish 40 Wall Street by that date in 1930, workers laid foundations for the tower even before they had finished wrecking the old building on the site.

❽   In August 1929, Bascomb writes, rumors reached Severance that Van Alen had modified the Chrysler Building to exceed the official 808 feet. Severance made his building's pyramidal top steeper and added a 60-foot steel cap to push 40 Wall Street to 925 feet. With three shifts working seven days a week, builder Paul Starrett met the May 1930 deadline and set a speed record for completing a skyscraper.

❾   But Ohrstrom, Severance, and Starrett had jumped the gun in claiming the height prize. In November 1929, with the interior still unfinished, they invited the downtown elite to a ceremony. "The World's Tallest Building Raises the Stars & Stripes to the New York Heavens," said the headline in the *New York World*. Unknown to those assembled, Chrysler and Van Alen had tricked them.

❿   First Van Alen added an arch to the ornate steel dome, bringing the Chrysler Building to 860 feet. Then he ordered workers to assemble a twenty-seven-ton steel tip deep within the construction site. A few weeks before the Wall Street event, workers hoisted the spike—called a "vertex"—to the top. The Chrysler Building gained 186 feet instantly; at 1,046 feet, it surpassed 40 Wall Street and the Eiffel Tower, for forty years the world's tallest structure. No one noticed until the story broke four days after the downtown ceremony.

⓫   Chrysler, however, was soon overshadowed by Raskob, who had hired Al Smith, the former presidential candidate and New York governor as his representative. In December 1929, Smith announced to the press that the Empire State Building would rise 202 feet taller than the Chrysler Building. Most of the height would come from a mooring mast for zeppelins (airships). It soon became clear that zeppelins could not land at 1,250 feet, 102 stories above the street, because of the strong winds. That didn't bother Raskob: Topping the others was what counted.

⓬   Raskob and Smith hired Starrett, who embarked on a second all-out construction push. Another rental deadline loomed, eleven months away. To finish by May 1, 1931, he couldn't afford to let his 3,500 men come down from the higher floors for lunch, so he built them restaurants in the unfinished building. The Empire State Building opened on time in 1931, at less than half the projected $50 million cost.

❸   It hardly mattered: By then the nation was in the middle of the Great Depression. With a seventy-seven percent vacancy rate, critics began to call the world's tallest building the Empty State. Half of them seriously suggested turning it into a hotel for New York's one million homeless. Starrett suffered a nervous breakdown, Ohrstrom lost his stake in 40 Wall Street, and Van Alen never worked on another big commission. "… but at least something more than paper and dreams were left," Starrett later wrote in his autobiography. "The tall buildings remained. They would stand for a long time."

Adapted from Jeff Glasser, *US News & World Report*

Scanning

▶ Answer the following questions in note form and in your own words as much as possible.

1. What are the Chrysler Building and the Empire State Building symbols of?

   _____

2. a. Why was it hard to build skyscrapers in the past?

   _____

   b. What happened to make it possible?

   _____

3. In what way were later skyscrapers different from the earlier ones?

   _____

4. Why did skyscrapers look like "wedding cakes"?

   _____

5. Why was it economically beneficial to build skyscrapers?

   _____

6. a. What measures were taken to make 40 Wall Street higher than the Chrysler Building?

   _____

   b. Were these measures successful? Explain.

   _____

7. a. What structure was used to make the Empire State Building the highest in the world?

_____

b. Did that structure serve a purpose? Explain.

_____

8. What was done to make sure that the Empire State Building was completed by May 1, 1931?

_____

9. What was the effect of the Empire State Building on the people who constructed it?

_____

◗ Check your answers with your partner.

Recapping the Information

▷ Tip

The **information** for **one** main **idea** can be **in more than one place**. One main idea is "reasons for building skyscrapers." Information on this idea can be found in paragraphs 2 and 6. ■

◗ **A Note Taking** You are going to talk about this article to someone who read a different article. Before doing so, you need to make some notes and to practice telling the information.

To make notes, follow these steps:

◗ **1.** Make an outline using the main ideas you identified earlier.

2. Identify the supporting points (if any) for each main idea. (See model on pages 54–55.)

3. Highlight the information corresponding to each point.

4. Use what you highlighted to complete your notes.

◗ **B Telling the Information** Working with a partner, compare your notes. Discuss whether your notes have the right amount of detail. (Too much? Too little?)

◗ Using your notes, take turns telling each other the important information in the article. Make sure you explain the information and add any ideas of your own.

❯ Comparing the Readings

Retelling the Information

❯ Work with a partner who read a different article. Use the notes you made to retell the information. Explain the ideas clearly in your own words. Encourage your partner to ask questions about the information or write some of the important facts you explain.

Reacting to the Readings

❯ Keeping in mind the information in the readings and your own experience, share your ideas about these questions.

1. What are some of the characteristics that the people who were involved in building the Brooklyn Bridge, the Empire State Building, and the Chrysler Building have in common?

2. In what way were their reasons for building these structures different?

3. Which reasons do you agree with and why?

4. What benefits does a city get when it has a lot of impressive buildings?

5. Should there be a limit to the number of man-made structures in a city or country? Why or why not?

6. Skyscrapers are one way of accommodating a growing population. What are some other options?

❯ Exploring and Understanding Reading

Predicting

❯ The following article discusses one option for accommodating a growing population. Discuss the following with a partner or in a small group.

1. Where is Dubai?

2. Why would it need to expand in "all directions?"

Skimming

❯ Read the article quickly and bracket the sections that discuss the following:

a. Reasons for the construction boom

b. The Palms project

c. The Burj project

❯ Check what you bracketed with a partner. Discuss the reasons for the construction boom and then highlight the information on each project.

Dubai: Expanding in All Directions

1   When the definitive history of Dubai comes to be written—as a modern state it is barely thirty years old—the Emirate will either be hailed as an amazing feat of engineering, or displayed as a warning of the dangers of uncontrolled construction.

2   Unlike its oil-rich neighbor Abu Dhabi, Dubai's oil reserves are running out, forcing it to diversify aggressively into luxury tourism. By 2015, it hopes that its world-famous resorts and duty-free shopping facilities will attract forty million tourists a year—eight times the current figure. In addition, it is doing its best to attract foreign investors and residents. Dubai now has almost no taxes and when, in 2003, the Crown Prince declared that foreigners could buy freehold property in so-called "free zones" in the Emirate, it was an invitation to the world to come and play in his luxurious sandpit. This immediately started a massive boom in residential investment.

3   Since then it has been impossible to keep up with Dubai. Higher and higher go the skyscrapers. The Arabian desert has become a modern city as homes, hotels, golf courses, and financial and IT (information technology) centers have sprung up, driven by state-owned construction companies.

4   This meant that one of its other main resources—the pale sandy beaches with almost guaranteed sunshine—was also running out. By the 1990s, all the waterfront areas were developed. Crown Prince Sheikh Mohammed ordered Nakheel, Dubai's largest state-owned construction company, to come up with a solution. They did. "We decided to build more beaches," said Hamza Mustafa, the assistant sales manager for Nakheel. These beaches would be in the form of islands designed to look like palm trees such that they would have maximum water frontage. "Every grain of sand is used for beach," Mustafa said. It is estimated that about 250,000 homes will emerge in the next few years.

5   From the air, even from outer space, it's already an astonishing sight: two gigantic palm trees fallen flat on the sea, which on closer inspection turns out to be an intricate network of manmade islands. And beyond the palms there's more—300 artificial islets laid out like a map of the world. There's France, Florida, Ohio, even a mini-Antarctica baking in the 80°F heat. When the entire project is complete, in five years, there will be three "palms" linked to the mainland by causeways, plus the 6-by-4-mile "World," to multiply Dubai's beachfront tenfold to more than 400 miles (640 kilometers).

❻   Land reclamation for the Palm Jumeirah, the first and smallest of the archipelagoes, is finished, and construction of 4,000 apartments and homes on its 12 square miles is scheduled for completion in early 2006. A poetic verse by the Crown Prince will be set in the island. "It takes a man of vision to write on water; great men rise to great challenges," is to be spelled out in Arabic calligraphy by the island's exclusive Water Homes. The residences, built on stilts and visible from the air, are the second phase in the project; the first phase of homes forms Sheikh Mohammed's choice line, "Take wisdom from the wise. Not everyone who rides is a jockey."

❼   The US $30 billion project that is reshaping this segment of the Persian Gulf coast is the world's largest land reclamation effort (75 miles of land have already been reclaimed from the sea) and the focus of one of its most fanciful land rushes. It's also part of Dubai's ambition to rival Singapore and Hong Kong as a business hub, and Las Vegas as a leisure capital. And it seems to be succeeding.

❽   The wealthy are already snapping up the homes on offer, even though few have been built, none has been occupied, and some exist only on maps of what is still open sea. Home buyers include British soccer icons David Beckham and Michael Owen, and what Mustafa described as a list of "actors, singers, and politicians" whose names he refused to disclose. Three-quarters of the buyers are foreigners, he said.

❾   Thirty-three islands in the archipelago called The World, 2.5 miles offshore, have already sold for US $7 million to $35 million each. The largest, 31-square-mile Palm Deira, has yet to rise above the sea and won't be done until at least 2009, but 4,500 of its projected 7,000 homes have already sold, according to the developer, Nakheel.

❿   Not satisfied with just spreading outward, Dubai is also soaring upward. The craze for height has already hit hard in industrializing Asian countries such as Taiwan, Hong Kong, and China, where seven of the world's ten tallest buildings are located. The world's current tallest, Taipei 101 in Taiwan, tops out at 1,671 feet and 101 floors. (The tallest structure, Toronto's CN Tower, stretches 1,814 feet into the sky, largely because of a huge antenna.) Having already built its fame on ambitious construction projects such as The Palms, Dubai now wants to join the competition.

⓫   It already has the world's tallest hotel—Burj Al Arab—a billowing sail-shaped structure soaring 1,053 feet above the Arabian Gulf, and overlooking the Wild Wadi, one of the world's top water parks. But Burj Dubai will be one of the more extreme projects attempted so far. Developers say the Burj Dubai will soar 2,300 feet above the desert—dozens of stories taller than skyscrapers in Taiwan, Chicago, or anywhere else. But they are keeping the exact height a secret to confuse would-be competitors in the world's furious skyscraper race.

❿❷ "We're going to records never approached before. Not only will it be the tallest building, it will be the tallest manmade tower," said Robert Booth, a director at Emaar Properties, the local construction giant developing the pointed, spire-shaped building. Booth joked that the $900 million Burj— due for completion in 2008—will sport a movable spire to keep observers from ever gauging the true height. "Only the chairman will know how tall it is," he joked. He refused to reveal the total number of stories, but a mock elevator at the site held a button for a 189th floor. The building's 10-foot sway in the wind means designers need to prevent whiplash in the ultra-long cables hauling up fifty elevators.

❿❸ The tower owes its shape to American architect Adrian Smith, of the Chicago firm Skidmore, Owings & Merrill. The Burj—"tower" in Arabic— is a silvery pinnacle in a style resembling the futuristic designs of the 1920s: a group of stair-stepped steel-and-glass cylinders that fall away as the central tower reaches into the clouds. A hotel will occupy the lower 37 floors, with 700 private apartments—sold in just eight hours by the developer—taking floors 45 through 108. Corporate offices and suites will fill most of the rest, except for a 123rd-floor lobby and 124th-floor observation deck—with an outdoor terrace for the brave. The spire will also hold communication equipment.

Burj Al Arab Hotel

❿❹ In the past, tall buildings sprouted in cities such as New York where the lack of land meant there was nowhere to go but up. In Dubai, there is no shortage of empty desert for construction. The tower, like other projects here, is aimed at putting the booming city on the map. "It's image, clearly," said Richard Rosan, president of the Washington-based Urban Land Institute. "There is no practical reason for having a building this tall."

❿❺ Developers say the building will return to the Middle East the honor of hosting the earth's tallest structure. That designation was lost in 1889 when the Eiffel Tower upset the 43-century reign of Egypt's Great Pyramid of Giza, at 481 feet high.

⓰   Whether the Burj can keep its title as the world's tallest remains to be seen. "We'll definitely hold the title for a couple years, perhaps longer," Greg Sang, project manager, said. "But someone, somewhere will come along and build a taller building. It's just a matter of time and money."

⓱   The frantic pace of development has utterly transformed Dubai from a sleepy trading and pearl-diving village of the 1960s to one of the world's flashiest metropolises. Other projects include an underwater hotel, an indoor ski slope, and a gargantuan theme park supposed to be nearly as large as the city itself. Hence the plans for Dubailand, a theme park to make Disney World look like Mickey Mouse. Dubailand will have within it Dubai Sports City. When completed—the first parts are due to be ready in 2007— Sports City will encompass 8,000 homes; they will be surrounded by state-of-the-art stadiums and luxurious facilities for golf, tennis, cricket, and football.

⓲   Wahid Attalla, Nakheel's operations director, says there's no reason to slow down. "The world isn't going to wait for you," Attalla said. "There's demand now, so why wait?"

Adapted from many international news sources

Retelling

◉ Use what you highlighted to describe the two main construction projects to a partner. Take turns telling the information.

What's Your Opinion?

◉ Read the following statements and quotes and decide whether you agree (A) or disagree (D). Be prepared to support your choices.

1. A   D   There should be no limit on the amount of construction in a city/country.

2. A   D   People should be allowed to own property anywhere they want even if it is not in their own country.

3. A   D   It is an honor to be able to have the earth's tallest structure.

4. A   D   By the 1990s, all the waterfront areas were developed … "We decided to build more beaches."

5. A   D   "There is no practical reason for having a building this tall."

6. A   D   "The world isn't going to wait for you," Attalla said. "There's demand now, so why wait?"

◉ Discuss your opinions with a partner or in a small group.

Vocabulary Building

Word Form

▶ **A** Study these five words and their forms. Then choose the correct form for each part of speech in the chart below. These words are commonly found in general and academic texts.

sustain (v.)	create (v.)	demonstrate (v.)	economize (v.)	shift (v.)
sustainability (n.)	creative	demonstrator	economical	shifting
sustenance (n.)	creator	demonstrative	economics	shift
sustainable (adj.)	creation	demonstrable	economically	
sustaining (adj.)	creatively	demonstrably	economist	
	creativity	demonstrating	uneconomical	
		demonstration	economy	

Verb	Noun	Adjective	Adverb
create	1. 2. 3.	1.	1.
demonstrate	1. 2.	1. 2. 3.	1.
economize	1. 2. 3.	1. 2.	1.
shift	1.	1.	

▶ Compare your lists with a partner.

▶ **B** Write three sentences using words from the list. Use different parts of speech.

Using Quotations

▶ Writers can use a variety of ways to support a point. They can use explanations, examples, statistics, and sometimes direct quotes. Find the following quotations and write down the point that the writer is supporting. The first one has been done as an example.

1. "It was a fortunate thing that his engineering engagements kept him away for prolonged periods, otherwise his children all would have died young." (High and Mighty)

   John Roebling was a tyrant.

2. "… she was very good at public relations." (High and Mighty)

   _____

3. "The bridge would fall down, the wind would blow it down, it would never pay, nobody would ever use it, it damaged the shipping interests, it was too long to walk over it, it would never compete with the ferries, the cost would be so great that the cities would be ruined, etc." (High and Mighty)

   _____

4. "No copyings of arches and columns and moldings! Me, I'm new! Avanti!" (Race to the Sky)

   _____

5. "The tall buildings remained. They would stand for a long time." (Race to the Sky)

   _____

6. "Every grain of sand is used for beach." (Dubai: Expanding in All Directions)

   _____

▶ Compare your answers with your partner.

Defining Special Terms

▶ Often writers include special terms that are not commonly understood. They identify them by putting them between quotation marks and give the definition either just before or just after the term. Find the following special terms and write down what they mean.

1. "caissons" (High and Mighty)

   _____

2. "cage design" (Race to the Sky)

   _____

3. "wedding cake" style (Race to the Sky)

_____

4. "free zones" (Dubai: Expanding in All Directions)

_____

▶ Compare your answers with your partner.

Expanding Your Language

Speaking

▶ **A Oral Presentation** Choose a construction either from the list on page 143 or any other that you are interested in. To prepare for your presentation, follow these steps.

▶ **1.** Find some information on the item you chose either at your local library or from the Internet.

2. Pick 4–5 main points/ideas that you would like to talk about.

3. Make notes for a five-minute presentation using the format on pages 54–55.

4. Show your notes to your teacher.

5. Practice delivering your presentation until you are comfortable explaining without reading your notes.

6. Make your presentation to others in a small group.

▶ **B Giving Your Opinion** The reading "Dubai: Expanding in All Directions" begins with the statement, "the Emirate will either be hailed as an amazing feat of engineering, or displayed as a warning of the dangers of uncontrolled construction." Which do you think is true?

▶ Make a list of 4–5 points in support of your opinion.

Writing

 **A Expository Writing** Use the notes from your oral presentation to write a report on the item you chose. Your report should consist of at least five paragraphs: an introduction, three body paragraphs on three of the ideas that you talked about, and a conclusion. Keep the following in mind:

- The introduction should include some general information and a clear thesis statement. (A thesis statement is one or two sentences at the end of the introduction that clearly state what the rest of the article is about.)
- Each body paragraph should be about one idea only and it should have a clear topic sentence. (A topic sentence comes at the beginning of a paragraph and clearly states what the paragraph is about.)

B Reaction Writing Write one page summarizing your opinion about the following information about "Illinois Sky City." If this project had gone through, would you like to have been one of the 112,000 tenants? Why or why not?

Illinois Sky City

In 1956, at 89, visionary architect Frank Lloyd Wright designed what was to be his final masterpiece: a mile-high skyscraper on the Chicago lakefront. Dubbed "Illinois Sky City," the 528-story building was to accommodate 112,000 tenants, sped aloft by atomic-powered elevators. Residents of lower floors might see rain falling while those at the top saw snow. Although it was technologically feasible, the building was never constructed due to economic and safety considerations.

Online Study Center   For additional activities, go to the ***Reading Matters*** Online Study Center at *college.hmco.com/pic/wholeythree2e*.

Sustainable Technology

Chapter Openers

Prioritizing

Technology has advanced very fast but not everybody is able to benefit, either because they are poor or because they live in a developing country. For example, there are many parts of the world where most people do not have access to electricity or own a car.

A Make a list of 8–12 services or goods that are generally available in the developed world but not in the developing world.

robots

computers

radios

_____   _____

_____   _____

_____   _____

Compare your list with a partner. Add to or modify your list.

B Discuss the following and be prepared to give reasons for your choices.

1. Which of these services or goods are essential and should be made available?
2. Which of these would be nice to have but are not essential?

List the ones that you decided were essential in order of their importance with the most important first.

Compare your list with another pair of students. Be ready to support your choices.

What's Your Opinion?

▶ **1.** Read the following statement and decide which side you agree with.

Many people feel that the developing world should one day have access to the same things as the developed world. But many disagree because the number of people in the developing world is so high that reaching the same level as the developed world would be too destructive of our natural resources.

2. Make a list of your reasons.

3. Discuss your reasons with someone who has a different point of view.

4. Is there any other alternative besides the two given above? If yes, what is it?

◗Exploring and Understanding Reading

Definitions

◗ When reading about an unfamiliar topic, it is important to first get a general understanding. Use the following steps to understand what is meant by "sustainable technology."

▶ **1.** Give a definition for each of the following words. Do not use a dictionary.

sustain _____

technology _____

2. Check your definitions first with a partner, then against a dictionary. Using your two definitions, agree on a definition for:

sustainable technology _____

_____

3. Check your definition by reading the following three paragraphs. Make any changes to your definition that you feel are necessary and discuss these changes with your partner.

Sustainable Technology

The number of people living on Earth has doubled over the last century. At the moment, a small number of these people use huge amounts of the Earth's resources such as land, energy, and water. Furthermore, the majority of technological innovation occurs in industrialized countries. But the technologies that result are not necessarily affordable, appropriate, or accessible for people in developing countries. On the other hand, traditional technologies used by communities in developing countries are frequently inefficient and unproductive, and increasingly threatened by the pace of technical change.

The solution is to behave in a way that not only makes our lives better today, but also ensures that people in the future will be able to live well. This is called sustainable development. Technology is important because our lives are shaped by technology. Not just new technologies such as cellular phones and computers, but also the traditional technologies that we use to make food, homes, and clothes. So if we are going to live in a sustainable way, the technology that we use has to be sustainable. In the developing world this means finding an "appropriate" technology that falls between the capital-intensive advanced technologies of the "West," which are driven by large-scale production and profit, and the traditional subsistence technologies of developing countries.

Intermediate or "appropriate" technology is intended to build upon the existing skills, knowledge, and cultural norms of women and men in developing countries, while increasing the efficiency and productivity of their enterprises and domestic activities. By and large, it also seeks to sustain the local environment.

Predicting

▶ The following reading is about a solution to a problem that exists in many parts of the world. Work with partner or in a small group. Using the information you have so far, as well as what you know of developing countries, predict the answers to these questions.

1. What are some of the problems that exist in developing countries?
2. Why do so many parts of the world lack electricity?
3. What effect does this have?
4. What do people use when they do not have electricity?
5. What are some of the negative effects of these alternatives?
6. Can the solution come from one man alone? Explain.

Previewing

▶ Read the title and subtitle and answer the following questions.

a. What problem will this article focus on?
b. Where is this problem taking place?
c. Who is providing the solution?

Skimming

▶ Work with a partner. Break the article into approximately four parts. Skim each part and tell each other what you remember without looking back at the article.

Not all articles are **well organized**, especially if they are the narrative type. They may **consist** of a mixture of **long and short paragraphs** and each **paragraph may not provide** all the **details** about one main **idea**. ■

Giving Light, Spreading Hope

Nearly half the homes in the developing world are without light. This Calgary engineer wants to change that.

❶　Dave Irvine-Halliday carefully picked his way along the Alpine trail, heading downhill on a clear spring day in 1997. The then 54-year-old Canadian and his Nepalese trekking guide, Babu Ram Rimal, were hiking the Annapurna Circuit of the Himalayas, working their way back toward the town of Pokhara, which they hoped to reach in a few days. First, though, they planned to spend a night in the village of some of Babu's relatives. Athletically built, with salt-and-pepper hair, Irvine-Halliday was thoroughly enjoying his unexpected Himalayan adventure. A leading fiber-optic specialist, the Scottish-born professor in the electrical engineering department at the Schulich School of Engineering, University of Calgary, was on sabbatical and had just finished a month at the Institute of Engineering (IOE), Tribhuvan University in Kathmandu, helping to set up a lab in its engineering department.

② But when he agreed to extend his stay to do a lecture, it meant missing his flight, leaving him with some time on his hands. So the keen climber decided to do something he'd always dreamed of. He arranged a Himalayan trek.

③ The afternoon light fading, Irvine-Halliday and Babu entered the mountain-shadowed village of Manang and headed for a modest stone-and-mud hut. A middle-aged man and woman greeted the trekkers warmly, invited them inside, and put a pot of water on the wood fire to make tea. The dwelling was so dimly lit and heavy with smoke from the fire pit that when Irvine-Halliday reached for the mug the woman handed him, he could hardly see it or the old couple.

④ They all chatted excitedly, Babu interpreting for Irvine-Halliday. "It would be nice to see their faces," the Canadian thought, smiling and squinting through the acrid smoke. But this remote area was not on a power grid. Only when the group ventured outside a little later that evening was Irvine-Halliday able to see his hosts clearly.

⑤ A few days later, near the end of the trek, Irvine-Halliday, walking ahead of Babu, came upon a stone schoolhouse and stopped to peer through its small windows. It was remarkably dark inside. "How can the children see to read and study?" he wondered, and this thought was immediately followed by another: "I am a photonics engineer; is there any way I can help them?"

⑥ It niggled at him for the rest of the trek and the flight home. "Without light, these people can't read," he thought. "Their children can't do homework. And those kerosene lamps they're using are a fire hazard." He had to find a better way to light up the villages of Nepal.

⑦ "I'm going to see what I can do for them," he told his wife, Jenny, when he got home, and he set to work in his lab at the university. He knew he'd need not only a source of light but also a source of power for the light. Whatever he came up with would have to be simple, durable, very energy efficient, and affordable.

⑧ For his light source, he concentrated on working with light-emitting diodes (LEDs)—a solid-state type of lighting like the red "on" light on a stereo—because they require very little energy. As far as he knew, they were available only in colors, and his prolonged attempts to blend a few together to create white light, which someone could read by, failed miserably because of their limited optical output.

⑨ He moved on to coming up with an energy source to power a light. But to do so would cost money. He asked Jenny, who loved his idea of bringing light to those who needed it, for advice. She said, "Let's put some money into it ourselves."

⑩ The former nurse had a small clothing-design business with a line of credit, and the couple decided to finance the equipment Irvine-Halliday needed with their savings and three credit cards, and use the line of credit to pay off the cards.

⑪ For hours in the evenings and on weekends over the next several months, Irvine-Halliday experimented. He ruled out alkaline and dry-cell batteries: not only do they die quickly but they're expensive and hazardous to the environment when they're discarded. And he carefully considered wind and solar power, but ruled out both as infeasible and overly expensive at that time.

❷ One day nearly two years after his Nepal trip, Irvine-Halliday sat at his computer typing random words like "illumination" and "LED" into search engines. When he put in "illumination products," up popped the web page of a Japanese company called Nichia which immediately caught his interest. There was a photo of a diode, and a banner that read "White LED." Irvine-Halliday read that the company had invented the 0.1-watt WLED light three years earlier.

❸ He grabbed the phone to call the company's U.S. office in Detroit. On the other end of the line, a representative listened to his proposed developing-world lighting project and then said Nichia would be happy to send him a dozen diodes to check out. "Will they be bright enough to read by?" he wondered.

❹ When the package arrived at the university a few days later, Irvine-Halliday grabbed his friend and colleague, technician John Shelley, and the two rushed to his photonics lab. They took one of the tiny diodes and connected its two wires to the positive and negative terminals of a power supply. Irvine-Halliday put a single sheet of typed paper beside it, and then Shelley closed the lab's door and turned off the lights. Not knowing how bright the white LED might be, they waited in the dark for ages to allow their eyes to be as sensitive as possible to low-light conditions. When they switched on the lamp, the tabletop was bathed in a soft, bright light. "Good God, John," Irvine-Halliday exclaimed, "a child could read by the light of a single diode!" The original idea of using LEDs to

bring the gift of light to the developing world may have been conceived in Nepal, but this moment in Canada was definitely the "eureka" moment. To light up a bigger area, he'd need only to bunch a few diodes together. But there was still the problem of how to power the lights efficiently and inexpensively. "What about pedal power?" the professor wondered. Anyone could pedal a stationary bike for a short time each day, he reasoned, to charge, or top up, a 12-volt lead-acid battery of the type used in motorbikes; these batteries could last up to five years powering a low-energy lighting system.

❺ He got to work building a pedal generator, adjusting it until he could pedal at a leisurely pace seated in a chair while reading a book in his hands. Then Irvine-Halliday ensured the rotating shaft didn't go to waste by connecting it alternately to a bobbin, for spinning wool or cotton, or a grinder, for sharpening knives or axes. It was a highly efficient, multi-functional invention.

❻ Irvine-Halliday created the Nepal Light Project and bought about 400 LEDs from Nichia. With these, he made some experimental lamps, and then he and Jenny journeyed back to Nepal in May 1999.

❼ About 6:30 one evening, high up in the mountains, Dave and Jenny Irvine-Halliday sat at the supper table in a powerless guest house with their host. They all had to shout above the roar of the pressurized kerosene lantern set in front of them. Irvine-Halliday strung up one of his WLED lamps and connected it to a fully-charged battery he'd brought along. He asked his host to turn off the lantern, then flicked the switch on the LED lamp. In the quiet, illuminated room, there were big smiles all around the table. "Can you please leave that lamp here?" his host pleaded as the family and guests enjoyed their meal of lentils and rice. What Dave and Jenny were learning was that the villagers truly disliked kerosene lamps of all kinds, as they were expensive to operate, smelly, unhealthy, and very dangerous.

⓲   "After we'd gone to a few more villages and gotten similar overwhelmingly positive responses," recalls Irvine-Halliday, "I realized that this was so much bigger than simply Nepal, so we renamed our initiative Light Up The World (LUTW).

⓳   When he returned to Nepal in the spring of 2000 with Jenny and their son, Gregor, and a large supply of lamps and pedal generators and lit up their first village, it was an "unbelievable feeling." Since then, the LUTW Foundation (www.lutw.org) and subsequent affiliates have provided light for over 14,000 homes in, among other countries, Nepal, Sri Lanka, India, Pakistan, Philippines, Dominican Republic, Guatemala, Bolivia, Ghana, South Africa, China, and Mexico. Around 100,000 or more people have been impacted directly and possibly as many more indirectly.

⓴   The recipients are responsible for generating power for their lamps (most now use solar photovoltaic power, followed by hydro and pedal power) and must pay a minimal fee into a village maintenance fund. But they now have light systems that will last decades, for a total cost of $90 to $110 each—much cheaper than the worldwide average of $100 for a year's supply of kerosene and candles.

㉑   Today, Irvine-Halliday uses a California-based WLED manufacturer called Lumileds to supply LUTW with the diodes at discount prices.

㉒   The Irvine-Hallidays just paid off the money they owed on their credit cards. (The foundation has a Board of Directors, three full-time employees—not including Irvine-Halliday, whose only income is his professor's salary—and half a dozen volunteers.) These days, LUTW's lighting projects are funded by donations from organizations and individuals in Canada and the United States, and by award money it has received for its humanitarian initiative.

㉓   LUTW projects have brought tangible gains to communities in the areas of health and safety, local education, economic infrastructure, and protection of the environment.

㉔   What's Dave Irvine-Halliday's ultimate goal? "Just look at the name of our foundation," he says. "I want us to light up the world by being a facilitator of knowledge. The reality is that most of the developing world can afford to light itself up—all it needs is the appropriate microfinance infrastructure to allow the poor to borrow the money."

Adapted from Bonnie Munday, *Reader's Digest*

Tracing the Development of an Idea

▶ With your partner, outline the steps that led to the establishment of the Light Up the World Foundation.

1. Dave Irvine-Halliday is invited to spend a month at the Institute of Engineering (IOE), which is part of Tribhuvan University in Kathmandu, Nepal.

2. _____

3. _____

4. _____

5. _____

6. _____

7. _____

▶ Check the steps you outlined against the article to make sure you did not miss any.

Note Taking

▶ Read the article more carefully and find support for the following ideas.

1. The need for lighting in the villages of Nepal

_____

2. Obstacles to finding a solution

_____

3. Irvine-Halliday and his wife's dedication and persistence

_____

4. Success of the solution

_____

▶ Work with a partner. Use the brief notes you made to talk about the article. Then discuss the following topics.

1. In what way could LUTW have brought gains to:
   a. health and safety?
   b. local education?
   c. economic infrastructure?
   d. protection of the environment?
2. Do you think Dave Irvine-Halliday is exaggerating when he says, "I want us to light up the world"?

Verifying Your Opinion

◑ The following reading lists the various benefits of using LED lamps. Divide up the benefits equally with a partner. Read the ones you chose. Highlight the important information. Take turns explaining each benefit to your partner.

Lighting the World with LEDs

Solid-state lighting is the lighting of the Third Millennium for the entire world. The technology eclipses conventional lighting, permits independent power production, and dramatically lowers energy requirements.

1. Reliable and Safe Lighting for the Poor

Fuel-based lighting is inefficient, expensive, dangerous, and unhealthy. Burning kerosene and wood fires produce noxious fumes, and because many houses are unventilated, this poses a serious health hazard in the form of respiratory and eye problems.

Kerosene lamps are also a safety risk. Many families cannot afford a proper lamp and rely on a fragile glass bottle with a piece of rope for a wick (Molotov cocktail). Such lighting has more probability of causing fires than all forms of electric lighting.

Light-emitting diodes (LEDs) are ideally suited to the harsh conditions that can exist in the developing world. With no delicate glass or filaments, LEDs can withstand severe shock and vibration—a common cause of premature failure with traditional light sources.

2. Energy and Cost Effectiveness

Providing electricity for lighting and other energy services is extraordinarily expensive in terms of transmission and distribution. Using kerosene is not much better. Supplies of kerosene are subject to restrictions and the price can escalate rapidly because villagers often must buy from the black market. Although the Nepalese government has an official subsidy scheme, when demand outstrips supply, the official price has little relevance. In Nepal, men and women often must trek for several days only to stand in line for several more days. Kerosene can be extremely expensive in remote areas, if it is available at all. Because an average family in Nepal consumes 51 liters of kerosene a year, the cost could be anywhere from US $15–$51 per year. This means that much of the family's funds are spent on poor, unreliable lighting rather than on food and clothing.

On the other hand, LEDs use less than 25 percent of the energy of a regular incandescent bulb. This simple but revolutionary technology can light an entire rural village with less energy than that used by a single conventional 100-watt light bulb. An LED also has an ultra-long life (100,000 hours). This translates into over forty years at six hours per night.

At a current one-time cost of approximately US $100 per installation, WLED lighting systems can provide vastly superior lighting that can be available on demand—unlike fuel, which must be carefully rationed by families.

3. Reducing Environmental Impacts

When families can't afford kerosene, or it is unavailable, they rely on dung or wood to produce fires to light the home. Burning dung is a source of pollution, and laying bare the landscape in search of wood fuel for lighting is recognized as a primary environmental problem in the developing world. It is responsible for habitat loss, mudslides, loss of forest production, soil erosion, and water pollution.

Another example of the benefits lies in the use of LEDs in flashlights. Conservative estimates indicate that the Nepalese use and throw away over 200 million "D" cell batteries every year—straight into the environment. The resulting pollution to streams, groundwater, and fields threatens to be immense. The use of LEDs in place of the conventional incandescent bulb can reduce the number of batteries thrown away to less than 20 million; the use of rechargeable batteries together with LEDs can decrease the throwaway numbers to a few tens of thousands.

4. Other Benefits

Fuel-based lighting is inadequate to conduct classroom instruction after daylight hours. When a home is properly illuminated at night, children can continue studying, which is especially important in areas where, during the day, they are required to help their parents. Lighting at night also allows for men and women to establish small businesses. Indeed, one such business is charging up the batteries that are required to power the LEDs.

LEDs have also found a place in the markets of the developed world. They now claim twenty percent of the traffic-signal industry in North America, up from just eight percent a year or two ago. Replacing conventional lamps with LEDs in the United States alone will bring energy benefits of up to $100 billion by 2025, saving up to 120 gigawatts of electricity annually. If used globally, they can create reductions of 1,100 billion kilowatt-hours per year of electricity ($100 billion per year) thus saving about $50 billion in construction costs and reducing global carbon emissions by 200 millions tons per year.

Adapted from Light Up the World Foundation, *Lighting the World with LEDs*

Applying the Information

▷ Keeping in mind the information in the readings above and your own experience, share your ideas about these questions.

1. What kind of person is Dave Irvine-Halliday (founder of LUTW)?
2. Do you know of or have you met anybody with the same qualities? If yes, share what you know about this person.
3. What are some of the important characteristics that technology suitable for the developing world must have?
4. Is it only individuals that can come up with such technology?
5. Why do companies such as General Electric or Sony not seem to be involved?
6. What changes would such companies have to make to their products if they wanted to sell them in developing countries or to low-income people?

Using the Introduction

▷ The following reading is about a company that altered its product in order to distribute it in developing countries.

Read the first three paragraphs and determine:

- the company.
- the product/name.
- where it is being distributed.
- the main difference between this product and its U.S. version.

Building a Better Washing Machine

❶ Silvia Oliveira calls her "my second mother." Lourdes Silva caresses her contours adoringly. The two Brazilian housewives aren't fawning over a person. The object of their adoration is a washing machine.

❷ Whirlpool Corporation has launched what it bills as the world's cheapest automatic washer, with an eye on low-income consumers who never thought they could afford one. "Before she came along I spent hours bent over the washing tub," says Mrs. Oliveira, a mother of six whose husband, a freelance mason, earns about $200 a month. Referring to the washer by its name in Brazil, she adds, "Now, I can put Ideale to work and do other things, like tend to my children, cook dinner, and even visit my sick mother."

❸ Whirlpool invested $30 million over eighteen months to develop the washing machine in Brazil. But the Ideale is a global project because it is also being manufactured in China and India. The washer was launched in October 2003 in Brazil and China (where its Chinese name means Super Hand-Washing Washer). It made its debut in India in early 2004, and quickly thereafter in other developing countries. The target retail price: $150 to $200. That compares with an average washer price of $461 in the United States, Whirlpool says.

❹   The people's washing-machine project shows how Whirlpool has decentralized its operations, shifting more design work to developing countries. Brazil boasts some of Whirlpool's most advanced factories and a growing technology staff, where highly-skilled, low-cost engineers and industrial designers not only "Latinize" U.S. designs, but create entirely new products for consumers worldwide. "It's the second wave of globalization," says Nelson Possamai, manufacturing director of Whirlpool's refrigerator plant in the southern Brazilian city of Joinville, where products are developed for Indian homes as well as U.S. college dormitories.

❺   Just about a quarter of Brazilian households have an automatic washing machine, and penetration is only about 8 percent in China and 4.5 percent in India, according to Euromonitor International, a consumer-goods research group in London. In Brazil, the Benton Harbor, Michigan, company believes that sales of Ideale will boost the use of washing machines by about 20 percentage points in two years. So far, sales are strong: In the first fifteen days on the market here, Whirlpool says it shipped more than twice as many Ideales than it expected to sell in the first full month. Initial reception in China has been similarly promising, the company says.

❻   Whirlpool has long dominated the appliance market in Brazil thanks to its purchase of two established brands, Brastemp and Consul. But its products catered mainly to well-to-do Brazilians. Sales of a basic washer launched in 1998 didn't take off because the model, which cost about $300, still was unaffordable to low-income consumers.

❼   Whirlpool persevered. Despite declining appliance sales in Latin America's largest market in recent years, there was apparent demand among Brazil's thirty million low-income households, which account for about one-third of all national consumption. Independent surveys indicated that automatic washers are the second-most coveted item by low-income consumers, after cell phones. Whirlpool researchers delved into the washing habits and mind-set of poor Brazilian homemakers through focus-group discussions and visits to households. Whirlpool engineers "adopted" dozens of consumers to give them feedback during the development of Ideale.

❽   Whirlpool was convinced that it had to start from scratch to make a product that was affordable and appealing to the average Brazilian worker, who earns about $220 a month. "It wasn't a matter of stripping down an existing model," says Marcelo Rodrigues, Whirlpool's top washing-machine engineer in Latin America. "We had to innovate for the masses," said Mr. Rodrigues, who is director of laundry technology at Multibras S.A. Electrodomesticos, the Brazilian unit of Whirlpool.

❾   His team developed a cost-effective technology, for which it has applied for patents in key markets. Washing machines normally work a bit like cars, shifting gears for different functions. But for Ideale, Brazilian engineers built a single-drive system by which clothes are washed and spun without switching gears. That is the biggest cost-saving device. To be sure, the spinning is slower than in more sophisticated machines, so clothes may be a bit damper, but Whirlpool studies show that it is good enough for the target consumers.

❿ Focus groups confirmed that the washing machine's capacity could be small, at nine pounds, because low-income Brazilians do laundry more frequently. A Brazilian habit of washing floors underneath furniture and appliances prompted Whirlpool to make Ideale stand high on four legs. Brazilian housewives said they want to see the machine operate, so Whirlpool made a transparent, acrylic lid that is cheaper than glass. In China, families prefer foldable tops because they often have shelves above their washers. In India, the machines are a source of pride so they have wheels for easy mobility.

⓫ Then there were the finer design points. Studies showed that low-income consumers were insulted that less-expensive appliances generally were less attractive. "We realized the washer should be aesthetically appealing; it's a status symbol for these people," says Emerson do Valle, vice president of Multibras. In China, researchers found that appearance is important for another reason: space constraints mean that many families keep appliances in the living room.

⓬ Whirlpool found that Brazilians prefer cheery and rounded styling over sleek and square. Housewives approved when the company changed a gray-and-black control panel to one that incorporated color, such as a yellow start button and blue lettering. Like wealthy Brazilians, however, low-income women also strongly associate white with cleanliness; Ideale comes only in white, as does the vast majority of appliances in Brazil. In China, white is disdained because it dirties easily. There, the washer comes in light blue and gray. In India, it is produced in green, blue, and white.

⓭ In addition to design, Whirlpool looked at special wash requirements in each country. The Brazilian Ideale has "soak" as part of the traditional main cycle to give the perception of improved cleaning. The Chinese Ideale has a "grease-removal" cycle for the vast number of bike riders, as well as up to seven rinse options, while in India there is a Sari cycle for the delicate wash of women's wraparound fabrics.

⓮ In the end, Whirlpool hopes that catering to a new and growing customer base will mean more profits for the company and, hopefully, more resources to continue tailoring products for customers in new and developing markets.

Adapted from Miriam Jordan and Jonathan Karp, "Machines for the Masses," *Wall Street Journal*

Scanning

▶ **A** Answer the following questions in note form and in your own words as much as possible.

1. a. What does Whirlpool have in Brazil?

   _____

   b. What happens there?

   _____

2. How successful have sales been in Brazil?

   _____

3. Why was the 1998 model unsuccessful?

   _____

4. What are the two items most desired by low-income families in Brazil?

   _____

5. How did Whirlpool find out exactly what kind of washing machine Brazilian consumers wanted?

   _____

6. a. What did Whirlpool do to lower the cost of Ideale?

   _____

   b. What effect did this have on the machine?

   _____

▶ Check your answers with a partner.

▶ **B** **Tabulating Information** Using paragraphs 10–13, complete the table on the next page to show how the machines for India, China, and Brazil were tailored to the particular requirements of consumers in each country.

Country	Design	Reason(s)	Special Feature	Reason(s)
Brazil				
China				
India				

Reacting to the Information

▶ Use the information in the readings and your own experience to answer the following questions.

1. Would you consider these washing machines to be a form of appropriate technology?
2. Are there any differences between appliances that you have in your own country and the ones you can find here?
3. Do you agree with what Whirlpool has done? Why or why not?

▶Vocabulary Building

Word Form

▶ **A** Study these five words and their forms. Then choose the correct form for each part of speech in the chart below. These words are commonly found in general and academic texts.

access (v.)	construct (v.)	consume (v.)	design (v.)	persevere (v.)
accessibility (n.)	construction	consumer	designer	perseverant
accessible (adj.)	constructively	consumption	designer	perseverance
inaccessible (adj.)	constructive	consuming	design	
	reconstruction	consumable		

Verb	Noun	Adjective	Adverb
construct	1.	1.	1.
	2.		
consume	1.	1.	
	2.	2.	
design	1.	1.	
	2.		
persevere	1.	1.	

▶ Compare your lists with a partner.

▶ **B** Write three sentences using words from the list. Use different parts of speech.

Grouping Related Terms

There are several ways in which related terms are grouped together. One way is by using commas. Another is by using words such as *such as* and *and*, as in the example below.

(From "Sustainable Technology" on page 167): "people use huge amounts of the Earth's resources *such as land, energy, and water*.

The use of the words *such as* and *and* and the commas show that *land*, *energy*, and *water* are several forms of the Earth's resources.

▶ Match a term from Column A with a group of related terms from Column B.

Column A

_____ 1. benefits of using LEDs

_____ 2. environmental effect of using wood as fuel

_____ 3. unsuitable energy sources for Nepalese villages

_____ 4. light sources for Nepalese villages

_____ 5. traditional technologies

_____ 6. new technology

Column B

a. inefficient and unproductive, and increasingly threatened by the pace of technical change

b. cellular phones and computers

c. habitat loss, mudslides, loss of forest production, soil erosion, and water pollution

d. reduction in electricity, saving on construction costs, and reducing global carbon emissions

e. alkaline and dry-cell batteries, wind and solar power

f. simple, durable, and economical

▶ Expanding Your Language

Speaking

▶ **A My Hero(ine)** Think of someone you admire that has had a strong impact on his/her surroundings. It could be someone that you know personally or that you have just heard of. Using your own information as well as information from a library or the Internet, make notes on the following aspects of that person.

1. Background information
2. Accomplishments
3. Impact on surroundings
4. Why you admire this person

▶ Use your notes to talk about this person to a partner or a small group.

▶ **B Finding Solutions** One of the first people to promote the idea of "appropriate technology" was Dr. Fritz Schumacher, a radical economist and philosopher. He was very interested in the problems of developing countries and especially in the idea of using low cost, appropriate, small-scale development to help people to help themselves. In 1965 Dr. Schumacher, together with three friends, founded the Intermediate Technology Development Group (ITDG). Since then, ITDG has become an international organization that employs 300 people on four continents and has worked in over sixty countries.

What follows is an example of the problems this organization has been involved with.

▶ Read the problem and then discuss it with a partner or in a small group.

Pump as You Play

The Problem

The Context Water is vital for life—without it, nothing could survive on Earth. As human beings, we depend on water like all other creatures. We use water:

- to maintain a balance of fluids in the body (at least five liters a day).
- for cooking.
- to keep ourselves and our clothes clean and hygienic.
- for farming.
- in industry.

It has been estimated that, in total, every person needs at least 50 liters of clean water a day to keep healthy and avoid water-related diseases such as dysentery and cholera. In over fifty countries around the world, people have less than this critical level. Yet in the United Kingdom, each person uses an average of 200 liters of water a day, and in the United States, this figure rises to over 500 liters per person.

Collecting and Carrying Water About two-thirds of the world's families do not have a water supply in the home. Instead they have to collect water from standpipes, wells, or rivers, and then carry it back to the house for use. It is usually the responsibility of women and children to collect and carry a family's water.

As people often live several kilometers from their nearest water supply, collecting water can be a time-consuming, difficult job. Some women spend many hours a day walking to a well or standpipe, waiting their turn, filling containers, and then walking back home. On average, a woman collects 15 to 20 liters of water on each trip—the equivalent of four bags of potatoes—which she then carries home on her head, back, or hip. Backache, inflamed joints, and even permanent deformities caused by neck and spinal damage are common.

> To make the job of collecting the water even harder, it often has to be pumped up from many meters below the ground. To do this, a deep, narrow hole called a borehole is dug down to the water level. Women and children then pump up the water they need from the borehole, usually using a hand pump. It takes about ten minutes of pumping to produce 25 liters of water. Diesel, gasoline, or electric-powered pumps can be used, but these are very expensive to buy and run, and they use up valuable fossil fuels.

Problem Solving

▶ With your partner or group, try to come up with some form of appropriate technology to solve the problem. Keep in mind the following criteria.

Appropriate technology:
- meets the needs of both women and men.
- enables people to generate income for themselves and their family.
- can be designed, improved, managed, and controlled by local people.
- is affordable.
- uses local skills and materials as much as possible.
- has a limited impact on the environment.

▶ Present your solution to another pair or group. Compare and discuss each other's solutions.

Analyzing the Information

▶ Read about the solution that was actually implemented, then answer these questions.

1. What are the direct benefits of this solution?
2. What are the indirect benefits?
3. Does this solution meet the criteria for appropriate technology?
4. Can it be applied in other parts of the world? Why or why not?

> ### The Solution
>
> *The Play Pump* Roundabout Outdoor, a South African company, introduced an innovative solution to the problem of pumping water from a borehole: the play pump.
>
> It came up with the idea of putting a merry-go-round near a borehole and connecting the water pump to the merry-go-round. As local children play happily on the merry-go-round, their energy is harnessed and used to power the pump. Water is pumped up from the borehole into a large, sealed storage tank near the playground. When families need water from the tank, they simply have to use a tap.

The play pump merry-go-round is almost as easy to push as a normal merry-go-round and children have great fun playing on it. Local families can now collect their water quickly and easily, leaving the women more time to earn money for the family and the children more time for education.

How Does the Play Pump Work? A drive mechanism below the merry-go-round is used to power a cylinder that pumps water up the borehole to the storage tank. The cylinder pumps about 4 liters of water for every rotation of the merry-go-round. The mechanism has just two moving parts, making it easy to operate and maintain.

The pump is much more efficient than a traditional hand pump and can move up to 1,400 liters of water per hour, depending on the depth of the borehole. This means that the storage tank can be filled in just two to three hours. After this, it can be topped up as necessary. If more water is pumped up when the tank is full, it is diverted back to the borehole so that none is wasted. Because both the tank and the pumping system are sealed units, the water supply is protected from the risk of contamination.

Get the Message! The play pump's water storage tank is raised up in the air on a twenty-foot-high stand, making it a noticeable local landmark. The designers decided to make the most of this by fixing advertising boards to the side of the tank.

Advertising space is sold to companies and the money made is used to:
- pay the initial costs of installing the equipment.
- train local people in the skills needed to maintain the pump and keep it working well.

There are also plans to use the advertising boards to display HIV and AIDS awareness posters.

Writing

▶ **A Reaction Writing** Comment on the quotation given on the title page of this unit:

"Technology made large populations possible; large populations now make technology indispensable."

▶ **B Position Writing** Think about the following statement:

"It is the duty of the developed world to help the developing world reach the same level of technological development."

▶ **1.** Decide if you agree or disagree.
   2. Make a list of ideas in support of your position.
   3. Work with a partner who has the same position and share your ideas.

4. Make an outline by listing your ideas in order of importance.

5. Add some details to support your ideas. Examples, statistics, and explanations are all good ways to support an idea.

6. Use your notes to write a one-page essay explaining your position.

▶Read On: Taking it Further

➤ Tip

Because this text is transcribed from an actual interview, you might find some unfamiliar terms and sentence structures. Ask your teacher for clarification. ■

▶ What follows is an interview with the cofounder of a Canadian aid organization and an engineering student that volunteers for the organization. As you read, think about whether you would like to volunteer for such an organization and be ready to discuss your reasons.

Engineers Without Borders

Host: Dan Matheson

Guests: George Rotor and Sara Ehrhardt, *Engineers Without Borders*

Dan: You have no doubt heard of Doctors Without Borders. Now Canadian engineers are launching their own international aid program to help developing nations. And joining us now: one of the cofounders, George Rotor, and member Sara Ehrhardt. They're right here. Good morning.

George: Good morning.

Dan: George, what is this thing? How did it get started? What was the inspiration?

George: Well, I guess myself and the cofounder, Parker Mitchell, were fairly aware of some of the challenges in the developing world as we were going through our bachelor's degrees and in school together ...

Dan: At which school?

George: We were at the University of Waterloo. And that was really where the seed was planted for the organization. The idea was there. We understood that technology could have an effect on improving the quality of life of people living in the developing world by attacking some of the basic livelihood challenges.

Dan: For people who don't know what engineers necessarily do, just give us some of the ideas.

George: Some of the ideas of the projects that we would be undertaking are allowing water to be purified, removing land mines, sanitation, and electricity. These are some things that we take for granted here in

Dan: And what you would bring to the project, then, is not necessarily your brawn, but your brain.

George: Right. And in a lot of cases that's exactly it.

Dan: [to Sara] So, when you hear of this concept, what do you think?

Sara: I think, great, really exciting. I'm an engineering student. I really wanted to get involved.

Dan: And how would you use a person like Sara?

George: Well, Sara has been wonderful. She is right now doing a lot of our organizing for our internship program. But other students that get involved would either be doing research in Canada on some of the solutions, making prototypes, like building a water purifier that runs by solar energy and costs under $10, for example. And then they would take these projects or work on other projects in the developing world. For example, installing a computer network in the Philippines.

Dan: So, you go from the birth of just a good idea, to an organization in place, with people already in the field. Tell us about some of the projects that are under way.

Sara: There are some great projects going on right now. We are doing a project that is called Light Up the World. We have interns that are in Nepal, in India, and also in Sri Lanka. And they're lighting up small communities that don't have access to electricity.

Dan: Oh, they don't have any electricity?

Sara: They don't have electricity. And what they're using is a white-light-emitting diode (LED) technology to create lamps.

Dan: They're using a *what* technology?

Sara: They're basically making low-power lamps. And then they're wiring them up. And they're using pedal generators to light up the communities. And it's a really great project.

Dan: Who are the people that go overseas? Are they young people? Are they still students?

George: Right now what we have on the majority of our projects are students going overseas and working with existing nongovernmental organizations like Care Canada, who have been working in the developing world for twenty or thirty years. So there are a lot of experienced people there, at least in developing-world projects. And then often there are engineers on those projects who act as mentors. And our next-stage projects—and we have already begun this with the Light Up the World project—are putting together groups of students

	going over there with professional engineers to implement some of these technologies.
Dan:	And what do these people report back to you? What do they say? Are they having a good time? Are they being productive? Are they making a difference? Is it rewarding?
Sara:	They love it. They come back with renewed interest, a renewed sense of vigor. And they come back and they tell us just how neat a group like Engineers Without Borders is. There was one intern that had gone to India, to the state of Gujarat, and came back and told us about a community of about three million people—so like the size of Toronto. And because of drought, they're trucking their water in every day. So every day they have these trucks coming in and bringing in water for the whole community. So, just try to imagine Toronto with all that water being trucked in. That is a real engineering problem. And engineers need to go in and help to solve these problems.
Dan:	So where do you go from here? You have had a couple of successful projects. You have a lot of interest. What do you do? What's your vision for this thing?
George:	Well, our vision is big. I like to think big and so do the people who are involved in the organization. Right now we have almost a thousand members across Canada, fourteen groups coast-to-coast right now. So we're growing. And we want to continue that growth and then start to expand in the United States and in Britain and in Australia.
Dan:	And how do you find the funding?
George:	We have some great corporate citizens who stepped up and took the lead on this. Suncor Energy Foundation and Ontario Power Generation, for example, and a few other similar-type organizations have given us the seed funding to keep this going. What we need to do now is to start approaching individuals in the community who are willing to support this project, as well as other corporations and government funding for development relief.
Dan:	Do you want to go in the field yourself?
Sara:	Yeah, I've gone to the field before. I can't wait to go back again.
Dan:	Well, nice seeing both of you. Good luck.
Sara:	Thanks a lot.

Adapted from "Engineers Without Borders," *Canada AM—CTV Television*

Online Study Center   For additional activities, go to the *Reading Matters* Online Study Center at *college.hmco.com/pic/wholeythree2e*.

Health Matters

Health is a
blessing that
money cannot
buy.

—*Izaak Walton*

Introducing the Topic

Scientists and physicians have made a lot of progress in diagnosing and dealing with many human health problems. Today, however, advances in health are raising many social and ethical issues. This unit deals with those issues in two areas in particular. Chapter 9 looks at the problems caused by epidemics and Chapter 10 focuses on issues related to advances in medicine such as organ transplants and other new medical procedures.

Points of Interest

Discussion

▶ Think about the following questions. Share your ideas with a partner or small group.

1. What health problems have you or people you know experienced?
2. What do you know about the symptoms and treatments of each of the following diseases?

   - Influenza
   - Heart disease
   - Hepatitis
   - Diabetes
   - AIDS
   - Cholera

3. Has your experience with medical doctors in general been positive or negative? Give examples to support your answer.
4. The American writer Mark Twain wrote, "Be careful about reading health books. You may die of a misprint." What kind of attitude do you think he would have toward health information on the Internet?
5. Are diseases now easier or more difficult to prevent or cure than they were in the past?

Proverbs

▶ The following proverbs are from different parts of the world. Discuss what each means with a partner or in a small group.

1. Early to bed and early to rise makes a man healthy, wealthy, and wise. (American)
2. He who has health, has hope, and he who has hope, has everything. (Arabian)
3. Sickness comes on horseback and departs on foot. (Dutch)
4. However broken down is the spirit's shrine, the spirit is there all the same. (Nigerian)

9 Epidemics

Chapter Openers

Discussion

The word epidemic carries with it all of the emotions of fear and worry over events that we may feel powerless to stop. Although we have treatments to use today that we didn't have in the past, we may still be unable to stop a disease that spreads so quickly that the rate of infection frightens us. Today, as certainly as in the past, epidemics can have a widespread effect on many aspects of our daily lives. In this chapter, we look at epidemics of the past and examine the issues of epidemics today.

▶ Think about the following questions. Share your ideas with a partner or in a small group.

1. What are some contagious diseases? How are they spread?
2. How can you best protect yourself against an infectious disease?
3. Can medical treatments such as vaccines protect against all infectious diseases today?
4. Why have some infectious diseases become epidemics in the past?
5. Are we vulnerable to epidemics today? Give some examples to explain why or why not.

Getting Information from a Chart

> Reading Tip

Reading to find information in a chart is an important study skill. ■

▶ Following is some important information about epidemics. Use the definitions and the information in the chart on the next page to answer these questions.

1. Why is a pandemic worse than an epidemic?
2. What areas of the world have been affected by the bubonic plague?
3. What areas of the world have been affected by cholera?
4. What areas of the world have been affected by influenza?
5. During which time period did the world's most destructive pandemics take place?

Definitions

- **Epidemic:** Any excessive and related outbreak of a particular disease above what is normally expected in a population.
- **Pandemic:** An epidemic that extends beyond the confines of a wide area, typically a continent, and becomes a more widespread problem affecting different parts of the world.

Important Epidemics and Pandemics

1300s

- The Black Death (bubonic plague) wiped out approximately one-third of the population of Europe and Asia, then spread to northern Africa.

1542 to 1560s

- Bubonic plague started in Egypt, then killed forty percent of the population of Constantinople, Turkey, before spreading to Europe. In London, one-quarter to one-third of the population died. It recurred in London at least six more times in the 1560s, killing thousands each time.

1500s to 1600s

- Smallpox devastated native peoples in Mexico, Peru, and North America, causing the deaths of millions. Outbreaks recurred from time to time for several centuries.

1817 to 1823

- The first great cholera pandemic of the nineteenth century traveled from India to Southeast Asia, Japan, China, Russia, and the Middle East, where an exceptionally cold winter stopped it from expanding into western Europe. There were worldwide cholera pandemics in 1830–1833, 1836–1837, 1849, 1863–1866, and 1881–1896.

1830 to 1832

- An influenza epidemic began in Asia and spread to the Philippines, Indonesia, the Malay peninsula, and back into Asia. From there, it went to Russia and spread westward, eventually arriving in North America.

1889 to 1890

- A worldwide influenza epidemic was the most destructive in its time, with 250,000 dead in Europe alone. The global death toll was two to three times that.

1917 to 1919

- The world's most lethal influenza pandemic occurred in these years. The World Health Organization said more than twenty million died. Troop movements in the last months of the First World War spread the disease.

1907 to 1953

- Polio outbreaks occurred repeatedly until the introduction of the Salk vaccine in 1955. In the United States each year from 1951 to 1954, there were an average of 16,316 paralytic polio cases and 1,879 deaths from polio.

❯Paired Readings

▶ People have known for some time that epidemics can grow quickly and then be very difficult to stop. In the past, epidemics took a large toll—affecting the lives of the sick and healthy alike. The readings that follow are about two such diseases: cholera and the 1918 Spanish influenza epidemic. Choose one of these readings. Work with a partner who is reading the *same* article.

❶A Deadly Bacteria Strikes

Skimming

▶ Read the article quickly and answer the following questions about cholera.

1. In what part of the world did the disease originate?

_____

2. How does it affect people?

_____

3. How does it spread?

_____

4. How is it treated?

_____

5. Is it still a problem today? If so, where is it present?

_____

▶ Compare your information with your partner. Refer to the reading to support your answers.

Cholera

The Origins of the Disease

❶   "Asiatic cholera," as it was sometimes called, has existed in southern Asia, especially the Ganges Delta region, from the beginning of recorded history and, as such, is endemic to the region. It was always much feared because it regularly occurred as an epidemic with high death rates. In Calcutta, a temple was built for protection against the disease. In 1817, the first cholera pandemic began as the disease spread outside the Indian subcontinent along trade routes to the west as far as southern Russia. A second pandemic started in 1826 and reached major European cities by the early 1830s. In 1831, the pandemic reached Great Britain. The response to the disease in England led to the establishment of local Boards of Health and a "Cholera Gazette," which served as a clearing-house for tracking the epidemic.

The Spread of Cholera

❷   At the time, cholera was thought to be spread by a "miasma" (a vapor like a fog) coming from rivers. But a study in London by John Snow in 1854 showed the association of the disease with contaminated drinking water, even though this was before any bacteria were known to exist. Three more cholera pandemics between then and 1925 involved Africa, Australia, Europe, and all the Americas. America's eastern seaboard states were hit hard not only in 1832, but again in 1845 and 1866, the year before Joseph Lister introduced the so-called "germ theory" by demonstrating that infections cannot occur in the absence of microbes. The bacteria that causes the disease, *Vibrio cholerae*, was not identified until 1884 in Calcutta during the fifth pandemic. Why the earlier pandemics began and how they ended is not known. Cholera did not persist in any of the new geographical areas that it had invaded but it continued as an ever-present disease in the Ganges Delta.

❸   In the United States, because of the large numbers of cases and deaths during these pandemics, the disease was viewed as a major public-health disaster requiring governmental intervention. The New York cholera epidemic led to the first Board of Health in the United States in 1866, and cholera became the first "reportable" disease, one for which the numbers of cases reported are officially documented.

Symptoms and Transmission of the Disease

❹   Cholera typically begins with the victim simply not feeling well. Soon after, sometimes in only a matter of hours, there comes a violent wave of vomiting and diarrhea. The victim experiences intense, painful spasms of the abdominal muscles. The diarrhea soon gives way to dehydration and shock. The victim's face appears blue and tight; the eyes are deeply sunken; the mouth and lips are parched and cracked. The cholera victim's energy decreases as the diarrhea increases. A clouded sense of reality, painful muscle spasms, seizures, and coma then follow. Between thirty and eighty percent of all cases of cholera during the nineteenth century resulted in death. Even today, untreated cholera continues to carry a mortality rate approximating sixty percent, and no one is spared the pain and suffering it brings.

❺   Cholera well deserves its reputation as a disease of the poor. For example, the bacteria that causes cholera thrives in the unsanitary conditions of places where there is inadequate plumbing. It finds its way into the intestine when human waste contaminates the water supply. Whether it enters in drinking water or on the surface of washed foods, when significant numbers of microbes have entered the gut of even a perfectly healthy individual, the bacteria begins to attack. It eats away at the intestinal lining until it is shredded. Not much more than four to six hours after the onset of symptoms, a vigorous man in perfect health will frequently lapse into shock and die. Most victims who die do so within twenty-four hours.

❻   Cholera is commonly associated with water but the bacteria also can be transmitted by contaminated food; contaminated water is frequently mixed with food, allowing either to act as a vehicle. In more developed countries, cholera is carried by contaminated food (especially undercooked seafood); contaminated water is the more common vehicle in less developed countries. Cholera is usually a warm season disease. In Bangladesh, where the disease is endemic (or naturally recurring in the environment), two peaks occur each year corresponding to the warm seasons before and after the monsoon rain. In Peru, such epidemics only occur in the warm season. Other than shellfish and plankton, animals do not carry it. In areas where cholera is present, the annual rates of disease vary widely, probably as a result of environmental and climate changes. Understanding the relationship between cholera and climate would allow public-health officials to plan better for epidemics.

Treatment is Effective

❼   Cholera can be easily and effectively treated. The key is to replace fluids as fast as they are being lost. Replacement fluids should have an electrolyte composition (chemical balance) similar to the fluids being lost. So a mixture of sufficient salt and sugar is needed. Oral rehydration therapies (ORT) that restore electrolytes have been used throughout the developing

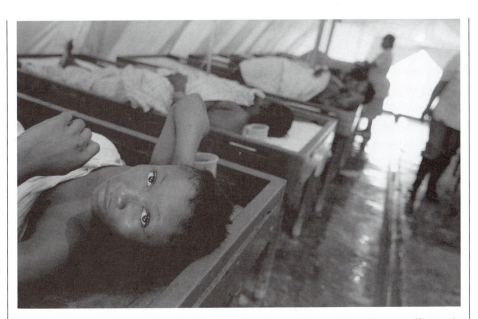

world since the early 1980s. Initially, the fluids must be given sufficiently rapidly to make up for the volume that has already been lost and to restore circulating blood volume. Additional maintenance fluids must then be given to continue to replace losses as they occur. If fluids are given promptly, nearly all deaths are avoided. The World Health Organization estimates that these therapies have saved the lives of millions of children. However, effective treatment is not always available in remote areas where cholera occurs; thus, cholera deaths are still common.

The Cholera Pandemic

8 In the eighty-five years between its initial appearance in Europe and 1902, cholera burst forth in huge intercontinental pandemics no fewer than six times. The current (seventh) pandemic now has involved almost the whole world.

9 The seventh pandemic began in Indonesia, not the Ganges Delta, and a new type of cholera bacteria was first isolated in 1905 from Indonesian pilgrims traveling to Mecca at a quarantine station in the village of El Tor, Egypt. It was found again in 1937 in Sulawesi, Indonesia. In 1960, for unknown reasons, this strain began to spread around the world. It invaded India in 1964, Africa in 1970, southern Europe in 1970, and South America in 1991. The disease has now become endemic in many of these places, particularly southern Asia and Africa. Since 1973, a type of cholera bacteria similar but not identical to the pandemic strain has persisted in the Gulf of Mexico and in the United States, causing sporadic cases of summertime, seafood-associated cholera.

Conclusion

 At the beginning of the twenty-first century, cholera remains an epidemic disease in much of the world. Scientists know a lot about the bacteria that causes the disease and have come up with simple and effective treatments. But new strains of the bacteria are likely to develop, evolve, and spread. Cholera will never be wiped out. So we have to try to keep it away from people and make sure that those affected are diagnosed quickly and treated immediately.

Scanning

▶ **Underlining Specific Information** Look back at the reading and underline the answers to the following questions.

The Origins and Spread of the Disease

1. How was cholera spread from areas where it is endemic to other parts of the world?
2. Where and when did the disease appear during the 1800s?
3. What is the cause of the disease?
4. What was the basis of Lister's germ theory?
5. What was the response to the disease in the United States?

Symptoms and Transmission

6. How does cholera begin and how do symptoms progress?
7. What percentage of people died from this disease in the past? Now?
8. How and in what places is the disease spread?
9. When do outbreaks of the disease occur in Bangladesh and Peru?

Treatment

10. To be effective, what treatment is administered and how is it done?
11. Why do people continue to die from this disease?

Pandemic

12. How many cholera pandemics have occurred?
13. What areas of the world are affected by the current pandemic?
14. Where is the disease now endemic?

Conclusion

15. Why will cholera continue to be a problem?
16. How can it be addressed?

▶ Compare what you underlined with your partner. Try to agree on what you think is important information. Make any changes that are necessary.

Recapping the Information

▶ **Note Taking** Fill in the following outline using the information you underlined. Write the key points for each main idea and the related details below each key point. Use your own words as much as possible. The key points for the first main idea have been provided as an example.

Main Ideas	Key Points / Details
The Origins and Spread of the Disease	Where & when originated
	How it spread
	Cholera in England
	Other pandemics
	Cause of disease
	Cholera in the United States
Symptoms and Transmission	
Treatment	
Pandemic	
Conclusion	

▶ Use your notes to discuss the article with each other. Explain as much as possible.

Reacting to the Information

▶ Based on your ideas, discuss the following questions.

1. Is it easy or difficult to avoid contracting cholera? Give the reasons for your answer.

2. What makes reporting a disease that could become an epidemic or a pandemic difficult?

3. Can cholera be better treated in countries where it occurs? What would have to be done for this to happen?

2 A Deadly Virus Strikes

Skimming

▶ Read the article quickly and answer the following questions.

1. In what part of the world did the disease originate?

_____

2. How did it affect people?

_____

3. Where and how did it spread?

_____

4. How was it treated?

_____

5. Is it still a problem today? Explain why or why not.

_____

▶ Compare answers with your partner. Refer to the reading to support your answers.

The Spanish Influenza

1   Flu, short for influenza, is an infection of the nose, throat, and lungs. Flu is highly contagious and is spread by coughing and sneezing. After a few days or maybe a week of feeling sick, the victims are back to normal. But the Spanish Flu of 1918–1919 was different. In two years, the Spanish Flu infected one billion people, half the world's population at that time, and killed approximately twenty-one million people around the world. In the United States, 675,000 died from the flu in less than a year, ten times more than the number of Americans killed in World War I. In Philadelphia, where 4,597 died in one week, the city ran out of coffins. San Francisco passed a law that everyone had to wear a surgical-type mask in public. At the Paris Peace Conference in April 1919, President Woodrow Wilson caught the flu and nearly died. "It had a worse impact than the black plague of the Middle Ages," says Dr. Edwin Kilbourne of New York Medical College. The Spanish Flu was a pandemic because it circled the globe. "Pan" means "all" or "everyone." It swept through North America, Europe, Asia, Africa, and Brazil in South America. In India, for example, the death rate was especially high, with 16,000,000 Indians dying of the disease.

The Origins of the Disease

❷   The Spanish Flu arrived in 1918 at the end of the First World War in Europe. The war was coming to a climax. Soldiers were moving all over the globe, carrying the Spanish Flu with them. It was called the Spanish Flu for two reasons; first, because it was first reported in Spanish newspapers in the spring of 1918, second, because it killed so many people there. Approximately eight million Spaniards died. The origin of the Spanish Flu is not exactly known, but scientists think it started in rural China. There it

passed first from ducks to pigs and then from pigs to humans. It infected pockets of people that spring and summer. But between the months of August and November of 1918, Spanish influenza spread quickly from country to country, brought by ships passing through major ports around the world. It caused illness among the troops of France, England, America, and Germany. There are even accounts of battles in Europe where soldiers stopped fighting because of the effects of the flu.

The Spread of the Flu

❸   Flu viruses circulate and mutate (or change) constantly, but usually cause little more than a bad cold. Every so often, a completely new strain of influenza appears. Human immune systems don't recognize the virus, so it can cause severe illness and higher-than-usual mortality. The Spanish Flu was the most dangerous strain ever. It spread easily and hit quickly. Spanish Flu began as a normal flu—runny nose, sore throat, and a few aches and pains. Then the symptoms turned vicious—a huge rise in body temperature followed by total physical collapse. The disease killed quickly, sometimes within hours as it traveled throughout the body, finally making it impossible for its victims to breathe. People were healthy one day and died from suffocation, unable to breathe, the next. So much fluid would fill the lungs that, after a person died, a red froth would still pour from the nose.

❹   The Spanish Flu was deadly, twenty-five times more deadly than ordinary flu. Normally, just one-tenth of one percent of flu victims die, and usually the disease kills only the young and the old who cannot resist disease as well as healthy young adults. But, the Spanish Flu killed two and a half percent of its victims. And the majority of its victims were young adult males aged 20–35.

Disease Without a Cure

❺   There was no cure during the pandemic. Doctors could do little to help. The only treatments available at that time were bed rest and aspirin. Most men kept working and resisted staying home in bed until it was too late. Today, antibiotics could combat many of the cases of pneumonia the flu brought on, but in 1918 antibiotics did not yet exist. There were no vaccines to inoculate the healthy against the flu. All a doctor could do was offer advice and comfort. To make matters worse in the United States, there was a shortage of doctors and nurses. Medical students had to stop their schooling so that they could work in the hospitals. They were given jobs as interns and nurses. In some cities, the Red Cross asked businesses to allow workers to have the day off if they volunteered to work in the hospitals at night. Emergency hospitals had to be set up to handle the number of flu victims.

❻   The pandemic led to a shortage of coffins and, consequently, families were forced to bury their own dead. Some insurance benefit checks bounced simply because the insurance companies had too little time to shift cash into the right accounts. Banks honored the checks anyway because they knew the companies had more than enough funds to cover any temporary shortfall. Losses to the insurance companies from the pandemic were substantial. New England Mutual Life Insurance Company said it paid more on influenza death claims in October 1918 than it had on war-related claims during all of World War I. Life insurance companies paid out a total of $125 million in influenza death claims. Inflation statistics show the payout amounted to 0.5 percent of the 1918 U.S. gross domestic product (GDP). Today, a 0.5 percent slice of U.S. GDP would be worth about $30 billion.

❼   Some cities tried quarantine—making it illegal to appear outdoors and out of one's home for forty days. Some towns made it illegal to gather in public places. Some states banned the opening of theaters, bars, schools, churches, and public meeting houses. These closings were an effective way of controlling the disease within the small town population. Because the influenza outbreak was highly contagious and easily spread by coughing, it was a good idea to keep people from coming together in large groups. Quarantines were hard on individuals and, though useful, were only partially effective. Once the quarantine period was over, the people were exposed to the disease. Ultimately, it was more effective to keep people from meeting in large numbers while still allowing them to go outside when it was necessary.

Spanish Flu Vanishes

8   The Spanish Flu ravaged the world for eighteen months. In cities and towns almost everywhere in the United States, October was the worst month of 1918. By November, the pandemic began to ebb. On November 11, World War I ended. People ran into the streets to celebrate and kiss. That gave the flu a brief second wind. Then, the number of cases dropped off. It died out in the fall of 1919. It was the most deadly epidemic the world had seen in 150 years and is still regarded as the worst epidemic of modern times.

9   Today, most people have forgotten about the terrible effects of the Spanish Flu. This is probably because we now have vaccines to use against influenza. But, while scientists are not sure what kind of virus it was, they are always on the alert for deadly diseases, and they worry about the effects that a deadly flu epidemic could have.

Adapted from *USA Today, National Underwriter,* and *Erlanger*

Scanning

▶ **Underlining Specific Information** Look back at the reading and underline the answers to the following questions.

The Origins of the Disease

1. How widespread and deadly was the Spanish Flu?
2. What was the cause of the disease?
3. What effect did the disease have on the troops in Europe?

Spread of the Disease

4. How do flu viruses become deadly?
5. How were people killed by this disease?
6. Who was affected by this outbreak?

Disease Without a Cure

7. What treatment was available at the time? How effective was it?
8. What measures did some cities take? Why were these measures taken?

The Spanish Flu Disappears

9. How did the pandemic end?
10. What happened to have the disease recur?
11. How serious is the epidemic considered today?
12. Why have people forgotten about this epidemic?
13. What are scientists still concerned about?

▶ Compare what you underlined with your partner. Try to agree on what you think is important information. Make any changes that are necessary.

Recapping the Information

▶ **Note Taking** Fill in the following outline using the information you underlined. Write the key points for each main idea and the related details below each key point. Use your own words as much as possible. The key points for the first main idea have been provided as an example.

Main Ideas	Key Points / Details
The Origins of the Disease	When it originated
	How widely it spread
	Effects in the United States
	The Spanish Flu—a pandemic
	Start of the Flu in Europe
	Reasons for its name
	Its origin and effects
Spread of the Disease	
Treatment	
Conclusion	

▶ Use your notes to discuss the article. Explain as much as possible.

Reacting to the Information

▶ Based on your ideas, discuss the following questions.

1. Could a flu virus become a pandemic today? Explain the reasons for your answer.
2. What measures would a government have to take in the face of an epidemic like the Spanish Flu today?
3. What would be the effect of these measures on people's lives?
4. What can be done to prevent this kind of outbreak today?

Comparing the Readings

Retelling the Information

▶ **Tip**

It is very helpful for the listener if you first introduce all the main ideas before talking about each main idea in detail. ▪

 Work with a partner who took notes on the other story. Use your notes to retell the information. Explain the ideas clearly in your own words. Encourage your partner to ask questions about the information or write some of the important facts you explain.

Reacting to the Readings

 Think about the following questions. Free write your ideas on the topic of epidemics. Share your ideas with a partner or in a small group.

1. What are some epidemics that exist today? What are the causes, treatments, and effects of these diseases?
2. Compared to the past, has our ability to fight epidemics improved? Why or why not?
3. What should be done to eliminate or minimize the spread of epidemics?

Evaluating the Information

▶ **Reading Tip**

Remember to skim for specific information. This is especially useful when looking for information in a newspaper article that has very short paragraphs. ▪

 The author of the following article is proposing one way to reduce the spread of contagious diseases. Skim the article and find out what solution she is proposing. After reading, discuss your opinion of this proposal with a partner. In doing this, consider the questions below.

1. What advice is she giving?
2. In her opinion, what are some reasons for new public health risks in North America?
3. Why don't people routinely do what she recommends?
4. How easy is it to follow this advice?
5. How likely is it that people will follow this advice? Give reasons for your answer.

Modern Risks and Old Habits

❶   Modern medicine, complacency, and a generation of parents who aren't nearly scared enough of disease are presenting some new public health risks. Hepatitis A and "hamburger disease" (caused by *e. coli* bacteria carried in improperly handled and cooked meat) are entirely preventable illnesses. Their appearance in North America can be directly blamed on completely preventable situations: lack of sanitation, lack of purified or clean water, and abysmal standards of personal cleanliness and hygiene. Mother was right: wash your hands. Keep your hands out of your mouth. Don't touch that. In North America, we've just seen the results of ignoring Mother's rules: an outbreak of Hepatitis A in which one man died.

❷   We've become complacent because we've been so successful in eradicating and controlling diseases that used to kill children—diseases that were spread by close contact and that formed part of the fear with which my mother's generation lived. It wasn't only good manners to wash regularly; it could be a lifesaver.

❸   Even with some new and virulent infectious diseases, however, there will never be another polio epidemic. There won't be another generation of parents terrified of infantile paralysis or measles or any of the childhood killers that have been slowly and systematically eradicated—almost in one generation.

❹   The legacy of Edward Jenner has freed us almost completely of fear. Jenner discovered vaccinations and how they work in 1796, through his observations of milkmaids. Those infected with cowpox did not subsequently get the more serious smallpox. In 1980, the World Health Organization declared smallpox eradicated. It took only 184 years.

❺   Now we are on the brink of declaring this continent polio-free. We have nearly wiped out diseases such as measles, rubella, and mumps. Vaccinations, inoculations, and public health and safety standards, combined with modern sanitation, clean water, and personal hygiene have given us the healthiest generation of children ever to live on the earth. We are victims of our own success.

❻   Mostly, though, we are victims of complacency. We assume the water is clean, that food is uncontaminated, that other people's standards mirror our own. We presume that what looks clean is clean. Most of the time, we're right. Most of the nastier diseases caused by lack of sanitation and hygiene just don't get a place to start.

❼   Yet incidents such as an outbreak of Hepatitis A show exactly how vulnerable we are. Unlike developing countries and isolated communities in North America where sanitation standards are limited or non-existent, almost no young adult has been infected with the virus. Thus, almost nobody has immunity. That's why more than thirty people came down with the disease over Christmas. We are vulnerable to forgotten lessons.

❽   We spend billions of dollars each year on shampoo, deodorants, and sweet-smelling soap. Millions of us shower every day. Not quite enough of us, though, practice the simplest method of disease prevention—washing our hands, often and well.

❾   The Hepatitis A outbreak was traced to the poor personal hygiene of a food handler. That any person employed in the food industry could even be suspected of not washing after using the toilet is a horrifying thought—but not a surprising one. Restaurants post signs in the restrooms reminding employees to wash their hands. That anyone handling food would need to be reminded is chilling. It's proof that too many parents aren't nearly terrified enough of disease, because personal hygiene isn't something you learn on the job, it's drilled into you day after day at home. You don't need a sign in a toilet.

Reprinted with the permission of *The Calgary Herald.*

Applying the Information

▷ **Making a Decision** You are on a committee that has to decide whether to declare a traveler's alert informing people that a dangerous disease is spreading in a location. Use the information from all three readings, as well as any ideas of your own, to decide if a traveler's warning should be issued for one or more of the following places.

a. A city in a country where most of the population has easy access to doctors and hospital care and can travel easily from one part of the country to another. The hospitals are very careful to regularly report the instances of contagious disease to the government. Only a few cases of the disease have been reported, none of them in this city.

b. A city in a country where most of the population has easy access to doctors and hospital care but rarely travels from one part of the country to another. The hospitals are very careful to regularly report the instances of contagious disease to the government. Only a few cases of the disease have been reported, two of them in this city.

c. A city in a country where only a small percentage of the population has easy access to doctors and hospital care but the population can travel easily from one part of the country to another. The hospitals are very careful to regularly report the instances of contagious disease to the government. Only a few cases of the disease have been reported, most of them in this city.

◐Vocabulary Building

Word Form

▷ **A** Study these five words and their forms. Then choose the correct form for each part of speech in the chart below. These words are commonly found in general and academic texts.

eliminate (v.)	guarantee (v.)	philosophize (v.)	proceed (v.)	resolve (v.)
elimination (n.)	guaranteed	philosopher	proceeding	resolutely
eliminating (adj.)	guarantee	philosophically	proceeds	resolution
eliminated (adj.)	guarantor	philosophical	procedure	resolved
		philosophy	procedural	resolute
			procedurally	resolve

Verb	Noun	Adjective	Adverb
guarantee	1. 2.	1.	
philosophize	1. 2.	1.	1.
proceed	1. 2.	1. 2.	1.
resolve	1. 2.	1. 2.	1.

▷ Compare lists with a partner.

▷ **B** Write three sentences using words from the list.

Vocabulary in Context

▶ **A Defining Specialized Vocabulary** Refer to the Paired Readings to find the words in context. Match the words in Column A with the definitions in Column B.

Column A

_____ 1. fluids

_____ 2. therapy

_____ 3. fatality rate

_____ 4. diagnose

_____ 5. microbe

_____ 6. endemic

Column B

a. death rate

b. something to drink such as water

c. occurring in and limited to a particular area

d. a germ

e. identify a disease

f. a course of treatment

▶ Choose three additional medical terms from the readings and write a definition for each. Compare your answers with a partner.

▶ **B Matching General Information and Specific Facts** In English, general information given in one sentence or clause is often followed by sentences or clauses that contain specific facts about—or examples of—that general idea. Often, the language used in the examples helps you understand the ideas in the general statement and vice-versa.

Match each general sentence in Column A with the one that best follows from Column B.

Column A

_____ 1. Cholera well deserves its reputation as a disease of the poor.

_____ 2. The Spanish Flu was deadly.

_____ 3. Cholera is usually a warm-season disease.

_____ 4. The Spanish Flu was a pandemic because it circled the globe.

Column B

a. It swept through North America, Europe, Asia, Africa, and Brazil in South America.

b. For example, the bacteria that causes cholera thrives in the unsanitary conditions of places where there is inadequate plumbing.

c. Normally, just one-tenth of one percent of flu victims die, but the Spanish flu killed two and a half percent of its victims.

d. In Bangladesh, where the disease is endemic (or naturally recurring in the environment), two peaks occur each year corresponding to the warm seasons before and after the monsoon rain.

▶ Check your answers. Work with a partner to read the pairs of sentences.

▶ **C Signal Words that Introduce Examples** There are words or phrases that are often used to introduce examples. One of these is *such* or *such as*. Scan the readings and circle the uses of *such* or *such as*. Then, in the chart that follows, list the idea and the examples that *such* or *such as* introduces.

Idea	Example
1.	
2.	
3.	

❯Expanding Your Language

Reading

▶ **Reading in the News** The following is a report on the AIDS crisis in Africa. Before beginning to read the report, read the following questions. After reading the report, answer as many as you can based on the information in the text. Highlight the information for each question. Compare your answers with a partner.

1. What are two concerns in the report from the United Nations AIDS program?
2. What is the purpose of the report?
3. What is the size of the current and future AIDS epidemic in Africa?
4. Why did the United Nations report prepare three different scenarios of possible responses to the AIDS crisis?
5. Which of the three scenarios:
   a. is the costliest?
   b. focuses most on prevention?
   c. focuses on drug treatments?
   d. focuses on changes to improve the health system?

Fighting AIDS in Africa

❶   According to a new report from the United Nations AIDS program, billions more dollars will be needed to curb the spread of AIDS in Africa. But as countries increase their donations, the amounts will be less important than how well they are spent and in what context. Pouring more money into programs to combat AIDS could do more harm than good unless they are effectively coordinated, stated the report, "AIDS in Africa," released at a meeting in Addis Ababa, Ethiopia.

❷   The United Nations said the report was intended to improve decision-making and deepen public understanding of the possible course of the AIDS epidemic in Africa by 2025 when, "no one under the age of fifty in Africa will be able to remember a world without AIDS." By then, under the worst circumstances, 89 million more people in Africa could be infected with HIV, the United Nations said. An estimated 25.4 million people in Africa are infected now. "The death toll will continue to rise, no matter what is done," the United Nations report said. "There is no single policy prescription that will change the outcome of the epidemic."

❸   The report describes three possible situations in which the AIDS pandemic could play out across Africa by 2025. The situations were told as stories that were prepared over the last two years and were intended to be thought provoking, not to provide all the solutions.

❹   In one outline, African countries would adopt tough long-term measures in which leaders would focus on prevention. By 2025, the numbers would grow but then fall to today's levels and continue to fall. But the number of orphans would double. This plan would cost an estimated $100 billion, with the United States spending $5 billion a year until 2015 and $6 billion a year thereafter.

❺   In a second situation, which would be medically focused, prevention measures would not be stepped up, so anti-retroviral drugs would be easier to obtain than good nutrition and clean water. In this approach, government leaders would fail to get ahead of the AIDS epidemic, and Africa's poverty and underdevelopment would deepen. Keeping such services at today's level would cost $4 billion a year by 2025.

❻   A third outline envisioned investments in health systems, agriculture, education, electrification, water, and roads to change fundamentally the ways donors provide aid and recipient countries deal with the donations to avoid inflation and not promote dependency. Such a situation would provide anti-retroviral drugs to seventy percent of people needing them by 2025. That effort would be expected to halve the number of people living with HIV and AIDS, despite an anticipated population growth of fifty percent. The cost would be $200 billion, with the United States increasing its contribution to $10 billion a year by 2014 and sustaining that amount until 2025, when it would begin to decrease.

Reacting to the Reading

▶ Free write your ideas to the following questions and discuss your ideas with a partner or in a small group.

1. What are the different approaches to AIDS in different parts of the world?
2. Why are there differences in the responses to the AIDS epidemic in different parts of the world?
3. Which of the three possible scenarios would you recommend and why?
4. What can be done to better respond to the AIDS epidemic in developing countries?

Writing

▶ **Opinion Writing** Your friend has asked you whether or not it is better to introduce quarantines and prohibit travel in the face of a new disease that could become a pandemic. Before you write your response, make an outline using the following steps.

▶ **1.** Choose a position.
  2. Think of two reasons for this position.
  3. Write them out in note form.
  4. Think of examples or explanations for each reason.
  5. Write them out in note form.

▶ Now write your opinion, which should consist of the following:

• A short introduction (three or four sentences), in which the last sentence states your point of view
• One paragraph for each reason (eight to ten sentences)
• A short conclusion (one or two sentences)

▶ Give your writing to your teacher for feedback.

 *Online Study Center*   For additional activities, go to the *Reading Matters* Online Study Center at *college.hmco.com/pic/wholeythree2e.*

10 Medical Miracles

❯Chapter Openers

Discussion Questions

❯ Think about the following questions. Share your ideas with a partner or in a small group.

1. What is a transplant?
2. Which parts of the body can be transplanted?
3. What are some problems associated with transplants?
4. What has made transplanting organs possible today?
5. Have you or anyone you know had a transplant? If yes, describe what happened.
6. What difficult questions or issues remain about transplanting organs today?
7. What can be done for premature babies today that wasn't possible fifty years ago?
8. What are the possibilities today for reattaching or replacing body parts?
9. What medical advances do you think will be possible in the next fifty years?

Getting Information from a Chart

 Tip

The information in the chart may be important for more than one type of development. Use key words in the information to help you decide. ■

❯ **A** Skim the chart on the next two pages and look for information about *one* of the following types of development.

1. The Development of Organ Transplantation
2. The Development of Human Blood Use
3. The Development of Genetic Science

❯ **B** As you skim, mark the number of the development type you chose in the last column of the table and highlight the information related to the type you chose. One has been done as an example.

❯ **C** Check your answers with someone who chose the same development type. Use the highlighted information to tell the history to your partner.

❯ **D** Relate the history of the development type you chose to a partner who looked for information about a different type.

Time	Event	Type
1900	Karl Landsteiner, an Austrian-American immunologist, discovers that blood can be classified into four ABO types: A, B, AB, and O.	2
1900s	Genetic engineering originates based on work done in the mid-1800s by Gregor Mendel.	
1905	The first human cornea transplants are attempted.	
1908	A knee joint transplant is successful.	1
1913	A kidney from a Japanese monkey is transplanted into a young girl with mercury poisoning.	
1914	Storage of blood first becomes possible with the addition of citrate and a nutrient sugar.	
1921	The first voluntary blood-donor program is established in London, England.	
1936	The world's first blood bank is founded in Chicago.	
1944	DNA is determined to be the hereditary material of all organisms.	3
1951	The first consistently successful cornea transplants are achieved.	
1952	A tadpole is cloned, making history as the first cloned animal. Cells from a tadpole embryo are used to create tadpoles identical to the original. Twenty-seven tadpoles develop.	
1953	The structure of DNA is determined.	
1954	The first kidney transplant from a live donor occurs between identical twins.	
1960s	Researchers start investigating blood transfusions.	
1967	The first liver transplant occurs.	
1970s	Scientists develop ways to isolate individual genes and then reintroduce them into cells.	
1972	Scientists successfully clone the first gene in a yeast cell.	
1977	An American researcher claims to have cloned mice, using the cells from early mouse embryos.	

Time	Event	Type
1978	Cyclosporine is discovered. It will become the most commonly administered drug to prevent organ rejection.	
1978	The gene for human insulin is cloned.	
1980s	Patients begin banking their own blood in case it is needed during their operation (autologous transfusions).	
1980s	Stem cells, the source of all blood cells, are isolated.	
1986	The first successful double lung transplant is reported.	
1988	The first patent on a genetically engineered animal is issued on a type of mouse developed for cancer research.	
1990s	Many advances in bone marrow transplantation occur. Unrelated transplants become more common.	
1990	Human gene therapy is first successfully attempted. The international Human Genome Project to map the entire human genetic makeup is created.	
1996	Ian Wilmut and his colleagues pioneer the technique of cloning mammals from the cells of adult animals, creating "Dolly," the world's first cloned sheep.	

Exploring and Understanding Reading

Previewing

▶ Look at the title and subtitle of the following article and make a list of three ideas you expect to find in the reading.

1. _____

2. _____

3. _____

▶ Share your ideas with a partner.

Surveying

▶ Read the first two paragraphs (introduction) and the first sentence of every paragraph after that. Underline the key words in each sentence. Using these key words, write the main idea of each paragraph in the margin. Try to use as few words as possible for each idea.

Using your previewing and your surveying, fill in the following table.

Paragraph	Main Idea
1, 2	Introduction: The beginning of modern organ transplantation
3	
4	
5	
6	
7	
8	
9	
10	Conclusion: The challenges we face today

▶ Share your ideas with a partner or in a small group.

Fifty Years of Transplants

Many advances have occurred since the first successful transplant, but hurdles remain. Key among them is a shortage of donor organs.

❶ Washington, D.C.—For hundreds of years, physicians knew that otherwise healthy patients were dying for lack of a functioning part. But the transplantation of a healthy organ from a body that could spare it to one that was needy remained a fantasy until, in 1954, a team of surgeons in Boston showed that it was possible. Joseph E. Murray, MD, John Hartwell Harrison, MD, and John P. Merrill, MD, pulled off the astounding act. They successfully transplanted a fit kidney from Ronald Herrick into his identical twin, Richard, who was dying of kidney disease. Before then, "the dogma was that it would never be possible and we were told we were playing God and shouldn't do it," said Dr. Murray, still writing and speaking at local high schools at age 85. The first step was resolving these kinds of very basic ethical challenges. Thus, the actual surgery followed not only years of laboratory work and research, but also lengthy debate over moral questions. "We discussed it with clergy of all denominations, with surgeons from other hospitals, and with the general public. Many were critical. But we felt we were on proper medical, moral, and ethical grounds," said Dr. Murray, a 1990 Nobel laureate.

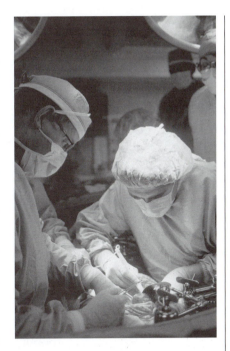

❷   Organ transplantation continues to inspire debate now, but the issues are different. They center on philosophical concerns, such as fairness in awarding precious organs to those most in need and the risk to live donors who may be family members, coworkers, or even strangers. But fifty years ago, when all signals seemed to finally point to yes, the kidney was deemed a good starting place "because the good Lord has given us two," Dr. Murray said. The fact that identical twins were the patients also influenced the decision to proceed. Their compatibility was almost guaranteed, and the calculation was that the transplanted kidney would not be rejected—and it wasn't. It also was known that a person could live a long, healthy life with one kidney. But the quest to overcome the immune system's innate rejection of a transplanted organ was the next, and perhaps even greater, hurdle for this new medical field.

Immunosuppression

❸   The quest for tolerance—the body's acceptance of a transplanted organ—is still a goal transplant surgeons strive to achieve. Most patients must follow a regimen of medications for the rest of their lives to prevent rejection of the transplanted organ by the immune system. In the earliest years, radiation was used to subdue the immune system so that it wouldn't reject the transplant, often with fatal consequences to the patient. Thomas Starzl, MD, PhD, a professor of surgery at the University of Pittsburgh School of Medicine, found an alternative while working on transplantation at the University of Colorado in Denver. "Everyone knew that transplantation as a true service was going to shrink and die unless better immunosuppression came along." Dr. Starzl began working with Imuran (azathioprine), one of the first drugs of this kind. He took it one step further and combined it with the steroid prednisone. "To everyone's surprise, and perhaps far exceeding my own expectations, we had one year survival of kidney transplants from live familial donors, not twins, of about eighty percent. The transplantation field exploded," he said. "Suddenly what had been an idiosyncratic procedure was a real service, overnight." That advance also paved the way for the transplantation of other organs. Dr. Starzl performed the first successful liver transplant in 1967. Soon after, the first heart, pancreas, lung, and bone marrow transplants were performed.

❹   Since then, the field's greatest advances have continued to occur in immunosuppressant drugs, said Norman Shumway, MD, PhD, who chairs the Department of Cardiothoracic Surgery at Stanford University. Dr. Shumway transplanted the first heart in the United States in 1968, following closely after the first such procedure by Dr. Christian Barnard in South Africa.

❺   But that early burst of successes was followed by a period of disillusionment. "Most of the people around phase one were burned out because of the generally poor results the patients had to suffer in order to survive," he said. The need was still great for effective immunosuppressive medications. "We were all rescued by the arrival of cyclosporine in 1980," Dr. Starzl said. For the first time, expectations of success were more realistic. "To me, it's been a climb to the top of the mountain to achieve the perfect transplant," said Oscar Salvatierra, MD, professor of surgery and pediatrics at Stanford University School of Medicine.

❻   Dr. Salvatierra has performed kidney transplants for thirty-two years and has seen survival rates rise dramatically. Imuran and prednisone were the only two immunosuppressants available when Dr. Salvatierra began his work. Survival rates for cadaveric kidneys were then fifty percent for one year, and the best living donor matches produced one-year survival rates of seventy percent. Transplants also brought complications. "Now we have survival rates that are generally close to ninety percent after five years, with a marked decrease in complications," he said.

❼   And there are ongoing improvements. Dr. Salvatierra has been working on a steroid-free immunosuppressant for children to allow for normal growth and appearance. The change in medications has resulted in a greater adherence to medication regimens and a drop in rejection rates. "With the body disfigurement, particularly in adolescence, they stopped taking their medications," Dr. Salvatierra said. He also pointed to the 1984 National Organ Transplant Act as a great advancement on a social scale. The legislation put in place a national organ procurement and transplantation network. "What that did was provide for maximum utilization of all organs acquired, equitable distribution of those organs, and a national registry," he said. Dr. Brian Pereira, president of the National Kidney Foundation, also points to the 1968 Uniform Anatomical Gift Act, which allowed people to give permission for their organs to be used for transplantation, as another great gain that resulted in the widespread use of donor cards. "When we look at all these scientific discoveries, we have to remember that the government and public have also kept pace."

Getting More Organs

8   While successful transplant operations number in the hundreds of thousands, there could be hundreds of thousands more if donors were more plentiful. There are more than 83,000 people on the waiting list, and most of those, 56,560, are awaiting a kidney. By 2010, the overall list is expected to reach 100,000. Thus, a key area of research is focused on furthering methods to ease the shortage. Experiments in transplantation between humans and animals have been occurring for decades with mixed results. For xenotransplantation to work, researchers must find a way to block the human body's ability to recognize an animal organ as foreign and attack it. Scientists also must develop methods to keep viruses possibly carried by these organs from entering the human population. On another path, some believe that stem cells could hold the key. The cells, which have the ability to adapt and regenerate into different cell types in the body, have the potential to replace tissues damaged by disease. It is even hoped that such tissue engineering might someday eliminate the need for many transplants and the anti-rejection drugs that go with them.

9   Researchers also continue to look for ways to eliminate transplanted patients' need for immunosuppressant drugs. Current medical thinking holds that pre-conditioning a transplant candidate before surgery might play a key role in this process. It is also believed that low doses of immunosuppressant administered immediately after the transplant might allow the fighter cells to attack, become exhausted, and eventually enable the body to accept the foreign organ as its own.

10   But the biggest challenge faced by those in the transplant field remains a shortage of donors. "I think we are probably not using half of the possible donors available today," Dr. Shumway said. "So I look for there to be a bigger use of donor material, a bigger fraction of those possible donors. But it will take time and education."

American Medical News

Scanning

 Reading Tip

Marking the question number in the margin of a text is another way to locate the information for your answers quickly. ■

▶ **Explaining the Issue** Scan for the answers to these questions. Mark the question number in the margin of the reading. Write your answers in note form.

1. What preparations did the team of Boston surgeons have to make so that the first organ transplant would be accepted on moral and medical grounds?

    _____

2. What issues concern people today that didn't concern them before?

    _____

3. a. After the first successful kidney transplant, what problem still remained?

    _____

   b. Has that problem been completely resolved today?

    _____

4. List the results of doctors' attempts to find a way to make the immune system accept an organ transplant.

Technique	Result
Radiation	_____
Imuran and steroid prednisone	_____

5. What was Dr. Starzl able to do by the end of the 1960s?

    _____

6. a. According to Dr. Starzl, what had happened in transplantation by 1968?

    _____

   b. Why were people discouraged at that time?

    _____

   c. What is cyclosporine and why was its discovery so important?

    _____

   d. How have the survival rates for kidney transplants improved over the thirty-two years of Dr. Salvatierra's career?

    _____

7. a. What improvements has Dr. Salvatierra been working on?

   _____

   b. Why are they important?

   _____

8. According to Dr. Salvatierra, what has been the benefit of the National Organ Transplant Act?

   _____

9. a. What problem are doctors currently concerned about?

   _____

   b. What three possible paths are doctors pursuing to solve this problem?

   _____

10. According to Dr. Shumway, what should be done to increase the number of organ donors?

    _____

▶ Work with a partner to ask and answer the questions. Compare the information you marked in the margin.

What is Your Opinion?

▶ Read the facts about transplants and, in light of this information, the reading you have done, and your own knowledge, decide if you agree or disagree with the ideas in the two groups on the next page.

Transplant Facts

- More than 83,000 people are on the national waiting list for organs, including more than 2,000 younger than eighteen.
- Each day an average of 106 people are added to the nation's organ transplant waiting list; 68 receive transplants from living or dead donors, and 17 die waiting for a suitable organ.
- There is no national registry of organ donors. Those with donor cards are urged to discuss their wishes with family members.
- People of all ages and medical histories should consider themselves potential donors.
- Fifty-four percent of families consent to a request that a deceased family member's organs be donated.

The Organ Procurement and Transplantation Network

▶ Circle *A* if you agree or *D* if you disagree with each statement.

1. The demand for organs has always been higher than the supply. As a result, certain choices have to be made. The following statements deal with some of these choices.

   a.   A   D   Young people should be chosen before old people.

   b.   A   D   A patient who has had an unsuccessful transplant should be placed at the bottom of the list.

   c.   A   D   People whose disease has been caused by their life styles (for example, alcoholics, smokers, addicts) should be given the same chance as everybody else.

   d.   A   D   People who suffer from a mental disability should not be allowed a transplant because they will not be able to follow the required steps after the operation.

   e.   A   D   A system should be established for identifying people who want to be organ donors.

2. Because the supply is so low, certain solutions have been suggested. The following statements deal with solutions for increasing supply.

   a.   A   D   People should be able to sell their organs.

   b.   A   D   Organs of a dead person should be used automatically unless that person has stated otherwise.

   c.   A   D   The brain is the most important organ in the body, so when people are brain dead, they should be considered dead and their organs used (instead of being kept indefinitely on life support).

   d.   A   D   Medical researchers should be allowed to freely develop ways to generate new organs.

   e.   A   D   Doctors should be allowed to transplant organs from animals to humans when there are no other organs available.

▶ Work with a partner or in a small group. Compare your ideas. Be ready to support your positions with reasons and explanations if possible.

Skimming

▶ The following article is taken from a weekly news magazine that gives information about people and ideas. Read quickly and then answer the following questions. Highlight the information in the article that will help you to explain the information.

1. Why did Chet Szuber need a heart transplant?
2. Why did Patti Szuber want to study medicine?
3. Why did Patti Szuber die?
4. Who benefited from receiving Patti's organs?
5. How do these people feel?

▶ Work with a partner to discuss your answers. Take turns explaining the facts to each other.

His Daughter's Gift of Life

A few years ago, Chet Szuber received the heart of his youngest child, Patti, who had been killed in a car accident; now, with each passing day, he celebrates her spirit.

By Bill Hewitt

❶ Friendly but taciturn, Chet Szuber is not one to show much emotion. Yet even now, long after an event that changed virtually everything for him and his family, he cannot help choking up when discussing it. At a gathering for surviving members of the families of organ donors, Szuber, a sixty-three-year-old Christmas tree farmer, gets up to thank the next of kin of those who died, on behalf of all organ recipients. "Without you," he says with emotion, "there wouldn't be any people like me." It is an equation Szuber understands only too well. For as he stands there with tears in his eyes, his daughter Patti's heart beats in his chest.

❷ It has been five years since Chet Szuber made the most tragic sort of history, becoming the first person ever to receive the heart of his own child. Having suffered for years with chronic cardiac problems, he got the transplant on August 22, 1994, four days after Patti, then twenty-two and an aspiring nurse, died from injuries sustained in a car crash while she was vacationing in Tennessee's Smoky Mountains. Since then, he has tried to honor her memory as best he can by becoming an evangelist for organ donation. "Medical people tell me that they can speak all they want about donation," says Szuber, "but until you have somebody who has experienced it, it doesn't have the impact."

❸   Patti was only a year old in 1972, when Szuber, then thirty-six and a salesman at Sears, had his first heart attack and was out of work for nine months. In the years that followed, he had two more attacks and had to quit his job. By the time she was twenty, Patti was often her father's chauffeur, driving him from their home in the Detroit suburb of Berkley up to the tree farm he had started on family land in northern Michigan. In 1990, Szuber was put on the waiting list for a heart transplant, which seemed to offer his last hope for survival. But as years went by and no heart came his way, he got to the point where he could barely move around during the day. "I had kind of given up," he says, "I had waited so long." Her father's problems profoundly affected Patti, who decided to go into the medical field, her family believes, because of all she had seen him go through. In 1994, she set her sights on getting a degree as a surgical assistant.

❹   She was scheduled to start classes within days when she went on her last vacation with childhood friend Todd Herbst, then twenty-four. Early on August 18, their car skidded off a curving road in the Smokies and Patti, not wearing a seat belt, was thrown from the vehicle. By the time the Szubers— Chet, his wife Jeanne, now sixty-three, and their five other children—got to the University of Tennessee Medical Center at Knoxville, to which Patti had been airlifted, she was on life support with no hope of recovery. Her family remembered that she had once casually mentioned that she had filled out an organ-donor card, so they gave the hospital the go-ahead to do whatever was necessary to get her organs to needy recipients. On August 21, Patti was declared brain dead. Susan Fredenberg Cross, a donor coordinator who had learned of Szuber's condition, gently suggested that he could get his daughter's heart, because donor families are allowed to direct organs to eligible friends and kin. Szuber refused. "I didn't think it was right," he says. "And I wasn't sure I could stand every heartbeat reminding me of Patti." Finally, though, Jeanne and his other children prevailed on him to accept. Patti's kidneys and liver were given to other recipients, and within twenty-four hours her heart was beating in Szuber.

❺   He missed his daughter's funeral back in Berkley, because he was in the hospital recovering from the operation. After that, there was a long period of physical rehabilitation and a longer time getting used to the idea of what had happened to him. "He was fine physically, but he was emotionally upset," says his son Bob, forty-one. "He felt he was going to be looked upon as a freak." Szuber, who is now able to hunt, fish, and play golf, decided that a way to deal with his lingering grief was to become an advocate, raising awareness of the need for organ donors. Every year he gives a dozen speeches around the country, imploring people to sign up and lobbying for

6 changes in donation procedures. Yet he remains haunted by Patti's tragedy. Unlike most other transplant recipients, Szuber has never celebrated the customary "second birthday"—the day on which recipients begin their lives anew with donated organs. "It's hard to celebrate a life and death at the same time," says Jeanne, "so we just kind of forgot about it."

But those who benefited from the generosity of Patti and her family cannot forget. Thanks to Patti's kidney, Mary Lawery, fifty-seven, a retired nanny in Nashville, now lives a relatively normal life, free of dialysis. Lawery, who has met the Szubers twice, knows she can never repay her debt to them. "It makes you sad because they loved her so much," she says. Meanwhile, Shirley Cobb Dotson, twenty-one, from Memphis, perhaps gained the most from Patti. She had suffered from liver trouble from the age of thirteen and, in August 1994, she had been given only seventy-two hours to live when Patti's donor liver arrived—"I pray every morning and night," says Dotson, "and I keep thanking God for this miracle." It is a feeling Chet Szuber knows well but always with that heartbreaking twist. "It's such a bittersweet situation. I certainly appreciate the good health," he says, "but I sure do miss that kid."

Bill Hewitt and Cindy Dampier/*People Weekly.* © 1999. All rights reserved Time Inc.

Reacting to the Information

▶ Discuss the following with a partner.

1. Imagine that there had been another patient in the same area, but in a much more serious condition than Patti's father. Who should have priority?

2. One person died and that person's organ donation allowed three others to live normal lives.
   a. How does this affect the way we look at organ donation?
   b. How does this affect the way that organ recipients lead the rest of their lives?

Free Writing

▶ Based on your readings and discussions, write your reaction to the issue of transplants. Consider these questions as you write.

1. Would you agree to be an organ donor?
2. What kind of transplants do you think will be possible in the future?
3. What kinds of medical problems do you hope doctors find cures for in the future?

Vocabulary Building

Word Form

▶ **A** Study these five words and their forms. Then choose the correct form for each part of speech in the chart below. These words are commonly found in general and academic texts.

affect (v.)	advocate (v.)	consist (v.)	impact (v.)	restore (v.)
affected (adj.)	advocate	consistence	impact	restoration
affecting (adj.)	advocative	consistent	impacted	restored
affective (adj.)	advocacy	consistently		restoring
affectively (adv.)	advocating			

Verb	Noun	Adjective	Adverb
advocate	1.	1.	
	2.	2.	
consist	1.	1.	1.
impact	1.	1.	
restore	1.	1.	
		2.	

▶ Compare lists with a partner.

▶ **B** Write three sentences using words from the list.

Vocabulary in Context

▶ **A** **Expressions in Context** English, like many other languages, has some common expressions. These expressions are best understood when read in context. Use the following contexts to find the meaning of the boldface expressions. Explain each in your own words.

1. The dogma was that it would never be possible and we were told **we were playing God** and shouldn't do it.

   _____

2. Most of the people were just **burned out** because of the generally poor results.

   _____

3. To me, it's been **a climb to the top of the mountain** to achieve the perfect transplant.

_____

4. In 1994, Patti **set her sights** on getting a degree as a surgical assistant.

_____

▶ Check your answers with a partner or with your teacher. Practice using these expressions by putting each into a sentence of your own. Find other expressions in the readings.

▶ **B Using Quotes** In English, quotes are almost always used to support a point that has already been made.

Example: In paragraph 1 of the article "His Daughter's Gift of Life," the quote "Without you, there wouldn't be any people like me" is used to support the idea that Szuber is thanking the relatives of organ donors.

▶ In your own words, write the points that the following quotes support.

1. _____

"Medical people tell me that they can speak all they want about donation, but until you have somebody who has experienced it, it does not have the impact." (paragraph 2)

2. _____

"I had kind of given up, I had waited so long." (paragraph 3)

3. _____

"I didn't think it was right. And I wasn't sure I could stand every heartbeat reminding me of Patti." (paragraph 4)

4. _____

"He was fine physically, but he was emotionally upset." (paragraph 5)

5. _____

"It's hard to celebrate a life and death at the same time, so we just kind of forgot about it." (paragraph 5)

6. _____

"I pray every morning and night and I keep thanking God for this miracle." (paragraph 6)

▶ Check your answers with a partner. Refer to the reading if necessary.

❰Expanding Your Language

Reading

▶ The following is a personal story of how one person's life was changed by the use of a medical procedure that wasn't available fifty years ago. Before beginning to read the story, read the following questions. As you read the story, highlight the information for each question. Compare your answers with a partner or others in a small group.

▶ Think about the following questions. Share your ideas with a partner or with a small group.

1. What happened to Woosik Chung when he was three years old?
2. What did Chung's father do after the accident?
3. How did Chung recover from the accident?
4. What were his early school experiences like?
5. What were his later educational experiences like?
6. What did Chung's teachers think of him?
7. What skills does Chung have?
8. Why does Chung want to be a doctor?

Miracle Hands

When Woosik Chung was a first-year medical student, a surgeon handed him a scalpel and told him to make the first cut during a routine knee operation. "It was quite a rush," says Chung, twenty-eight. "At that moment I understood that using my hands as a surgeon was an honor and a privilege."

And in his case, very close to a miracle. When Chung was three years old, both his hands were completely severed in an accident. Then, in a rare and risky operation, they were successfully reattached. "To have the function of his hands after having them severed is monumental," says Robin Schroeder, associate dean of student affairs at UMDNJ—New Jersey Medical School, from which Chung graduated in May. "But to have the dexterity to be a surgeon is amazing."

Chung's against-all-odds saga started in 1978 as he played hide-and-seek with pals in Uijungbu, South Korea, near Seoul. Ducking behind a tractor, the curious toddler reached out to touch the whirring engine. In a split second, the fan blades severed both his hands at the wrists. Chung's horrified father saw the accident from his apartment window. He and his wife filled a bucket with ice and ran to their screaming son. Both hands lay on the ground; the left was intact, but the right thumb had been cut off.

The boy's parents carried him to a hospital just blocks away, but it was a national holiday and no specialists could be found. So Chung's father, John, an Army surgeon, reattached Woosik's hands himself. With his wife, Haewon, fifty-three, a nurse, and other staff assisting, John operated on his son for more than nine hours. "I had never completed a surgery like that," says John, fifty-five. "But I was desperate. I prayed to God and did my best."

His best, it turns out, was superb. Although Chung couldn't move his hands when the casts were removed two months later, he did regain full motion a couple of years later. For that Chung bows to his maternal grandfather, Byungdal Gong, a *tae kwon do* grand master, who used the martial art as the boy's sole physical therapy program. Chung trained for several hours a day. "He was firm, but it was never like I was afraid of him," says Chung. "Discipline took root, and when it did, I thrived." His scars, now mostly faded, brought taunts from schoolmates in Uijungbu—who called him Frankenstein—and again in the southern African nation of Malawi, where the family moved when he was seven. Says Chung, "I was in fights every day."

At fourteen he moved with his family to the United States, where Chung attended the Lawrenceville School, an elite New Jersey boarding school. He went on to Yale University—where he was a *tae kwon do* champ, ranking second in the United States in his weight class—and earned a degree in molecular biophysics in 1997. He considered trying out for the 2000 Olympics, but opted for medicine instead. "When he told me," says his father, now in private practice in Trenton, "I was very happy."

Chung's professors were wowed. "This kid, even as a first-year student, had skills equivalent to someone with six years' experience," says Howard Kiernan, an orthopedic surgeon at Columbia-Presbyterian Medical Center in New York City. "And he's great with patients too." Chung's professors had no inkling of his ordeal until last summer, when he described it in an application essay for the residency program at Columbia-Presbyterian. When the story came out, says associate dean Schroeder, "I told my children about him, I was so impressed."

When he finishes his five-year residency, Chung knows exactly what he wants to be: a hand surgeon. "The best way I can thank my dad," says Chung, "is to help others in similar situations."

Christina Cheaklos/*People Weekly*. © 2003. All rights reserved Time Inc.

Speaking

▶ **Debate** Choose one of the following statements from the Opinion statements on page 220, such as "People should be able to sell their organs," or "Organs of a dead person should be used automatically unless that person has stated otherwise."
Debate the statement, using the following steps as a guide.

▶ 1. Choose the debate topic.

2. Choose the side you will argue.

3. Make a list of ideas in support of your position.

4. Work with a partner arguing the same position and add to your list of ideas.

5. Divide the ideas between you and your partner and decide what each person is going to say.

6. Predict what the other side will say and prepare to "attack" their ideas.

7. Practice your arguments.

8. Present and argue your position against a pair who prepared the other side.

Writing

▶ **A Persuasive Writing** In persuasive writing, writers choose a position and then support that position by stating one or more arguments that they support with facts.

Sample positions: We must find ways to continue and improve transplant surgery.
Transplant surgery is not a medical priority in today's society.

Before you write, make an outline as follows:

▶ 1. Choose a position.

2. Think of two arguments for this position.

3. Write out the reasons for these arguments in note form.

4. Think of examples or explanations for each reason.

5. Write them out in note form.

▶ Now write your opinion, which should consist of the following elements.

- A short introduction (three or four sentences), in which the last sentence states your point of view
- One paragraph for each reason (eight to ten sentences)
- A short conclusion (one or two sentences)

▶ Give your writing to your teacher for feedback.

▶ **B Journal Writing** Continue writing in your journal. Focus on ideas that you really agree with as well as ideas that you really disagree with.

▶ **C** **Free Writing** Write about one or more of the following questions.

- What limits should the government put on medical research?
- Can life be associated with a particular part of the body—for example, the brain?
- Should governments set rules and regulations about organ donations?

◗Read On: Taking It Further

Magazine Articles

▶ Find an interesting magazine article about some aspect of new advances in medicine. You could look for an article about new developments in cancer research, reproductive technology, organ transplants, or even the use of animals for research. Try to find an article that is no more than two pages long. Prepare to present the information to a partner or to a small group.

Follow these steps:

▶ **1. Skimming** Quickly read the article to get the general idea and to check whether the information is interesting.

2. Surveying Read the introduction (one or two paragraphs) and the first sentence of every paragraph after that.

3. Find the writer's point of view and the ideas he or she uses to support it.

4. Highlight the important information for each idea. Make notes from your highlighting.

5. Practice your presentation.

6. Make your presentation.

Reading Journal

▶ Write your reactions to the magazine article in your reading journal. You can also include your reactions to articles presented by your fellow students.

 ***Online Study Center*** For additional activities, go to the *Reading Matters* Online Study Center at *college.hmco.com/pic/wholeythree2e*.

Attitude Matters

An optimist is
a fellow who
believes what's
going to be, will
be postponed.
—*Kim Hubbard*

Introducing the Topic

Emotions affect how we experience so much in our lives—our relationships, our achievements, even our health. In this unit, we will explore the workings of powerful emotions and find out whether and how our emotions can be controlled and used in a positive way. Chapter 11 is about anger: what it is, what it results in, how we experience it, and how we can cope with it. Chapter 12 looks at our feelings of hope and optimism and how attitudes, desires, interests, and occupations affect our lives. Together, these chapters present part of the complex nature of human emotions.

Points of Interest

How do emotions, both positive and negative, affect our lives?

11 Anger: How to Manage It

Chapter Openers

Discussion Questions

▶ **A** Discuss the following questions with a partner or in a small group.

1. Have you ever been angry? How does anger affect your behavior and your relations with other people?
2. Do people get angry more often today than in the past? If so, why?
3. Can people stop themselves from being angry? What are some ways to do this?

▶ **B** **Expressions** Here are some sayings about anger. Read and ask yourself what the writer wants us to understand about the power of anger. Is anger a productive or a destructive force? Is anger something we control or does it control us?

1. Never go to bed angry.
2. Never try to pacify people at the time of their rage.
3. A just man is slow to anger and quick to forgive.
4. Anger robs a person of wisdom.
5. It is easy to be angry. But to be angry with the right person, to the right degree, at the right time, for the right purpose, and in the right way—this is not easy.
6. Anger is the only thing to put off 'til tomorrow.

▶ What sayings about anger do you know? Think of one to share with your classmates.

What's Our Anger Like?

▶ **Skimming** Every time we open a newspaper, we find news about examples of uncontrolled anger—road rage, plane rage, sports rage. Some examples of anger in everyday life are given in the two following news stories. Read each one quickly and underline:

- what happened.
- where it happened.
- why it happened.
- how people feel about the problem.

Road Rage in Beijing

Beijing—One day this year, cab driver Qin Wei steered his taxi into the right-turn lane, unknowingly forcing a Volkswagen sedan to slow. Angered by Qin's maneuver, the second driver accelerated around him and drew to a halt.

"They got in front of me and stopped, and two guys got out and started to curse at me," Qin said. "I didn't do anything. I didn't say anything."

The furious men screamed profane insults for several minutes as Qin, twenty-five, sat frozen in his red Citroen. With today's hair-trigger mood on the streets of Beijing, he feared the pair might smash his windshield or pummel him with their fists. Both types of assaults have occurred in recent weeks.

Eventually, the men spent their fury and drove away. But Qin's experience isn't unique. On the once even-tempered streets of Beijing, drivers increasingly are taking out their frustrations upon one another or other vehicles. "I see more and more conflicts on the streets now," Qin said.

An explosion of new car sales over the past year has transformed driving in the Chinese capital into an exercise in pulse-pounding frustration. Car sales in Beijing rose forty-five percent last year to 400,000 vehicles. Most of the people behind the wheel are inexperienced or poorly trained. Traffic laws often are ignored. And most city center roads were designed for a time when almost no private citizens owned cars.

In Xicheng, one of Beijing's 16 districts, authorities sentenced twenty-one people last year in cases of "car temper," according to *Beijing Youth Daily*.

David J. Lynch, *USA Today*

Angry Parents at the Game

Las Vegas—Coaches are being threatened, referees assaulted, and kids hurt more than ever by the parents of some of the estimated thirty million young players in organized sports.

From parents brawling at a T-ball game in Florida while four- and five-year-old children watched to a father being beaten to death at a hockey game in Massachusetts, anger is growing. "From road rage to airplane rage to cell phone rage, children in sports aren't immune to all of this," said Fred Engh, head of the National Alliance for Youth Sports. Lincoln Coverdale, a seventeen-year-old high school senior in Shaker Heights, Ohio, has played organized hockey for much of his life and knew many parents who put too much pressure on their children. "The kid just has to sit there and be mortified because all the people around him are watching him get yelled at by his parents," he said.

Overbearing parents are also getting to referees, according to a recent survey by the National Association of Sports Officials. Seventy-six percent of respondents from sixty high school athletic associations said increased spectator interference is causing many officials to quit.

The organization keeps a list of attacks, such as when the coach of a Nebraska peewee flag football team punched a sixteen-year-old referee during a game and a fan in Ohio threatened a soccer referee with a gun.

"The parent of today is much different than the parent of five years ago," said Engh, whose West Palm Beach, Florida-based association has 2,200 chapters across the United States. "It used to be maybe five percent of the people stepped over the line. It's grown now to about fifteen percent."

Excerpted from *Times-Colonist*

Discussion   ▶ Using what you underlined, discuss these questions with a partner or in a small group.

1. How were the people in these stories affected by what happened to them?
2. What are the consequences in each case?
3. What do you think could be the underlying cause(s) of the behavior described in these stories?

◗Exploring and Understanding Reading

Previewing   ▶ In North America, one response to angry behavior is anger management classes. What do you think these classes consist of and why are they becoming more common? Do you think they can be effective?

▶ Look at the picture, title, and subheadings of the next reading. List three ideas you think will be discussed.

1. _____

2. _____

3. _____

▶ Compare your ideas with a partner.

Surveying   ▶ Survey the reading. Read the introduction (paragraphs 1–3) and the first sentence of every paragraph after that. Check to see if your preview predictions were correct. If you think you were wrong, change your predictions.

Anger: The Neglected Emotion No More

❶   All over the United States, people are being sentenced to anger management classes as part of the punishment for the crimes they committed. Nowadays, that's just part of the phenomenon called anger management.

❷   Pam Hollenhorst, of the University of Wisconsin Law School, reviewed anger management and found that it starts with preschool programs teaching children how to control their behavior and extends beyond— reaching across every age group and socioeconomic class. It ranges from grade school programs teaching conflict resolution to teaching teenagers how to control their emotions as a condition of participating in different sports activities. It is becoming a popular tool for companies in which employees harass their coworkers or their subordinates by ridiculing, setting impossible goals, micromanaging, or spreading malicious rumors about them. It can even be recommended to celebrities. Tiger Woods received anger management training to improve his professional performance on the golf course. It generally covers a lot of people in different stressful professions, including doctors who are dealing with changes in the health care industry, people who are suffering from different diseases, police officers, correctional officials, and many others.

❸   Anger management is the solution to any number of problems. Every week, it seems, judges and courts are recommending it to people accused of violent crimes and workplace bullying. It's the subject of books, videos, and CDs. But as widespread as anger management programs have become, some central questions about them remain unanswered: What defines such programs? Do they actually work? What motivates employers to recommend them? And in the absence of concrete answers to those questions, why is anger management such a thriving phenomenon?

How Do We Measure Anger?

❹   In the 1970s, American academic researchers took up anger as a phenomenon worthy of study. Psychologist Charles Spielberger went into anger research at the University of South Florida. Strange as it might seem, around 1978 and 1980, there were no measures of anger within psychology. Anger had been a neglected emotion. Spielberger created the State-Trait Anger Expression Inventory, STAXI, a questionnaire that scores people according to how hotheaded they are. The scores are calculated on a ten-item questionnaire with four points for each item. "I feel angry: not at all, somewhat, moderately so, very much so. I feel angry: almost never, sometimes, often, almost always." You get a score that will vary from ten to forty. Scores of twenty-eight or thirty tend to be in the high-intensity and also in the high-frequency range. According to Spielberger, only about five or six percent of respondents in a survey score in that high range, suggesting that, for the most part, people don't get really angry very often.

❺   At Colorado State University, psychologist Jerry Deffenbacher says he stumbled into the field around the same time. He was supervising doctoral students in the University's clinic training program. They asked him to help them with helping their angry patients and wanted to know what he could do. Basically, he had to say that he didn't know. When he began to look in the literature, he found that there was relatively little to help people understand anger. That aroused his curiosity, so he put aside the anxiety and stress research that he was doing at the time and started looking at anger and anger reduction.

Methods for Managing Anger

⑥   Dr. Deffenbacher helped develop methods that are now widely applied: relaxation techniques and what are known as cognitive change strategies. What this involves is looking at what people *think* when they're angry. First, he found that people often make bad situations worse. "For example, let's suppose a person cuts you off on the highway on the way to work. If you say, 'That jerk! Where'd he get his driver's license, at a video arcade? What a fool,' you're going to be much more angry than if you say, 'Look, an accident looking for a place to happen. Just back off, slow down, get away from here, manage your anger. You know, there are bad drivers every day. You just met one.' Same circumstance, but a very different self-dialogue, if you will, or a self-talking-to."

Anger—The Justifiable Emotion

⑦   Dr. Spielberger and other researchers found that anger is a physiological condition. The most obvious aspects of intense anger are increased blood pressure, increased heart rate, and increased secretion of hormones such as epinephrine and norepinephrine. In addition, Dr. Deffenbacher says that mixed among those chemicals is a healthy dose of righteousness. Basically, you might think of anger as a kind of moral emotion. Something has or should have happened that did or didn't happen, and we often become angry at those kind of things. And anger doesn't have to be physical to hurt; anger can move people to exclude individuals from group activities or prevent people from getting information that they should have.

Aggression Management 101

⑧   Nowadays, people who throw temper tantrums at work may be told by an employer to take a course. People who throw punches or shout insults may be told to do so by a judge; likewise, people who are caught driving aggressively. Naturally, all those anger management programs need teachers, and there must be someone to teach them how to teach. A good example of such a training course is one run by Anderson & Anderson, psychologists in California. In fact, it's an example of the sizable enterprise that anger management has become. Anderson & Anderson have produced workbooks, videos, and interactive CDs and, of course, they run training sessions. Theirs is just one anger management outfit out of many and its founder, psychotherapist George Anderson, says he has trained 4,000 facilitators in the past seven years, most of them since 2001. Dr. Anderson says anger management is likely to become mandatory soon for California motorists who exhibit road rage. He is confident that people who go through an anger management course based on the principles of cognitive therapy that underlie his program—which include recognizing your behavior, becoming conscious of it, and controlling or changing it—are likely to emerge better able to control their anger. He concedes that there is virtually no research to demonstrate this, nor, he says, is there any definition of what an anger management course is or how long it should last.

Working Without Standards

⑨   Unfortunately, there are no standards to follow. Dr. Anderson has worked with the courts in California for about five years. The state asked him what the average length of stay in an anger management program should be and he recommended twenty-six sessions. Thus, that is the average that is being followed. But when it comes to dealing with companies, often they're not willing to accept twenty-six sessions. Instead, most of the companies prefer ten sessions or ten weeks of anger management. So when Anderson says that twenty-six weeks would be more effective, the answer is, "Yes, but we have to also be practical."

⑩   Judges seem to like anger management courses as a form of alternative sentencing, despite some notorious failures of anger management programs. The boxer Mike Tyson has been through anger management, apparently without success. Researcher Pam Hollenhorst found when she surveyed the literature on the topic that there is very little data showing that anger management works. Since there haven't been a lot of studies, they really don't know who it benefits. However, there's a generally held belief and a recognition that improved social skills will help people cope in society.

❶   The theory is that if we teach people social skills, they'll get along better and won't commit as many crimes. Nonetheless, given the reality of crowded jails and the newly defined offense of road rage, the outlook would seem to be that the numbers of Americans in anger management will only increase.

National Public Radio, *All Things Considered*

Scanning

▶ **Looking for Examples** In this reading, ideas are often explained by means of examples. Scan for the answers to these questions. Mark the question number in the margin of the page. Write your answers in note form.

1. a. What is STAXI ?

   _____

   b. What two things does it measure?

   _____

   c. What percentage of scores are in the high range?

   _____

2. Why did Dr. Jerry Deffenbacher get interested in anger and anger reduction?

   _____

3. a. What are cognitive change strategies?

   _____

   b. What is one example of this?

   _____

4. What are the two components of anger?

   _____

5. a. What is Anderson & Anderson?

   _____

   b. What is it an example of?

   _____

6. What is the reason that Anderson offers a different standard for training sessions in companies?

   _____

7. What example shows that there is a need for more research into the use of anger management as an alternative form of sentencing?

_____

8. What does the author imply about the need for anger management training?

_____

▶ Check your answers with a partner. If necessary, refer to what you have underlined.

Reacting to the Information

▶ Discuss the following questions with a partner or in a small group. Explain your answers.

1. What do you think people should do in an anger management course?
2. Is it important to evaluate the effectiveness of these courses? How could this be done?

Applying the Information

▶ Anger is an emotion that influences our behavior in unpredictable ways. Is it possible to teach people how to behave and, if we do so at an early age, will it affect their ability to control their anger? The reading that follows is about teaching manners to kids. Read it and keep in mind the idea stated in the previous reading: "There's a generally held belief and a recognition that improved social skills will help people cope in society."

▶ Would the author agree that teaching kids manners will help them cope later in life? Would you agree? Why or why not?

Skimming

▶ Quickly skim the reading and answer the following questions.

1. What does this program try to do?

_____

2. Why is this program important?

_____

Teaching Manners to Kids

1   It was a sight to gladden the hearts of the standard-bearers of civilized behavior. The children lined up patiently at the door of the conference room here at the Harrison Avenue Elementary School, each waiting to shake hands with Susie McNamee, the teacher, before entering the room. As they quietly put away their lunch boxes and settled at the conference table, Mrs. McNamee reprimanded one boy, "Don't keep your feet on the table. We eat food from there." The children then started writing letters to faraway friends and relatives.

2   There are no standardized tests in the subject, and no final exams on courtesy looming down the road. But teaching civility and good manners is time well spent, educators here say. "Our kids are really pretty nice," said Mark Solomon, the principal. "Fighting and bullying are not a concern. But we thought that maybe kids could use some work on their manners. One of the things I've noticed is that in the two months since the class started, there has been a fifty percent reduction in the number of children sent to my office for problems," he said.

3   About 280 of the school's 530 students have voluntarily enrolled in this class, which is offered to kindergartners through fifth graders as a lunchtime activity. The program, which costs about $3,500 to cover the instructional fee and supplies, is financed by the local Parent Teachers Association (PTA). Mr. Solomon said the manners class is part of an overall focus to support character education, which he called "a piece of a bigger pie."

4   Mrs. McNamee is a consultant who also offers the manners course at the Stanwich School, a coeducational independent day school in Greenwich, Connecticut, and will soon teach the course as an after-school activity at the Milton Elementary School in Rye, New York. "It adds to one's success to be gracious and polite," Mrs. McNamee said. "I'm trying to introduce the idea to the children that it's important to show people that you know how to act."

5   For Christina Loguidice, a fourth grader, "learning how to say please and thank you, set stuff at the table, how to eat politely, and how to be excused" have been worthwhile lessons. Nicole Barletta, another fourth grader, said, "We've learned how to greet people and how to pass things around the table and how to have nice conversation."

6   Mrs. McNamee teaches the class three days a week, and Dinah Howland teaches one day a week as a volunteer. A mother of three, including two at the Harrison Avenue School, Mrs. Howland said, "For the past two years, there has been a lot of talk about the need for character education. We talked about everything from anger management, bullying, and fighting to common courtesy. When we did a survey last spring, we found that people weren't interested as much in the big stuff, as in dealing with respect for others."

❼   The curriculum, given out in twenty-minute doses during a ten-week period, covers topics from meeting and greeting people, how-to's for setting a table, table manners (including what to do when you don't like the food or have to spit something out), to being a good sport, being respectful to those who are different, polite ways to answer the phone, acceptable field trip behavior, and helpful advice for how to write thank you notes.

❽   Even with just a few sessions so far, some parents find that there seems to be a difference in the children's behavior, specifically toward one another and adults. "I go to events like the Halloween party or the book fair, and parents come up to me and say, 'We're so glad you're doing this,'" Mrs. Howland said. "They talk about 'how nicely my son introduced his friends to me.' One mother said that her son wouldn't eat until she came out of the kitchen and sat down. The children will shake hands and make eye contact." To Sydney Hochman, whose three children attend the Harrison Avenue School and are enrolled in the manners course, the results are apparent. "There's such a vast improvement in their table manners," she said. "Everyone cut their own food. It's lovely. They're twirling spaghetti on the spoon. They really learn, and really enjoy it."

❾   Not everyone is convinced, at least not yet, of the course's effectiveness. "It's too early," said Chris Cowan, a fourth-grade teacher. "It's only been a few weeks. There are certain children where I felt it would be beneficial for them to take it. But they weren't the ones who elected to take part in the program."

Adapted from Merri Rosenberg, *The New York Times.* Copyright © 2003 by The New York Times Co. Reprinted with permission.

Scanning

◉ **Underlining Specific Details** Look back at the reading and underline the answers to the following questions.

Class in Civility

1. How did the students greet their teacher when they came to class?
2. What is one example of a behavior the teacher disapproves of?
3. What problems do these students not have?
4. What improvements have been achieved?

Voluntary Program

5. How many students participate in the program?
6. When is it offered?
7. Who pays for it?
8. How many schools is the program offered in?
9. What are the goals of the program?

Reaction from Students and Parents

10. Why do students like this program?
11. Who is Dinah Howland and what does she do?
12. What aspects of character education were discussed?
13. What did parents think was important?

The Curriculum

14. How are the classes organized?
15. What is taught in the classes?

Results

16. What have parents noticed?
17. What examples of good behavior are given?
18. What reservations does one teacher have?

▶ Compare what you underlined with your partner. Try to agree on what you think is important information. Make any changes that are necessary.

Giving Your Opinion

▶ With a new partner, use what you underlined to talk about the article. Make sure you explain as much as possible. Then discuss the following questions.

1. Would this kind of training make a difference to behavior later in life?
2. Whose responsibility is it to provide this kind of behavior training—the schools, the family, the community? Explain your reasons.

Vocabulary Building

Word Form

▶ **A** Study these five words and their forms. Then choose the correct form for each part of speech in the chart below. These words are commonly found in general and academic texts.

conflict (v.)	motivate (v.)	psychologize (v.)	recognize (v.)	survey (v.)
conflict (n.)	motivational	psychologist	recognition	surveying
conflicting (adj.)	motivator	psychological	recognizing	surveyor
conflictual (adj.)	motivated	psychologically	recognizably	surveyed
conflictingly (adv.)	motivation	psychology	recognized	survey

Verb	Noun	Adjective	Adverb
motivate	1. 2.	1. 2.	
psychologize	1. 2.	1.	1.
recognize	1.	1. 2.	1.
survey	1. 2.	1. 2.	

▶ Compare lists with a partner.

▶ **B** Write three sentences using words from the list. Use different parts of speech.

▶ **C** In English, the form of the word can change when it is used as a different part of speech. For example, a suffix (ending) can be added to change the verb *motivate* to the noun *motivation*. Some common noun suffixes are *-ness, -tion, -ment, -th, -ity,* and *-al.* Read each sentence and circle the correct word to use in the sentence. Write *N* if the word is a noun or *ADJ* if it is an adjective.

1. _____ There is a generally held belief and a **recognizing / recognition** that improved social skills help people cope in society.

2. _____ The **refusing / refusal** to listen to a parent or teacher is one of the behaviors that marks the adolescent years.

3. _____ Chris is feeling so angry that there is a very real chance for it to have a **devastating / devastation** effect on his life.

4. _____ It would be important to bring a satisfying **resolving / resolution** to this problem.

5. _____ There has been a fifty percent **reduced / reduction** in the number of children sent to the principal's office.

6. _____ There has been a very noticeable **improving / improvement** in the children's table manners.

7. _____ They introduced many key topics, such as how to reduce anger, how to control **negative / negativity** thinking, and how to change bad behavior.

Synonyms

▷ **Verb Phrases** Refer to "Anger: The Neglected Emotion No More" to find the words in Column A in context. Match them with the words in Column B that have the same meaning.

Column A

_____ 1. take (took) up

_____ 2. go (went) into

_____ 3. stumble(d) into

_____ 4. put aside

_____ 5. back off

_____ 6. throw a temper tantrum

_____ 7. survey the literature

_____ 8. get along

Column B

a. to lose control in anger

b. to be on good terms with someone

c. to develop an interest

d. to search for information

e. to undertake as a profession

f. to retreat

g. to begin something accidentally

h. to stop doing something

Vocabulary in Context

▷ Use your understanding of one part of the sentence to help you guess the word that is missing. Complete each sentence with one of the phrases from the list.

a. adjusting for   b. come out   c. hold in
d. how to let off steam   e. make room for   f. play a role in

1. Psychologists believe that expressing our emotions can _____ reducing our pain.

2. Teachers think that it is important to help children learn _____ in ways that are not destructive.

3. Many people try to _____ their anger rather than let it out.

4. They changed the schedule in order to _____ some additional classes.

5. The scientists knew that news of their discovery would _____ eventually.

6. Researchers found important results even after _____ the ages of the people in their study.

▶ Check your answers. Work with a partner to read the sentences.

The Language of Examples

▶ **A** In English, an important way to explain something is to give an example or two. Read these sentences. Write an *I* under the word that expresses the idea and an *E* under the word or phrase that contains the example.

1. The most obvious aspects of intense anger are increased blood pressure, increased heart rate, and increased secretion of different hormones.

2. Anger releases stress hormones such as adrenaline.

3. Acting out stresses—whether family or academic problems or emotional upheavals—is often the reason for teen anger.

4. Anger takes many forms, from indignation and resentment to rage and fury.

5. Some parents find that there seems to be a difference in the children's behavior, specifically toward one another and adults. One mother said that her son wouldn't eat until she came out of the kitchen and sat down. The children will shake hands and make eye contact.

▶ Check your answers with a partner. Take turns reading your sentences.

▶ **B** Write three sentences of your own that show how an idea is explained through examples.

1. _____

2. _____

3. _____

❰xpanding Your Language

Speaking

❏ **A Interviewing** Answer the questionnaire below on the topic of anger. Check your rating on page 276 in the "Exercise Pages" section. Interview two people who completed their questionnaires. Compare your information. Report on the similarities to and differences from others in your class.

How Hostile Are You?

Find out how hostile you are on the road, in a supermarket line, and at the office by answering these questions, devised by Dr. Redford Williams of Duke University.

1. I am in the express checkout line at the supermarket, where a sign reads, "No more than ten items, please!"

    a. I pick up a magazine to pass the time.

    b. I glance ahead to see if anyone has more than ten items.

2. My spouse, boyfriend, or girlfriend is going to get me a birthday present.

    a. I prefer to pick it out myself.

    b. I prefer to be surprised.

3. Someone is speaking very slowly during a conversation.

    a. I am apt to finish his or her sentences.

    b. I am apt to listen until he or she finishes.

4. Someone treats me unfairly.

    a. I usually forget it rather quickly.

    b. I am apt to keep thinking about it for hours.

5. The person who cuts my hair trims off more than I wanted.

    a. I tell him or her what a lousy job he or she did.

    b. I figure it'll grow back, and I resolve to give my instructions more forcefully next time.

6. I am riding as a passenger in the front seat of a car.

    a. I take the opportunity to enjoy the scenery.

    b. I try to stay alert for obstacles ahead.

7. At times, I have to work with incompetent people.

    a. I concentrate on my part of the job.

    b. Having to put up with them ticks me off.

8. Someone bumps into me in a store.

   a. I pass it off as an accident.

   b. I feel irritated at the person's clumsiness.

9. Someone is hogging the conversation at a party.

   a. I look for an opportunity to put him or her down.

   b. I soon move to another group.

10. There is a really important job to be done.

    a. I prefer to do it myself.

    b. I am apt to call on my friends or coworkers for help.

11. Someone criticizes something I have done.

    a. I feel annoyed.

    b. I try to decide whether the criticism is justified.

12. Another driver butts ahead of me in traffic.

    a. I usually flash my lights or honk my horn.

    b. I stay farther behind such a driver.

13. I see a very overweight person walking down the street.

    a. I wonder why the person has such little self-control.

    b. I think that he or she might have a metabolic defect or a psychological problem.

14. There have been times when I was very angry with someone.

    a. I have always been able to stop short of hitting them.

    b. I have, on occasion, hit or shoved them.

15. I recall something that angered me previously.

    a. I feel angry all over again.

    b. The memory doesn't bother me nearly as much as the actual event did.

Laura Mansnerus, *The New York Times Magazine*

▶ **B Discussion** Form a group with some classmates who are from different countries to exchange ideas based on the following questions.

1. What are some of the most common reasons that people get angry?

2. Is expressing anger the same in all cultures? If not, what are the differences?

3. Can anger be a positive force? Give some examples to support your opinion.

Reading   Read the following story and find out about one woman's reaction of anger. As you read the story, consider these questions: What made this woman angry? What was the result of her anger?

I'm Too Mad to Die!

By Bill DeFoore

A friend of mine named Dayna was on a backpacking trip in the Rockies when she learned the value of her own anger. She and her friend Lynn had been traveling around in an old Volkswagen bug for several weeks when they decided to hike up into the mountains and do some camping. Neither of them had much experience in this, but they were adventurous and carefree—a combination which almost proved deadly.

Lynn had seemed to be the one who had it all together during the trip. She was bold in talking to strangers, getting free meals, and finding places to stay. Dayna was more shy and reserved, holding back in many situations where Lynn seemed brave and daring. Lynn's bravado led to some pretty hairy situations, but nothing compared to their experience on the mountain.

It was Lynn's idea to keep hiking, even when it started getting cold and the sun was setting behind the nearby snow-capped peaks. Dayna protested, but as usual, Lynn insisted. Soon it became apparent that they were in trouble.

They came to a place on the mountain where they could not go any higher. There were no more trees to hold onto and the slopes were getting steeper. Both of them were amateur climbers at best. They were not equipped to spend the night on the mountain, even if there had been a place to put a bedroll.

Suddenly Dayna noticed a change in Lynn. She got quiet and started making little whimpering sounds. Her hands and legs were starting to tremble. When she looked into Lynn's eyes, Dayna could actually see her collapsing inside.

Lynn whispered in a small, weak voice, "Dayna, I have to tell you something. I have a fear of heights."

"Now she tells me," thought Dayna.

Just at that moment, the mountain seemed to push against Lynn's backpack and dislodge her sleeping bag. Before Dayna could reach it, it was tumbling down the mountain.

Unsteady on their feet, they watched in silence as the sleeping bag bounced all the way into the ravine that stretched into the blackness below them. There was a moment of silence that seemed to vibrate with their fear. They were suddenly aware that their lives were hanging by a thread. Little did they know the thread that would save them was Dayna's anger.

A light snow started to fall and the wind picked up a little, making a low moaning sound. There was a desolate, lonely feeling in the air. Lynn seemed to be fading into the side of the cliff. But not Dayna.

Dayna felt herself getting hot inside. At first she didn't know what it was. Then she suddenly realized. She was furious! Without knowing what she was saying or why, Dayna started screaming at Lynn, at God, and at the mountain. She told all three of them that her time was not up!

"I'm not ready to die!" she screamed, "And I sure don't plan to end my life on this cold, lonely mountain or tumbling down the side of it! I've come too far and been through too much to quit now!"

She stood up, grabbed Lynn's pack, and slung it over her shoulder with her own. In a voice she barely recognized as hers, she said to Lynn, "Get up! We're going down!" Lynn was whining by now and not making much sense. She was terrified of the situation, but she was even more afraid of the rage in Dayna.

She was still talking about being afraid of heights when Dayna took her by the arm and pulled her up until they were face to face. Looking hard into Lynn's frightened eyes, Dayna said in a forceful and confident voice, "We are going down, because I'm taking us down. You are going to be just fine. Hold on to me and shut up."

Dayna had not felt so powerful since the time she beat up the neighborhood bully when she was eight years old. Anger had been her ally before and it came to her aid now. Her body felt strong and steady as she helped her trembling friend down the side of the mountain in the cold windy twilight. She did not really know what had happened and she didn't question it. Only years later did she realize that her anger had saved her life.

Although her life had been far from wonderful, Dayna was determined not to lose it. The result had been an empowering anger that allowed her to do exactly what needed to be done. Dayna discovered the survival value of her anger.

Health Communications, Inc.

Reacting to the Story

▷ Work with a partner. Recount the details of this story to each other. Then discuss the questions you considered as you read. Finally, write two important questions of your own about this story for others to react to. Work in small groups to ask and answer each other's questions.

Writing

▷ **Journal Writing** Write your reactions to the ideas about anger that you read about in this chapter. What thoughts did you have about the information or in the discussions you had? Would you use any of this information in your life?

▷ **Topic Writing** Based on the information in this chapter and information of your own, write about the topic of anger, featuring three key points:

1. What researchers know about the emotion of anger
2. How anger can harm
3. How useful anger can be

Online Study Center

For additional activities, go to the ***Reading Matters*** Online Study Center at *college.hmco.com/pic/wholeythree2e*.

Succeeding in a Complex World

▶Chapter Openers

What's Your Opinion?

◐ Circle *A* if you agree or *D* if you disagree with these statements.

1. A   D   Most people are very happy most of the time.

2. A   D   Happy people are just born that way.

3. A   D   We can't change our basic personality.

4. A   D   People who are wealthy are happier than those with less money.

5. A   D   Most people expect to be happy in their lives.

6. A   D   People's feelings affect the amount of success in their lives.

7. A   D   Most people know what it is they want in life.

◐ Work with a partner or a small group. Compare your answers. Explain your ideas as completely as possible.

Free Writing

◐ Write as much as you can about any of the following ideas. Use examples you know about or have experienced in your own life.

1. What makes us happy? What doesn't?
2. Does our level of happiness change during our lives?
3. Does our attitude toward life affect how successful we are or not?

Exploring and Understanding Reading

Brainstorming

> Reading Tip

Brainstorming means **writing** or **saying everything** you know about a **topic**. It is a useful technique to use before reading because it helps you **think** of **ideas** that will **make** understanding the **reading easier**. ▪

 Read all the following quotes taken from the reading. Brainstorm a list of ideas that each quote makes you think of. Some possibilities include guessing at the meaning, deciding whether you agree or disagree, or giving an example you know of. Write these ideas in note form.

Quote	Ideas
1. "Students with high hopes set themselves higher goals and know how to work to attain them."	
2. "Having hope means you have the will and the way to accomplish goals, whatever they may be."	
3. "It's not enough to wish for something, you need the means too."	
4. "Hope can be nurtured."	
5. "Where there's a will, there's a way."	

 Discuss the ideas you brainstormed with a partner. Share your ideas with others.

Predicting

 Based on your brainstorming, check (✔) the ideas you expect to find in this reading.

1. _____ The need to have hope in order to be successful

2. _____ How successful people accomplish their goals

3. _____ The way to increase people's sense of hope

4. _____ Why hope is so important

 Read the selection, then check your predictions. Discuss your answers with a partner.

Hope Emerges as the Key to Success in Life

Introduction

Psychologists are finding that hope plays a surprisingly powerful role in giving people a measurable advantage in areas as diverse as academic achievement, bearing up in oppressive jobs, and coping with tragic illness. And, by contrast, the loss of hope is turning out to be a stronger sign that a person may commit suicide than other factors long thought to be more likely risks.

A Measure of Success

"Hope has proven to be a powerful predictor of outcome in every study we've done so far," said Dr. Charles R. Snyder, a psychologist at the University of Kansas who has devised a scale to assess how much hope a person has. For example, in research with 3,920 college students, Dr. Snyder and his colleagues found that the level of hope among freshmen at the beginning of their first semester was a more accurate predictor of their college grades than were their SAT scores or their grade point averages in high school, the two measures most commonly used to predict college performance. The study was reported in part in the November issue of *The Journal of Personality and Social Psychology*.

"Students with high hope set themselves higher goals and know how to work to attain them," Dr. Snyder said. "When you compare students of equivalent intellectual aptitude and past academic achievements, what sets them apart is hope."

In devising a way to assess hope scientifically, Dr. Snyder went beyond the simple notion that hope is merely the sense that everything will turn out all right. "That notion is not concrete enough, and it blurs two key components of hope," Dr. Snyder said. "Having hope means believing you have both the will and the way to accomplish your goals, whatever they may be."

Getting Out of a Jam: Ability and Attitude

Dr. Snyder's scale assesses the degree to which people think that they can cope with adversity by asking, for instance, whether they typically find they can think of many ways to get out of a jam or find ways to solve problems that discourage others. It then measures the idea of willpower, through such questions as whether people feel they have been fairly successful in life or usually pursue goals with great energy.

Despite the folk wisdom that "where there's a will, there's a way," Dr. Snyder has found that the two are not necessarily connected. In a study of more than 7,000 men and women from eighteen to seventy years old, Dr. Snyder discovered that only about forty percent of people are hopeful in the technical sense of believing they typically have the energy and means to accomplish their goals, whatever those might be.

The study found that about twenty percent of the people believed in their ability to find the means to attain their goals, but said they had little will to do so. Another twenty percent have the opposite pattern, saying they had the energy to motivate themselves but little confidence that they would find the means.

The rest had little hope at all, reporting that they typically had neither the will nor the way.

"It's not enough just to have the wish for something," said Dr. Snyder. "You need the means, too. On the other hand, all the skills to solve a problem won't help if you don't have the willpower to do it."

Portrait of Hope: What Does it Look Like?

Dr. Snyder found that people with high levels of hope share several attributes:

- Unlike people who are low in hope, they turn to friends for advice on how to achieve their goals.
- They tell themselves they can succeed at what they need to do.
- Even in a tight spot, they tell themselves things will get better as time goes on.
- They are flexible enough to find different ways to get to their goals.
- If hope for one goal fades, they aim for another. According to Dr. Snyder, "Those low in hope tend to become fixated on one goal and persist even when they find themselves blocked… They just stay at it and get frustrated."
- They show an ability to break a formidable task into specific, achievable chunks. "People low in hope see only the large goal, and not the small steps to it along the way."

In a ten-year study reported on in a 1987 article in *The American Journal of Psychiatry*, of 206 patients who reported thoughts of suicide but had not yet made an attempt, the patients' scores on the hopelessness scale was the single best predictor of whether they would go on to attempt suicide.

Dr. Snyder reported that people who get a high score on the hope scale "have had as many hard times as those with low scores, but have learned to think about it in a hopeful way, seeing a setback as a challenge, not a failure."

Nurturing Hope

Snyder and his colleagues are trying to design programs to help children develop the ways of thinking found in hopeful people. "They've often learned their mental habit of hopefulness from a specific person, like a friend or teacher." He has made a videotape for that purpose, showing interviews with students who are high on hope, to help freshmen in university better handle the stress of their first year. … Dr. Snyder believes that similar approaches might work to raise hopefulness among other groups, such as children in impoverished neighborhoods. "Hope can be nurtured," he said.

Daniel Goleman, *The New York Times*. Copyright © 1991 by The New York Times Co. Reprinted with permission.

Understanding Details

> **Reading Tip**

An inference is an idea that you might logically think could be true based on the information in a reading, even though it is not directly stated. Considering what can be inferred from a reading is an important critical reading skill. ▪

▶ **Inferences** Read each of the following statements. Write *T* if an idea is stated in the reading, *F* if it is not stated or is untrue, and *I* if you think the statement can be inferred. Mark the question number in the margin where you located the information.

1. _____ Having hope is important for success in a variety of life situations.

2. _____ Dr. Charles Snyder's scale for assessing hope would be a useful tool for university admissions officers to use.

3. _____ Dr. Snyder would like to test many more students at different universities.

4. _____ According to Dr. Snyder, you have to have both the will and the way to accomplish your goals.

5. _____ Hopeful people are friendlier than those without hope.

6. _____ Hopeful people are good at giving themselves positive messages.

7. _____ Successful people never give up trying to accomplish a goal even when it seems hopeless.

8. _____ Hopeful people see only the large goal.

9. _____ Dr. Snyder's scale can be used by crisis centers to determine if a person is a suicide risk.

10. _____ Dr. Snyder believes that hopefulness can be taught to children.

▶ Work with a partner to compare your answers. Refer to the reading to check where you found the information on which you based your answers.

Charting Results of Studies

> **Reading Tip**

Remember that most reports of studies include facts about the subjects (people who participated in the study) and the results of the study. ▪

▶ Making a chart is a useful way to critically analyze the information reported on in studies presented in this type of reading. Use the chart headings to help you locate the key information. Report on the results of the studies only. Write the information in note form. Some items are started for you.

Results of Studies that Show the Importance of Hope	
Study	**Results**
1. Research with 3,920 college students	
2. Research with more than 7,000 men and women	40% 20% 20% rest 6 attributes of hopeful people
3. Ten-year study of 206 patients	

▶ Work with a partner to take turns explaining the results of the studies.

Applying the Information

According to the information in "Hope Emerges as the Key to Success in Life," the most effective messages give specific information on the way to accomplish goals and to do so in a positive way.

▶ **A** Look at the following situations and circle the messages you think are the most effective.

1. Your friend, Sue Kwan, is in her freshman year of college. She is disappointed because she got a "C" on her first paper. Sue tells you that she is thinking of dropping the course. She thinks she's a bad student and that her writing is awful. You tell Sue:

   a. It's better to drop the course before the deadline.

   b. Don't worry, you'll do better on the next paper.

   c. Ask your professor why you got a "C" and find out what to you can do to improve.

2. Your friend, Roberto Sanchez, has started to study art. Roberto really likes it but his parents are afraid that it will take time from his math and science courses. He is worried that his parents will be disappointed in him if he continues in art. Roberto thinks that he could be a really good artist if he continues, but he also thinks that his parents may be right. You tell Roberto:

   a. Pleasing your parents is more important than doing something that pleases you right now.

   b. Studying art might not lead to a good job in the future. It's better to concentrate on math and science and find a more practical interest.

   c. Look at your weekly schedule and see how much free time you have. Decide if you could have time to do both art and your other studies. Then decide on a week-by-week basis.

3. Your friend, Judy Lee, has been feeling anxious and having trouble sleeping at night. She thinks she has heart problems but is afraid to see a doctor. You tell Judy:

   a. Don't worry. It's all in your mind. Have a glass of wine at dinner and relax.

   b. I would be worried if I were you. Your life is too stressful.

   c. I'll help you find a good doctor and schedule an appointment. If I'm free, I'll go with you to the doctor's office.

▶ **B** Discuss your choices with a partner or in a small group. Based on what you remember from the reading, give reasons for your answers or create an answer of your own.

◗Paired Readings

◖ In this section you will read about some tools that the authors think are useful for finding personal and professional fulfillment. The first reading is about a method people can use to identify the things in life that are important to them; the second reading is about how to find out what type of work you would like to do.

Choose one of these readings. Work with a partner who is reading the *same* article.

①Creating Your Personal Profile

Skimming   ◖ Read the article quickly and answer the following questions.

1. What are some of the important drives that motivate us all?
2. What research is Reiss's book based on?
3. What is the purpose of making your own desire profile?
4. What effect can it have on your relationship to others?

◖ Compare your information with your partner. Refer to the reading to support your answers.

Finding Out What Motivates You

The Sixteen Basic Desires

❶   Do you know—really know, with confidence—what makes you tick? Can you imagine how your life might be different if you had an inventory of the things that truly motivate you, and those that don't? Steven Reiss believes your life can be more meaningful and more satisfying. He has spent several years developing a method for people to find out for themselves what they really want in life. Reiss, a professor of psychology and psychiatry at Ohio State University, has written a book entitled *Who Am I?: The 16 Basic Desires That Motivate Our Actions and Define Our Personalities*. These specific desires "drive nearly everything we do," Reiss says. They are: power, independence, curiosity, acceptance, order, saving, honor, idealism, social contact, family, status, vengeance, romance, eating, physical exercise, and tranquility.

❷   Not that all of these things are important to everyone. Far from it. Some are very important to you, some are only of average importance, some desires don't rank at all. "The relative importance we place on each of the sixteen desires is what makes us individuals," Reiss says. "The way in which you prioritize these sixteen desires is what makes you uniquely you." These desires, he adds, are largely genetic in origin. How we satisfy them is up to us, but we cannot change what we inherently want. "I don't know how you can deliberately say, 'I'm going to be less ambitious,' or 'I'm going to be more curious.'"

Research on Self-Discovery

❸   Reiss describes the book as self-discovery based on original scientific research done by him and his colleagues, combining elements of psychology and philosophy. More than 6,000 people were surveyed to come up with the list of basic desires and values. Each of the sixteen basic desires is explained in detail, and readers are asked to decide for themselves whether or not each is very important or not important to them. For example, you'd rate romance as very important if you agree with this statement: "You spend an unusual amount of time, compared to other people you know who are about the same age as you, in the pursuit of romance." You would rate romance as less important if you agreed with this statement: "You spend little time pursuing or thinking about having a close physical relationship with others."

❹   By examining how you feel about each of the sixteen desires, you come up with your own "desire profile," showing your own ranking of strongest, average, and weakest desires. To help readers understand the concept, Reiss has analyzed the desire profiles of some celebrities. Jacqueline Kennedy Onassis had strong desires for saving, family, and status, and weak desires for idealism and social contact. Actor Humphrey Bogart was motivated most by independence, honor, idealism, and romance. Acceptance, curiosity, family, and status weren't important to him.

❺   The questions in *Who Am I?* can create more than forty-three million combinations of the sixteen desires. (A standardized psychological test Reiss has developed, the Reiss Profile of Fundamental Goals and Motivational Sensitivities, can assess more than two trillion different profiles.) Reiss says, "The point of finding out our desire profiles is to make our lives more meaningful. The nice thing about a test like this is that you're guaranteed to like the results. This is a test of what you want; you're going to get the results you want."

Uses of the Profile

❻   The theory is that once you have your own desire profile, you can start to make changes in your life to reflect it. Reiss shows readers how to go about fulfilling their basic desires to achieve "value-based happiness" in romantic relationships, family relationships, careers, sports, and spirituality. A person who recognizes she has a weak desire for order might decide to opt for greater spontaneity and uncertainty. Someone with a higher than average desire for vengeance might think about switching jobs to a more competitive environment.

❼   Reiss stresses that it's important to accept your basic desires for what they are. "If you're a person who is strongly independent, well, that's who you are. Don't let somebody tell you there's something wrong with that or try to get you to change. It's your life—make your life meaningful. Stand up for your values." If a strong desire for power makes you work long hours at your job, that's OK for you, as long as you honestly believe that being a workaholic makes you happy. Reiss also says that creating your desire profile can help you relate better to other people—by understanding that their desires differ from yours. You can also learn that you cannot change the desires of other people any more than you can change your own. People commonly miscommunicate by passing their desires off onto others, he says. The ambitious parent habitually battles a child who is naturally not ambitious. … Reiss says, "The underlying presumption is, 'If only you'd try it my way, you would enjoy it.' They're basing everything on their own personal experience." The profile helps you to realize that every individual has a different set of desires.

8   What is most important to you? The sixteen basic desires are:

- Power: the desire to influence. Manifests itself in leadership, achievement, and work.
- Independence: the desire for self-reliance. Manifests itself in doing things one's own way and resisting advice and guidance from others.
- Curiosity: the desire for knowledge. Manifests itself in truth seeking and problem solving.
- Acceptance: the desire for inclusion. Manifests itself in avoiding rejection and criticism.
- Order: the desire for organization. Manifests itself in making rules, planning, and a low tolerance for messiness.
- Saving: the desire to collect things. Manifests itself in frugality.
- Honor: the desire to be loyal to one's parents and heritage. Manifests itself in high character, morality, and principled behavior.
- Idealism: the desire for social justice. Manifests itself in devotion to causes, volunteer work, and giving to charities.
- Social contact: the desire for companionship. Manifests itself in socializing and the need for friendships.
- Family: the desire to raise one's own children. Manifests itself in making child rearing and day-to-day time with one's family a priority.
- Status: the desire for social standing. Manifests itself in a concern with reputation.
- Vengeance: the desire to get even. Manifests itself in competitiveness and aggression.
- Romance: the desire for sex and beauty. Manifests itself in courting and the pursuit of love.
- Eating: the desire to consume food. Manifests itself in eating, dining, and cooking.
- Physical exercise: the desire for exercise. Manifests itself in physical activity and participatory sports.
- Tranquility: the desire for emotional calm. Manifests itself in the avoidance of stressful situations.

Adapted from David Howell, *The Gazette*

Scanning

▶ **Underlining** Reread and underline the answers to the following questions.

The Sixteen Basic Desires

1. Who is Steven Reiss and what has he done?
2. What are the sixteen specific desires everyone shares?
3. How important are these desires to each individual?

Research on Self-Discovery

4. What is the basis for the information in Reiss's book?
5. What information is contained in the book?
6. How do people make their own "desire profile"?
7. How many combinations can be created?
8. What is the point of making your "desire profile"?

Uses of the Profile

9. What does Reiss show readers they can do?
10. What is important for people to accept?
11. How does the desire profile help you relate better to other people?
12. How does the profile help you to communicate better with others in your life?

▶ Compare what you underlined with your partner. Try to agree on what you think is important information. Make any changes that are necessary.

Discussing the Information

▶ Use the information you underlined to talk about the article to each other. Make sure you explain as much as possible. Then discuss the following questions.

1. Do you agree with the idea that knowing what is most important to you will help you to know yourself and relate to others better?
2. Do you think that you can change your basic desires? Why or why not?
3. From the list of sixteen basic drives, which do you think motivate you the most? Which motivate you the least?

②Creating Your Professional Profile

Skimming   ▷ Read the article quickly and answer the following questions.

1. Why are people unhappy in their jobs?
2. What should people do to avoid being unhappy in their jobs?
3. Who is Real World 101 designed to help?
4. What are some techniques people can use to find the right job?

▷ Compare your information with your partner. Refer to the reading to support your answers.

Getting More than a Good Job

What to Give Up On, When Not to Give Up

❶   Greed may have been the byword of the 1990s when it came to work and success, but experts urge college graduates in 2003 to consider a different, more enduring value as they set out on their careers—job satisfaction.

❷   "A lot of people stumble into their first job, and then they feel locked in," said Sandy Putnam, a longtime human-resources expert who now has her own career consulting firm, Back to Work Connection, in Yorba Linda, California. "They suddenly realize, 'I'm unhappy and can't get out.'"

❸   A survey by The Conference Board last summer shows that more and more people feel trapped in a job rut. About half of those surveyed—50.5 percent—said they were satisfied with their present job. That compares with 58.6 percent in 1995. Those surveyed who were 65 and older had the greatest job satisfaction at 55.4 percent, with the under-25 age group second at 55.2 percent. But satisfaction rapidly declined after age 25, with those 35–44 in the least satisfied group at 47.4 percent. Putnam and other experts say graduates can avoid that trap with a little thought in advance. "Don't look at the market frantically," said Putnam. "Step back just long enough to find out about yourself before you step into that first position."

A Counseling Program That Helps You Choose a Career That's Right for You

❹   Officials at DBM, an international human-resources consulting company, decided that job satisfaction was so important that they created a course last year, Real World 101, to help college graduates navigate the transition into the working world. "We kept seeing many people coming back (for career counseling), and they were already three or four jobs out and weren't happy," said Barbara Marchilonis, director of career services, who created the program. "Most of the time, they just jumped into the job market after graduation." Marchilonis cited the example of a recent accounting major. "When she got out of school and found out what she was going to do for eight or 10 hours a day, she said, 'Ooh, I made a mistake.'" Working with a career coach, DBM helped her redirect her skills into an entry-level management position where a knowledge of accounting would come in handy, but she wouldn't be doing accounting work all day.

❺   This approach even works for traditional social-science majors, who may feel they don't have any skills to offer most employers. "When someone goes into English or social science, they are usually highly gifted communicators who can write and read a lot," said Marchilonis. "Using these skills is highly valued to certain employers if you make a good case." She said graduates should really think about the job being offered. Is the environment very structured or does it leave workers on their own? Is it casual or formal? Is it high-pressured or no pressure? Is there a lot of travel or no travel? She also advises being patient—and realistic. "You are not going to get your ideal job in Round 1," she said. "But you want to get a job that will help put you on a very successful path."

Take Time to Look Around and Investigate

❻   Jeff Gunhus, author of *No Parachute Required*, a career guide for students, recommends doing informational interviews with people in industries you think you might be interested in. That's what he did when he graduated as a business/economics and political science major from the University of California at Santa Barbara. Wall Street was booming and he thought he wanted to be a stockbroker. So he talked to an investment firm to find out what being a stockbroker was like. Gunhus ended up with two job offers to become a stockbroker, but realized it wasn't the kind of work he wanted to do. Then he looked at the entertainment industry and interviewed a vice president at a major talent agency. Again he was offered a job, but realized that wasn't the place for him. Gunhus eventually went back to National Services Group, a company based in Orange, California, that uses college students to paint houses. He had worked for the company for several years while in school and decided it offered the kinds of entrepreneurial opportunities he wanted. He is now a general partner of the company, a job that leaves him enough time for his other passion—writing novels.

❼   Another way to test the waters, Gunhus said, is to think about how you would feel about the job in the future. He suggested that to a young woman who recently came to him for advice after being offered a management trainee job at Wells Fargo bank. "Can you imagine yourself waking up and saying, 'I can't wait to go to work today?'" he asked her, knowing her real passion was fashion. "She's now in the process (of getting a job in fashion)."

❽ Gunhus acknowledges that it's not always possible to hold out for the right job. "If you have to take a job to pay the bills, do it, but still set aside 20 hours a week to pursue the job (you really want)," he said. And it could take some time. "It's so much harder to find a career than to find a job," he said. Above all, Gunhus said, don't let people talk you out of pursuing your dreams. "Dream big and try to do the things everybody said you can't do."

Mary Ann Milbourn, *The Orange County Register*

Scanning

▶ **Underlining** Reread and underline the answers to the following questions.

What to Give Up On, When Not to Give Up

1. Who is Sandy Putnam and what does she do?
2. What advice does Ms. Putnam have for recent graduates?

A Counseling Program That Helps You Choose a Career That's Right for You

3. Why was Real World 101 created?
4. How did Barbara Marchilonis help one recent accounting major?
5. Why is this service useful for social science majors?
6. What questions does Ms. Marchilonis suggest that recent graduates should ask themselves?
7. What advice does she give?

Take Time to Look Around and Investigate

8. What advice does Jeff Gunhus offer students?
9. What experience did Mr. Gunhus have when he graduated from the University of California?
10. What job did he finally find and why did it suit him?
11. What advice does he have for those who can't hold out for the right job?

▶ Compare what you underlined with your partner. Try to agree on what you think is important information. Make any changes that are necessary.

Discussing the Information

▶ Use the information you underlined to talk about the article to each other. Make sure you explain as much as possible. Then discuss the following questions.

1. Why do you think people stay in a job they don't really like?
2. What advice would you give someone who doesn't like his or her job?
3. What advice would you give someone who is looking for a first job?

▶Comparing the Readings

Discussing the Stories

▷ Work with a partner who read the other story. Use the information you underlined to retell your story. Explain the ideas clearly in your own words. Encourage your partner to ask questions about the information or write some of the important facts you explain. Choose one of the discussion questions that followed your story to discuss with your partner.

▶Vocabulary Building

Word Form

▷ **A** Study these five words and their forms. Then choose the correct form for each part of speech in the chart below. These words are commonly found in general and academic texts.

analyze (v.)	approach (v.)	assess (v.)	presume (v.)	specify (v.)
analyst (n.)	approach	assessment	presumed	specification
analysis (n.)	approaching	assessable	presumptive	specifically
analyzed (adj.)	approachable	assessor	presumably	specific
analytical (adj.)	approachability		presumption	specified
analytically (adv.)				

Verb	Noun	Adjective	Adverb
approach	1.	1.	
	2.	2.	
assess	1.	1.	
	2.		
presume	1.	1.	1.
		2.	
specify	1.	1.	1.
		2.	

▷ Compare lists with a partner.

▷ **B** Write three sentences using words from the list.

▶ **C Adverbs** Adverbs are parts of speech that tell us about the *how* of things. Adverbs modify verbs, adjectives, or other adverbs. Many adverbs end in *-ly*.

▶ Read each statement. Circle the adverb. Write *V* if the adverb modifies a verb, *ADJ* if it modifies an adjective, or *ADV* if it modifies an adverb.

1. _____ Psychologists are finding that hope plays a surprisingly potent role in giving people a measurable advantage.

2. _____ In devising a way to assess hope scientifically, Dr. Snyder went beyond a simple notion.

3. _____ The scale assesses people … by asking whether they typically find they can think of many ways to get out of a jam.

4. _____ It measures will through such questions as whether people feel they have been fairly successful in life or usually pursue goals with great energy.

5. _____ Dr. Snyder has found that the two are not necessarily connected.

Vocabulary in Context

▶ Words you already know can help you understand the meaning of new words. Write the meaning of the words in boldface in your own words. Circle the words that helped you guess the meaning.

1. Psychologists are finding that hope plays a role in **realms as diverse as** academic achievement, bearing up in oppressive jobs, and coping with tragic illness.

Meaning: _____

2. "Hope has proven to be a powerful predictor of outcome in every study we've done so far," said Dr. Charles R. Snyder … who has **devised a scale** to assess how much hope a person has.

Meaning: _____

3. "When you compare students of **equivalent intellectual aptitude** and past academic achievements, what sets them apart is hope."

Meaning: _____

4. "Those low in hope tend to **become fixated** on one goal and persist even when they find themselves blocked."

Meaning: _____

5. They show an ability to break a **formidable** task into specific, achievable chunks.

Meaning: _____

6. "Hope can be **nurtured**," said Dr. Snyder, who has made a videotape showing interviews with students who are high on hope to help freshmen better handle the stress of their first year.

Meaning: _____

❋xpanding Your Language

Speaking

▷ **Role Play** To prepare for this simulation, work with others and choose one of two situations to work with. Choose Scenario A, which follows, or Scenario B in the "Exercise Pages" section on page 276.

▷ **Scenario A** Consider the following situation. Read the information and decide what action you would recommend and why. Compare your solution to that of others. Together, write out lines of dialogue to role play the situation and your solution.

You work at a bookstore. You work with someone who always seems to be in a bad mood. The person is sometimes rude when you ask a question, even though he has worked there much longer and knows the store better than you do. This coworker never wants to help you or to let you help. Although you try to be pleasant and begin conversations, your efforts are ignored. This person has even insulted you in front of the other workers in the store.

One day you find out that this person is being considered for a new and better job as a manager at the store. The company wants you to give your evaluation of this person as part of the decision-making process. You will be meeting with the head of personnel to give your recommendation. What would your evaluation be?

▷ **1.** Work with your partners and discuss your recommendation.

2. Prepare the lines of dialogue between the following people:

a. Pleasant bookstore worker

b. Unpleasant bookstore worker

c. Other employees

d. Personnel director

3. Use your lines to act out the story, but do not memorize the lines. Be creative.

4. Following your role play, ask the class to complete the following evaluation sheet for the personnel director, who will recommend the bookstore worker for a promotion or not.

The candidate would be:

_____ a. Outstanding in this position

_____ b. Good in this position

_____ c. Suitable in this position

_____ d. Unsuited for this position

5. After hearing both role plays, discuss the differences and similarities between your evaluations of this unpleasant coworker. Explain the reasons for your decisions.

Reading

▶ In "Hope Emerges as the Key to Success in Life," we learned that people achieve their goals when they have not only the will and the opportunity to do so, but also the following:

1. Encouragement of friends and family
2. Practical experience of carrying out a task
3. Ability to set high goals and a willingness to work for them
4. Development of positive mental habits

▶ **A** The reading that follows gives some statements about these ideas. Read the article, then reread it critically to see if any of these four ideas are found in the text. Look for any information that fits in the four categories. Mark the number of the idea in the margin next to the information.

▶ **B** Work with a partner. Compare the information you marked for each of the categories. Refer to the reading in cases where you disagree.

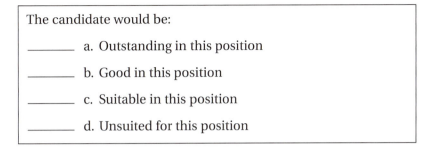

Practice, Not Talent, Produces "Genius"

By John Clare

❶ London—The notion that geniuses such as Shakespeare, Mozart, and Picasso were "gifted" or possessed innate talents is a myth, according to a study by a British psychologist. After examining outstanding performances in the arts and sports, Professor Michael Howe and colleagues at Exeter University concluded that excellence is determined by opportunities, encouragement, training, motivation, self-confidence, and—most of all—practice.

❷   The theory—a radical break with traditional beliefs—has been applauded by academics worldwide. It has significant implications for teachers and parents, not least because children who are not thought to be gifted are being denied the encouragement they need to succeed. The authors took as their starting point the "widespread belief that to reach high levels of ability a person must possess an innate potential called talent." They said it was important to establish whether the belief was correct because it had social and educational consequences affecting selection procedures and training.

❸   However, studies of accomplished artists and mathematicians, top tennis players and swimmers reported few early signs of promise prior to parental encouragement. No case was found of anyone reaching the highest levels of achievement without devoting thousands of hours to serious training. Even those who were believed to be exceptionally talented—whether in music, mathematics, chess, or sports—required lengthy periods of instruction and practice.

Mozart Received Training

❹   Mozart produced his best work only after a long period of training. It was not until he had been immersed in music for sixteen years that he first produced an acknowledged masterwork. "The early biographies of prominent composers have revealed that they all received intensive and regular supervised practice sessions over a period of several years," the study said. "The emergence of unusual skills typically followed, rather than preceded, a period during which unusual opportunities were provided, often combined with strong expectations that a child would do well."

❺   Research had shown strong correlations between the level of performance of student violinists and the number of hours they practiced. Even people who were not thought to have special talent could, after training, reach levels previously considered attainable only by gifted individuals.

❻   Research had shown that cocktail waitresses could regularly remember as many as twenty drink orders at a time, far more than a control group of university students. "It is conceivable that people who are employed as waiters gravitate to such jobs because of an inborn memory skill," the study said. "But the findings make it far more likely that employees excel in recording orders because of on-the-job practice."

❼   In sports, differences in the composition of certain muscles were thought to be reliable predictors of differences in athletic performance. "However, the differences in the proportion of slow-twitch muscle fibers that are essential for success in long-distance running are largely the result of extended practice in running."

⑧ The study said reasoning about talent was often circular. "She plays so well because she has a talent. How do I know she has a talent? That's obvious, she plays so well." Some children did acquire ability more effortlessly than others but that did not mean they were gifted.

Rare Performance Standards

⑨ Categorizing children as innately talented is discriminatory, the authors say, "preventing people from pursuing a goal because of the unjustified conviction of teachers or parents that certain children would not benefit from the opportunities given to those who are deemed to be talented." By the same token, a false belief that one did not possess the necessary talent could affect a person negatively. Talent is a myth and it is time it is demolished, say the authors, but they add that it would be wrong to assume that any diligent child could excel at anything, especially in the absence of expert teaching, encouragement, and unusual motivation.

⑩ Opponents of Howe's theory said practice and other factors were no doubt important contributors to outstanding performance, but not enough to explain great creative works. In the words of David Feldman and Tamar Katzir of Tufts University, Massachusetts, "Talent is essential."

The London Telegraph

Discussing the Information

▷ Discuss the following questions.

1. What positive points are explained in this article
   a. for children?
   b. for parents?
   c. for teachers?
   d. for athletes?
   e. for musicians?

2. Do you agree with the final statement that practice is necessary but "Talent is essential"? Why or why not?

Writing

▷ **A Journal Entry** Write in your journal about the topic of attitude. How do you feel your attitude has helped you or will help you to achieve your goals? Think about a person in your life who has inspired or encouraged you to be the best you could be. Think about the opportunities you believe exist for people to develop and maintain a positive attitude. Look for newspaper articles on this topic over the next few weeks and write your reaction to them.

◖ **B Topic Writing** Write about the importance of attitude in our lives based on your discussions and chapter readings. Follow these steps:

◖ **1.** Outline the ideas about (a) the importance of hope, (b) what hope is, (c) the areas of life that are affected by our attitude, and (d) how to nurture hope. Include at least three or four points under each of these ideas.

2. Write about each idea in a separate paragraph.

◖Read On: Taking It Further

Reading

You may know someone who is almost always upbeat and positive. It may be hard to understand how someone can be so happy—and if you know this person well, it may even be a bit annoying. The next reading is a very personal story of how one person learned about the importance of attitude.

◖ Read the story and prepare to discuss the following questions.

1. What was Jerry's answer to the question "How do you do it"? What is your reaction to this advice?

2. What are the feelings you experienced as you read this story?

3. What does this story tell us about the nature of life?

Attitude Is Everything

By Francie Baltazar-Schwartz

Jerry was the kind of guy you love to hate. He was always in a good mood and always had something positive to say. When someone would ask him how he was doing, he would reply, "If I were any better, I would be twins!"

He was a unique manager because he had several waiters who had followed him around from restaurant to restaurant. The reason the waiters followed Jerry was because of his attitude. He was a natural motivator. If an employee was having a bad day, Jerry was there telling the employee how to look on the positive side of the situation. Seeing this style really made me curious, so one day I went up to Jerry and asked him, "I don't get it! You can't be a positive person all of the time. How do you do it?"

Jerry replied, "Each morning I wake up and say to myself, 'Jerry, you have two choices today. You can choose to be in a good mood or you can choose to be in a bad mood.' I choose to be in a good mood. Each time something bad happens, I can choose to be a victim or I can choose to learn from it. I choose to learn from it. Every time someone comes to me complaining, I can choose to accept their complaining or I can point out the positive side of life. I choose the positive side of life."

"Yeah, right, it's not that easy," I protested.

"Yes it is," Jerry said. "Life is all about choices. When you cut away all the junk, every situation is a choice. You choose how you react to situations. You choose how people will affect your mood. You choose to be in a good mood or a bad mood. The bottom line: It's your choice how you live life." I reflected on what Jerry said. Soon thereafter, I left the restaurant industry to start my own business. We lost touch, but I often thought about him when I made a choice about life instead of reacting to it.

Several years later, I heard that Jerry did something you are never supposed to do in a restaurant business: he left the back door open one morning and was held up at gunpoint by three armed robbers. While trying to open the safe, his hand, shaking from nervousness, slipped off the combination. The robbers panicked and shot him. Luckily, Jerry was found relatively quickly and rushed to the local trauma center. After eighteen hours of surgery and weeks of intensive care, Jerry was released from the hospital with fragments of the bullets still in his body. I saw Jerry about six months after the accident. When I asked him how he was, he replied, "If I were any better, I'd be twins. Wanna see my scars?"

I declined to see his wounds, but did ask him what had gone through his mind as the robbery took place. "The first thing that went through my mind was that I should have locked the back door," Jerry replied. "Then, as I lay on the floor, I remembered that I had two choices: I could choose to live, or I could choose to die. I chose to live."

"Weren't you scared? Did you lose consciousness?" I asked.

Jerry continued, "The paramedics were great. They kept telling me I was going to be fine. But when they wheeled me into the emergency room and I saw the expressions on the faces of the doctors and nurses, I got really scared. In their eyes, I read, 'He's a dead man.' I knew I needed to take action."

"What did you do?" I asked.

"Well, there was a big, burly nurse shouting questions at me," said Jerry. "She asked if I was allergic to anything. 'Yes,' I replied. The doctors and nurses stopped working as they waited for my reply. I took a deep breath and yelled, 'Bullets!' Over their laughter, I told them, 'I am choosing to live. Operate on me as if I am alive, not dead.'"

Jerry lived thanks to the skills of his doctors, but also because of his amazing attitude. I learned from him that every day we have the choice to live fully. Attitude, after all, is everything.

Writing

 Reading Tip

Don't forget to write your reading journal and vocabulary log entries in your notebook. ■

▶ Write your reactions to this story in your reading journal.

 For additional activities, go to the *Reading Matters* Online Study Center at *college.hmco.com/pic/wholeythree2e.*

Exercise Pages

UNIT 1 **Fun Matters**

Chapter ❶ Challenges in Your Free Time

Speaking

▶ **A Interviewing** Give yourself one point each time your answer to the interview question agrees with the key below.

Key

1. F
2. F
3. T
4. T
5. F
6. T
7. T
8. F
9. T
10. F
11. T
12. F
13. T
14. T
15. F
16. T

Rating

13–16:	extremely comfortable with high-risk situations
9–12:	fairly comfortable with high-risk situations
5–8:	fairly uncomfortable with high-risk situations
1–4:	extremely uncomfortable with high-risk situations

Chapter ❷ Taking a Break Responsibly: Eco-Tourism

Applying the Information

◐ Compare your rankings on page 26 with the popularity of activities shown in the graph below.

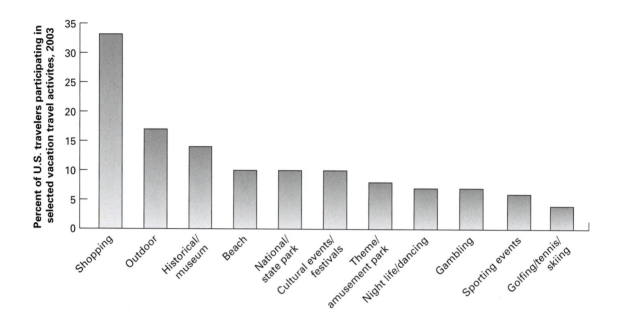

UNIT 4   **Technology Matters**

**Evaluating
What We Have**

▶ **A** The following items were all invented between 1900 and 2003.

1909	instant coffee
1947	cellular phone
1913	zipper
1903	airplane
1965	CD (compact disc)
1950	credit card
1942	computer
1971	VCR
1937	photocopier
1928	bubble gum
1901	vacuum cleaner
1954	McDonald's
1921	robot
1900	escalator
1945	atomic bomb
2001	self-cleaning window

UNIT 6   **Attitude Matters**

Chapter ⓫ Anger: How to Manage It

Speaking

▶ The questions on pages 246–247 are excerpted from the much longer test Dr. Redford Williams administers to patients. Responses to fifteen questions won't determine whether your hostility level is a health risk, but they can suggest whether you would benefit from defusing hostile thoughts.

Questions 1, 2, 6, 10, and 13 are designed to measure cynicism, which Dr. Williams describes as a "mistrusting attitude" toward people's motives and a tendency to be "constantly on guard" against others' misbehavior. If you answered two or more with the responses in parentheses—1(b), 2(a), 6(b), 10(a), 13(a)—your cynicism level is high.

Questions 4, 7, 8, 11, and 15 measure anger, the tendency to respond with "anger, irritation, or annoyance when faced with life's frustrations." If your answers match two or more of the responses in parentheses—4(b), 7(b), 8(b), 11(a), 15(a)—your anger level is probably quite high.

Questions 3, 5, 9, 12, and 14 measure aggression, the tendency to express your anger, either physically or verbally. A highly aggressive person would most likely choose the responses in parentheses two or more times—3(a), 5(a), 9(a), 12(a), 14(b).

Chapter ⓬ Succeeding in a Complex World

Speaking

▶ **Role Play** To prepare for this simulation, work with others and choose one of two situations to work with. Choose Scenario B, which follows, or Scenario A on pages 266–267.

▶ **Scenario B** Consider the following situation. Read the information and decide what action you would recommend and why. Compare your solution to that of others. Together, write out lines of dialogue to role play the situation and your solution.

You work at a bookstore. You work with someone who always seems to be in a bad mood. The person is sometimes rude when you ask a question, even though he has worked there much longer and knows the store better than you do. This coworker never wants to help you or to let you help. Although you try to be pleasant and begin conversations, your efforts are ignored. This person even insulted you in front of the other workers in the store.

One day you find out that this person is being considered for a new and better job as a manager at the store. The company wants you to give your evaluation of this person as part of the decision-making process. You will be meeting with the head of personnel to give your recommendation. You plan to give this person a terrible evaluation, but before your meeting you overhear a conversation between your unpleasant coworker and his brother. You find out that your coworker's mother is very ill and that he is the sole support of the family—working while he is trying to finish his degree. Your coworker is behind in his schoolwork and may fail his year as a result. What would your evaluation be?

▶ **1.** Work with your partners and discuss your recommendation.

2. Prepare the lines of dialogue between the following people:

    a. Pleasant bookstore worker

    b. Unpleasant bookstore worker

    c. Unpleasant bookstore worker's brother

    d. Other employees

    e. Personnel director

3. Use your lines to act out the story, but do not memorize the lines. Be creative.

4. Following your role play, ask the class to complete the following evaluation sheet for the personnel director, who will recommend the bookstore worker for a promotion or not.

The candidate would be:

_____ a. Outstanding in this position

_____ b. Good in this position

_____ c. Suitable in this position

_____ d. Unsuited for this position

---

5. After hearing both role plays, discuss the differences and similarities between your evaluations of this unpleasant coworker. Explain the reasons for your decisions.

Text Credits

pp. 6–8: "Life on the Edge," by Karl Taro Greenfield. Copyright © 1999 TIME Inc. Reprinted by permission.

pp. 12–14: "Jamie Clarke," from "High Drama," by Jamie Clarke. Reprinted with permission.

pp. 15–17: "Alan Hobson," from "High Drama," by Jamie Clarke. Reprinted with permission.

pp. 24–25: "The Rise and Fall of Vacations," by Felicia R. Lee. Copyright © 1999 by The New York Times Co. Reprinted with permission.

pp. 27–30: "Eco Tourism: Eco-Tourism project took off quickly; Spending our money in the world's threatened areas can help save them," by Larry Tye, *Boston Globe*, September 2, 1989. Copyright 1989 by Globe Newspaper Co. (MA). Reproduced with permission of Globe Newspaper Co. in the format Textbook via Copyright Clearance Center.

pp. 34–38: "Trouble in Paradise," by Adam Piore. From *Newsweek*, July 2, 2002, © 2002 Newsweek, Inc. All rights reserved. Reprinted by permission.

pp. 39–41: "Everest: From Mountain to Molehill of Litter," *USA Today*, May 10, 2001. Reprinted by permission.

pp. 44–46: "How to be a Responsible Ecotourist," *Earth Island Journal*, San Francisco, Summer 2003, Vol. 18, Issue 2, p. E5. Adapted from an article found on http://www.ecotravel.com.

pp. 55–56: "Modeling the Weather Gets Better," adapted from Cathy Nangini, "Computerized Models Aid Forecasters' Eyes in the Sky: 'We never imagined it would become so successful in producing forecasts,' says one scientist," *National Post*, Don Mills, Ontario, July 8, 2002. Reprinted by permission of the author.

pp. 60–63: "Signs of Thaw in Desert of Snow. Scientists Begin to Heed Intuit Warnings of Climate Change," by Deneen L. Brown, *The Washington Post*, May 28, 2002. © 2002, The Washington Post, reprinted with permission.

pp. 63–65: "Scientists Track Changes in Antarctica" from "Real Threat of Global Warming is Global Cooling (Final Edition)," by Gwynne Dyer, *Kingston Whig-Standard*, Kingston, Ontario, September 9, 2003, p.5.

pp. 68–70: "Students On Ice: Trips to the Poles," from "Forget Cancun …" by San Grewal, *Toronto Star*, Toronto, Ontario, March 9, 2004, p. C1. Reprinted with permission— TorStar Syndication Services.

pp. 75–77: "Preparing for Disasters: Natural No Longer," from "Unnatural Weather, Natural Disasters: A New U.N. Focus," by Elizabeth Olson, *The New York Times*, May 18, 2004, p. F2. Copyright © 2004 by The New York Times Co. Reprinted with permission.

pp. 81–84: "When the Weather Gets You Down," from "When the weather gets you down: A meteorologist joined forces with a doctor to create a weather map that predicts health problems," by Katie Jaimet, *The Ottawa Citizen*, November 26, 2001. Republished by permission of the Ottawa Citizen.

pp. 185–187: "Engineers Without Borders." Interview from *Canada AM-CTV Television*, Toronto, July 27, 2001. Reprinted by permission of CTV Television Inc.

pp. 193–196: "Cholera." Reprinted from *The Lancet*, Vol. 363, David A. Sack, R. Bradley Sack, G. Balakrish Nair, A.K. Siddique, "Cholera," p. 223, Copyright 2004, with permission from Elsevier.

pp. 203–205: "Modern Risks and Old Habits," from "Deadly Reminder," by Catherine Ford, *The Calgary Herald*, January 12, 1996. Reprinted with the permission of The Calgary Herald.

pp. 209–210: "Fighting AIDS in Africa," from "A U.N. Report Takes a Hard Look at Fighting AIDS in Africa," by Lawrence K. Altman, *The New York Times*, March 5, 2005, p. A2. Copyright © 2005 by The New York Times Co. Reprinted with permission.

pp. 221–223: "His Daughter's Gift of Life," Bill Hewitt & Cindy Dampier/*People Weekly* © 1999. All rights reserved Time Inc.

pp. 226–227: "Miracle Hands," Christina Cheakalos/*People Weekly* © 2003. All rights reserved Time Inc.

pp. 233: "Road Rage in Beijing," from "Flames of Road Rage Blister Drivers in China; Frustrations Boil into fits of 'car temper,'" David J. Lynch, *USA Today*, April 26, 2004, p. A11. Reprinted by permission.

pp. 233: "Angry Parents at the Game," from "Parental Rage Sweeps through Youth Sports," Tim Dahlberg, as found in *Times-Colonist*, Victoria, B.C. June 3, 2001, p. A2. Reprinted by permission of The Associated Press via Reprint Management Services.

pp. 234–238: "Anger: The Neglected Emotion No More," from "Profile: Anger Management Programs on the Rise despite lack of national criteria, oversight or evaluation of efficacy," *All Things Considered*, Washington, D.C., October 28, 2003. Reprinted by permission of National Public Radio.

pp. 240–241: "Teaching Manners to Kids," from "In Teaching Civility, It's Everyday Stuff," by Merri Rosenberg, *The New York Times*, November 23, 2003, p. 14. Copyright © 2003 by The New York Times Co. Reprinted with permission.

pp. 248–249: "I'm Too Mad to Die," from *Anger: Deal with It, Heal with It, Stop It from Killing You*, by Bill DeFoore. Copyright © 1991. Reprinted with permission of Health Communications, Inc.

pp. 252–254: "Hope Emerges as the Key to Success in Life," by Daniel Goleman, *The New York Times*, December 24, 1991. Copyright © 1991 by The New York Times Co. Reprinted with permission.

pp. 257–259: "Finding Out What Motivates You," from "16 Basic Desires Drive All that We Do," by David Howell, as appeared in *The Gazette*, Montreal, Quebec, September 11, 2000, p. E4. Reprinted by permission of the Edmonton Journal.

pp. 261–263: "Getting More Than a Good Job: Graduates should weigh their satisfaction as they pursue a career," by Mary Ann Milbourn, *Orange County Register*, June 9, 2003. Reprinted by permission of the Orange County Register, copyright © 2003.

pp. 267–269: "Practice, Not Talent, Produces Genius," by John Clare, *The London Telegraph*, September 11, 1998. Reprinted with permission of the Telegraph Group Ltd.

pp. 270–271: "Attitude is Everything," by Francie Baltazar-Schwartz. Reprinted with permission from Jack Canfield, ed., *Chicken Soup for the Soul at Work*.